THE SUPERVISOR'S SURVIVAL GUIDE

A PRACTICAL GUIDE TO SUCCESSFUL SUPERVISION

THE SUPERVISOR'S SURVIVAL GUIDE

A PRACTICAL GUIDE TO SUCCESSFUL SUPERVISION

KRIS COLE

Copyright © 2002 Pearson Education Australia Pty Ltd

First published 2002

Pearson Education Australia
Unit 4, Level 2
14 Aquatic Drive
Frenchs Forest NSW 2086

Acquisitions Editor: Nella Soeterboek
Project Editor: Kathryn Fairfax
Copy Editor: Jennifer Coombs
Cover and internal design: Ingo Voss
Typeset by Midland Typesetters
Printed in Malaysia

1 2 3 4 5 06 05 04 03 02

ISBN 1 74009 617 7

National Library of Australia
Cataloguing-in-Publication Data

Cole, Kris.
The supervisor's survival guide: a practical guide to successful supervision.

Includes index.
ISBN 1 74009 617 7.

1. Supervision of employees. 2. Personnel management.
I. Title.

658.302

An imprint of Pearson Education Australia

Sometimes, supervising can seem very much like an act of survival!

As anyone who has acted in a supervisory role will know, regardless of the size of their organisation, the greatest challenge that supervisors face is how to simultaneously motivate, manage, mentor and measure the performance of your staff, while also focusing on delivering a quality service and fulfilling customer expectations. Often, determining the most effective approach involves a mixture of experience, advice from others, research and good fortune.

I therefore welcome the publication of a book such as this, which brings together practical and comprehensive information on the spectrum of issues relating to supervision. By covering the various aspects of managing yourself, managing people and managing operations, Kris has produced a book which I believe will serve as both an instructional guide for new supervisors and a reference guide for experienced managers.

The Supervisor's Survival Guide reflects an understanding that successful supervising is above all about valuing your staff and communicating effectively with your colleagues and stakeholders. Healthy working relationships foster a cooperative, team-based approach, which in turn creates an environment that encourages trust, openness, commitment, creativity, accountability, high morale and continuous improvement. Such an environment provides the conditions for organisational results and objectives to be achieved— which makes supervising an enjoyable and rewarding challenge.

I hope that you enjoy reading and using this book and that it benefits both you and your organisation.

Christine Nixon, APM
Chief Commissioner of Police

CONTENTS

PART 3   MANAGING OPERATIONS

W hether you're a first-line manager, team leader, supervisor, superintendent, section manager, leading hand, coordinator, area manager, frontline manager or department head, your role is unique. It is also one of the most important, and most difficult, in any organisation.

Few jobs have changed as much in the last 30 years as the supervisor's. If you're new to this role, I hope this book will be your guide, mentor and reference. If you're an old hand, I hope it will support you in the changes you face and add to your toolbox of skills.

You'll discover how successful supervisors approach their jobs and increase their value to their organisation and how they communicate and work effectively with others.

You'll find out how to find and foster winners, bring out the best in people and maximise productivity, build a great team, lead meetings and deal with the 'tough stuff' such as poor performance and performance appraisals. You'll also find out how to use a range of systematic tools and techniques to keep getting better, solve those annoying problems that plague every supervisor, keep your customers happy, and introduce change successfully.

If you need a quick hit on how to deal with a problem, a puzzle or a predicament, you'll find it in this book. It's filled with practical, easy-to-do ideas, explanations and tips for increasing your value to your employer, building your career and boosting your earning potential.

Kris Cole

ACKNOWLEDGEMENTS

I would like to thank Sue McCormick and Carla Marsh of Melbourne-based recruitment consultants Lonsdale Carlson, Rosemary Wallage from Sheridan and Donny Walford from Business SA (formerly the South Australian Employers Chamber) for their helpful suggestions and information, particularly relating to Chapter 4.

Thanks also go to Amy Irving in Edinburgh, Scotland, for her great translation of Robert Burns's poem *To a Mouse* in Chapter 14, and Jane Hemstritch of Accenture who many years ago posed the question 'Why do people behave as they do?' which sparked the research which led to much of the information in Chapter 2.

The material for this book was drawn from a number of sources including practising supervisors and managers, my own experience and many excellent books and journals. I have also drawn on the works and research of numerous scholars including W. Edwards Deming, Rosabeth Moss Kanter, Michael Beer, John Adair, Henry Mintzberg, Peter Drucker, Roy Gilbert, Jean Hall and Margaret Wheatley. Their findings and ideas on modern management thinking and how to bring out the best in people and work systems are peppered throughout this book.

I am grateful to Pat Evans of Pearson Education, for her continued support and whose idea this book was, and to Nella Soeterboek and her team of terrific editors who have been, as usual, a priviledge to work with.

ABOUT THE AUTHOR: KRIS COLE
BSc (Hons), Post Grad. Dip., CTO, FAICD, ASM, AFAHRI, MAITD

A n industrial psychologist and manufacturing technologist with more than 25 years of experience on five continents, Kris Cole works with leading organisations to help them strengthen their most powerful competitive weapon—their people.

Her seminars and presentations show employees how to lead, communicate, and work more successfully with their colleagues and customers, manage their time, and juggle their priorities more effectively so they can achieve their goals and help their organisations flourish. She offers proven and practical ways for people to bring out the best in themselves and each other.

Further information is available at http://www.bax.com.au.

WHAT OTHERS HAVE SAID:

■ Kris you were the highlight of our conference!

■ I got a lot of great practical ideas to put to immediate use! Thanks!

■ The course was phenomenal—interesting and very thought-provoking and I have taken some valuable ideas from it to implement immediately.

■ An excellent course of immense value presented to perfection. Thanks Kris.

■ This is the most direct, down to earth, and nitty gritty course I've ever attended.

■ Kris's approach has been the most realistic and easily applied to 'day to day' work life I have ever attended. I really appreciated the explanations on applying the many skills covered rather than just explaining what they are.

■ This course was the most interesting and professional I've ever attended.

■ Kris is *awesome!*

OTHER BOOKS BY KRIS COLE

Kris is considered Australia's best selling business author, with books in six languages. They include:

Supervision: The Theory and Practice of Fist Line Management, the Australian standard tertiary level text in front line management. 814 pages, Prentice Hall, Sydney, 1998 and 2000. This is the most up-to-date book available in this diverse and developing field. It provides both the practical information and the theoretical grounding needed to develop the technical, conceptual and interpersonal skills required to be a successful supervisor and front-line manager.

Make TIME: Practical Time Management that Really Works! 222 pages, Prentice Hall, Sydney, 2001. This is a no-nonsense guide to practical time management that will last a lifetime. Also available in Malaysian.

Crystal Clear Communication: Skills for Understanding and Being Understood, 314 pages, Prentice Hall, Sydney, 1993 and 2000. This book covers the essential techniques of successful communication and provides practical, hands-on information to put to use straight away. Also available in German, Manadarin and Bahasa Indonesian, and an Indian subcontinent edition.

Office Administration and Supervision, 250 pages, Prentice Hall, Sydney, 1992, with Barbara Hamilton. This text for new managers combines the theory of first-line management with practical applications and office-based case studies.

PART ONE

MANAGING YOURSELF

If you can't manage yourself you will never successfully manage others or the operations you are responsible for.

CHAPTER ONE

BE A PEAK PERFORMER
Personal skills for supervisors

Would it surprise you to learn that up to 70% of managers feel like 'frauds'? That is, deep down, they wonder if they are up to their job. *Am I qualified? Am I the sort of person others respect? Will people follow my lead? Am I quick-witted and knowledgeable enough to make effective decisions?* Developing your personal skills can go a long way to reducing self-doubts like these.

MINDSETS FOR SUCCESS

The way we operate is critical to our success. In part this comes from our training and life experiences. At the core of the way we operate, however, are our **mindsets**. These are the lenses through which we view our world and the crayons with which we colour it.

Mindsets set apart the 'best' from the merely 'good'. They are our beliefs, views and opinions about ourselves, others and the world around us. What do you believe about yourself? About other people? About the way 'things work'? Whatever you believe, it will silently guide your behaviour and shape your success.

Here are five mindsets that will help you succeed.

High self-esteem

What do you think of yourself? Are you capable? Kind? Deserving of respect and good things? Do you like yourself? If you do, you probably have a positive self-esteem. Without high self-esteem it's difficult to achieve anything. After all, if in our own minds we're more worthless than worthy, more timid than confident, more dislikeable than likeable, how can we ever succeed at anything? We need to believe in ourselves first.

A sense of self-worth gives us the confidence to tackle challenging tasks, learn new things and make mistakes along the way, and communicate and work effectively with others. In fact, our ability to supervise effectively hinges on our level of self-esteem.

Set challenging goals

Do you routinely establish goals for yourself? People who stretch themselves and test and expand their skills are more likely to be successful in whatever they're doing. Set challenging goals for yourself and extend yourself. If a goal is so big or far away that you have trouble accepting you can achieve it, break it down into smaller, more 'believable' stages.

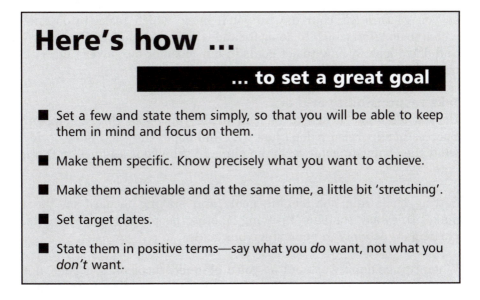

Here's how ...

... to set a great goal

■ Set a few and state them simply, so that you will be able to keep them in mind and focus on them.

■ Make them specific. Know precisely what you want to achieve.

■ Make them achievable and at the same time, a little bit 'stretching'.

■ Set target dates.

■ State them in positive terms—say what you *do* want, not what you *don't* want.

Set high standards

If we have high self-esteem, we naturally have high standards and expect the best from ourselves and for ourselves. Do you continually look for ways to do things better? Do you look for ways to challenge yourself and stretch your skills? You do if you expect the best from yourself.

Expecting the best also means that we expect those around us to perform, too. Who was the best supervisor you've ever had? Chances are it was someone who insisted on, and received, top performance. The best supervisors surround themselves with the best people. You can breed success all around you with positive expectations.

Focus

Staying focussed on our goals brings us closer to reaching them, step by step. Goals act as our guidepost, channelling our action and attention to what's important. The more we concentrate on them, the more likely we are to achieve them.

When we run into problems, focusing on our goal helps us overcome them. When we have too much on our plate, we can decide what to do based on our goals. When we have a decision to make, we can refer to our goals.

If we don't stay focused on our goals, our efforts and energies will be aimless and likely to achieve little. Keep your goals constantly in mind as you go through your day so you'll know which tasks to do now, which to do later, which to delegate and which to 'dump'. In Chapters 3 and 6, we look at how to set goals in our jobs, for ourselves and with our teams.

Take responsibility and act

Do you *wait* for things to happen or do you *make* things happen? Successful supervisors don't just wait and hope. They act! They decide what they want to achieve, make plans to achieve it and act on those plans.

Setting clear and challenging goals and staying focused on them makes this easy. Instead of relying on other people or random events, participate actively in achieving your goals.

When things don't work out as you'd planned, focus on solutions, not problems. Don't complain about the circumstances or people that caused the unwanted to happen, don't make excuses or 'give up and go home'. See what you can do about it. Focus on things you can influence or control, not on things you can't affect, such as the economy, senior management's decisions or a competitor's activities. Focusing on the former gives us power and energy; focusing on the latter drains it.

BOOSTING YOUR PERSONAL PRODUCTIVITY

The way we approach things makes all the difference. The latest psychological research into personal productivity confirms this. How we approach things underpins how much we achieve and how easily we achieve it. Here are three approaches you can adopt to support your mindsets for success.

4

Checklist for success

☐ Build your self-esteem.

☐ Set high standards and expect the best.

☐ Adopt a 'Can do!' approach and have faith you'll succeed.

☐ Keep extending your skills.

☐ Be a habitual goal setter and action planner.

☐ Stay focused on your goals.

☐ Take responsibility for making things happen.

☐ When things go wrong, see what you can do to put them right.

☐ Treat mistakes, your own and others', as learning opportunities.

☐ Look towards the future, not the past, and find ways to fix problems.

Enjoy what you do

Have you ever noticed that the jobs you like the best are the ones you do first—and best? If you really enjoy something, time seems to stand still. Wouldn't it be nice if that applied to 100% of everyone's job—we'd never have to worry about performance management, motivation or job satisfaction again!

Unfortunately we can't always do *only* what we like! Everyone has parts of their job they could do without. Does this give us an excuse to avoid the jobs we don't enjoy? No! It means we need to change our approach.

Do things because you **want to,** *not because you* **have to**

Instead of saying *'Ugh, I* hate *this!'* and doing something half-heartedly, resentfully, hurriedly or superficially, we can say *'I* want *to get this done because…'* It might be to get it out of the way, to allow you to make progress towards something that is important to you or to set a good example for your team.

Here's how ...

... to get the right approach

Instead of saying:	Say:
I have to work on this report.	I want to work on this report so I'm not forced to do it in a last-minute panic.
I've got to get this admin. done.	I want to spend an hour on my admin. so I don't fall behind.
It's time for performance appraisals. I hate them!	I want to use this year's appraisals as a way to strengthen relationships with my team and come to a clear understanding of what we're trying to achieve.
I suppose I should analyse these figures.	I'd like to analyse these figures to see if they highlight any problems or opportunities.
I have to speak to Sam about the meeting. I'm dreading it.	I need to speak to Sam about the meeting. I'll think of a way to make this discussion go smoothly.
A mediocre outcome.	**Result** An outcome of excellence.

Take a break and have some fun

Do you work hard all day? Try taking a break every once in a while to relax or do something you enjoy. Find ways to bring fun into your work, too. Breaks and fun help revitalise our brains, energy levels and thinking processes. Laughter helps us relax and improves our creativity while humour helps us lose ourselves in what we're doing.

Rest and reflect

Rest and reflection are crucial to productivity. Some of the most productive public figures took time to rest. Winston Churchill, for example, took one long nap almost every day, even during World War II. Albert Einstein 'discovered' the theory of relativity while daydreaming in a meadow. You can't work well when you're tired and you can't come up with new ideas if you have no mental room for them.

Exercise for energy

Do you wake up tired or full of energy? If you feel energetic, you'll have a go at tasks you might otherwise put in the 'too hard' basket. A sense of wellbeing can bolster productivity.

If you feel you could do with more energy to tackle those tough tasks, try a dose of regular exercise. We are in a better mood and think faster during and after exercise than at other times. Exercise increases levels of hormones called *endorphins*, which produce a sensation of euphoria, and *cortisone*, which wakes us up. These changes can help us get more done.

Be mindful not mindless

Do you ever feel you're in a rut with your job, that it's just the same old thing, day after day? Psychologist Ellen Langer of Harvard University calls this kind of rigid, automatic thinking *mindlessness*. We just go through the motions, blind to opportunities and solutions to recurring problems and hassles. We give up and never move forward.

Mindfulness, on the other hand, means keeping our goals in sight and our eyes open. This allows us to see the novel in the familiar and take a flexible and creative approach that turns stumbling blocks to building blocks. It helps us find solutions to almost anything. It encourages us constantly to examine what we're doing to find ways to do it better, differently, more efficiently, more easily, more quickly. How can I streamline this? How can I add more value?

Know where you're headed and be flexible on how to get there

Psychologists have found that goal setting increases productivity in terms of both quality and quantity more than any other technique, including pay increases! If you want to accomplish anything, set yourself a clear and challenging goal. Aiming for easy or vague goals will do little for your productivity. Make them important and worthwhile, too, so that you will be committed to them. Then chart your course with action plans.

Use these action plans to guide you, not rule you. Blind pursuit of an action plan can be counterproductive since the initial course you set to reach a goal may not turn out to be the most fruitful. Be mindful and keep an open mind. Goal-governed supervisors, for example, follow procedure to the letter, even if the procedure is cumbersome and even if it moves them away from their ultimate goal. Flexible supervisors listen and think.

Checklist for success

☐ Your mindsets are the building blocks with which you construct your world. Make sure they support you.

☐ Enjoy what you do. This will help you avoid procrastination, lack of satisfaction, mediocrity and apathy.

☐ Do things because you *want* to, even if it's only to get them out of the way.

☐ Exercise for stamina, strength and suppleness, to increase your self-confidence and self-esteem, to improve your mood and to reduce your stress levels.

☐ Commit to your aims and keep your eyes open for the best way to achieve them.

PROJECTING A PROFESSIONAL IMAGE

The impression others have of you can advance your career or curb it. With a bit of thought and effort, you can come across to others as positive and professional in the way you look and sound, and in the reputation you develop for integrity, 'delivering the goods' and 'doing the right thing', and for being open, honest and considerate.

Visual: look the part

Yes, the way we look does count. We need to know how to do the job and *look* like we can do it.

Dress for success

This means dressing in the manner considered appropriate in your organisation or for the job to which you aspire. Follow your organisation's expectations regarding dress: Is it stylish or conservative? Flashy or subdued? Casual, smart casual or 'corporate'?

Don't dress as if you're going to a disco if you want to be taken seriously. Buy a good set of basics and dress to suit your job's requirements, your personality and your body shape.

Stand tall
Your body language speaks volumes. Whether they're conscious of it or not, people read it and draw conclusions based on it. If you want those conclusions to be positive, mind your body language.

To look authoritative, sit or stand straight and pull your shoulders back and your stomach in. Cowering body language, with a caved-in chest, slouched back and hanging head, makes a poor impression. You'll look meek and timid and your professional image will be ruined.

Verbal: sound the part
How you look is a large part of your professional packaging. How you sound rounds it off.

Listen to yourself!
Nasal, whining, raspy, harsh or high-pitched voices detract from our professionalism. Clear, brisk, to the point, matter of fact voices sound more authoritative and confident.

Here's how ...

... to look and sound professional and confident

- See that your facial expression and other body language accurately reflect your feelings and what you are saying.

- Make appropriate eye contact and keep your hand movements open, emphasising key points.

- Keep your voice steady, clear and firm, neither too loud nor too soft.

- Avoid awkward hesitations and keep a steady, even pace in the way you speak.

- Slow down to sound more thoughtful and serious.

- Choose your words carefully.

- Pause before significant points so that people will take more notice of what you're about to say.

- Speak clearly.

- Use people's names.

Do you have an upward inflection? Overdoing the rising tone at the end of sentences, as if you're asking a question, makes you sound uncertain and insecure. To sound stronger and more convincing, go for a 70% to 80% falling inflection at the end of sentences.

Use positive words

Look at the phrases in the box below. Which would you rather hear? Which would attract your cooperation? It's pretty clear that the more positive words and phrases we use, the more people will take our message on board. If you can't make them positive, at least make them neutral.

Here's how ...

... to turn negatives into positives

Negative phrases	Positive phrases
You'll have to ...	I'll need you to ... so that ...
You never ...	How about ...?
You're not listening.	Let me run through that again.
No worries!	That's terrific; It's a pleasure.
What's the problem?	How can I help?

Be objective

If you want to sound more mature and level-headed, don't exaggerate or be overly critical. Compare the negative and disapproving with the more balanced and composed ways of saying the same thing in the box on the next page. Which would you rather hear?

Use specific and strong words

Why say 'I'll send it' when you could be more specific by saying 'I'll courier it' or 'I'll fax it'? Why say 'I'll contact you soon' when you could say 'I'll telephone you on Monday' or 'I'll e-mail you tomorrow'? Whenever you can, use precise words that say exactly what will happen. People won't need to guess, reach their own conclusions or

Here's how ...

... to turn criticisms into observations

Critical phrases	Objective phrases
You're wrong.	I see it differently.
These figures are rubbish!	I need to be clear about how these figures were arrived at.
This new guy has no idea!	We'll need to spend some time with Paul to help him understand how we do things.

assume what you will do. Accuracy increases people's 'comfort level' with you.

Here are some weak words:

may	could	might
possibly	probably	seems to

Here are some weak phrases:

Appears to be ...	That should be okay.
I'll do my best, but ...	I'll see what I can do.

If you water down your message with weak words and phrases like these, so will others.

Use strong and definite words. Instead of saying *'I'll try to have it for you by Friday'* say *'I'll have it for you by Friday'*, if that's what you mean. That's how it will be heard anyway. Qualifications weaken your message and people will ignore your verbal 'escape routes'.

Actions: do things 'right'
Here are six ways to present a positive image:

1. *Create winning teams.* Recruit high-calibre people, train them well and support their efforts. Generate enthusiasm, enhance

employees' self-esteem, and set and achieve realistic yet challenging goals.

2. *Develop a reputation as reliable and competent.* Deliver the goods, complete projects successfully, understand your industry and your organisation, manage people well and 'talk sense'. People will come to know they can rely on you.

3. *Communicate openly, honestly and tactfully.* An important part of a professional image is establishing a reputation for reliable and straightforward communication balanced with consideration for others. People will want to work with you.

4. *Be associated with success.* Have plans to improve things and discuss them with others. Give credit where credit is due and, without 'blowing your own trumpet', ensure that others know about your achievements. Make your team's successes known and talked about throughout the organisation and avoid empty publicity that you cannot back up with solid achievement.

5. *Build networks.* Try to be in the right place at the right time and build mutually supportive relationships. Demonstrate, by word and deed, your loyalty and commitment to your job, your department, your organisation and your customers. Being well known and considered trustworthy enthusiastic and dedicated is an important part of your professional image.

6. *Act the part.* Make sure your attitude is generally positive. Blend your personal style with your organisation's culture so it is clear to others that you belong in your job.

Of course, the most professional package in the world will soon crumble if it isn't backed up by professional behaviour and the ability to get results.

Talk about what you do
Don't expect people to recognise what a great job you and your team are doing if you don't mention it. Keep your manager posted on your progress and what you've accomplished. Without boasting, let others know about what you do, what projects you're working on, what you've achieved and how the organisation benefits. Keep it objective and factual to avoid bragging. If you 'hide your light', no one may think to look for it.

Do you feel uncomfortable telling others about your achievements? Here are some ideas to project a positive image without becoming boring or developing a reputation as a braggart.

■ Schedule a meeting every few weeks to update your manager on your work, what you've accomplished, what problems you have resolved or are working on and generally how things are going. Be objective and factual.

■ Aim to come up with one good idea a month to present to your manager. It doesn't have to be anything major. How can you serve customers better, smooth out the workflow, create a motivating atmosphere? If one a month seems too many or too few, adjust your target.

■ Prepare a summary to share with others about what you learned on a seminar or workshop you attended or from an article or book you've read. Put what you've learned into practice and let your manager know how well it worked.

Keep your promises, honour your commitments
Honouring your commitments builds trust; we can't operate effectively if others don't trust us. You'll do what you've said you'd do easily if you maintain the type of *To Do* list suggested in Chapter 3.

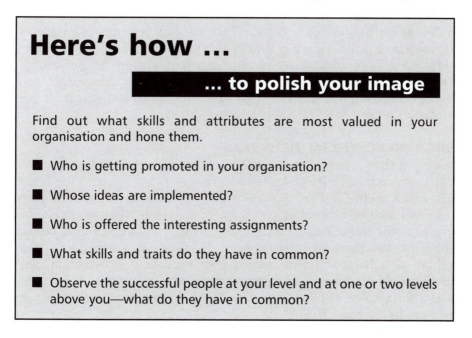

Here's how ...

... to polish your image

Find out what skills and attributes are most valued in your organisation and hone them.

■ Who is getting promoted in your organisation?

■ Whose ideas are implemented?

■ Who is offered the interesting assignments?

■ What skills and traits do they have in common?

■ Observe the successful people at your level and at one or two levels above you—what do they have in common?

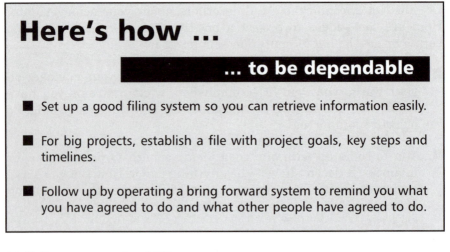

Here's how ...

... to be dependable

■ Set up a good filing system so you can retrieve information easily.

■ For big projects, establish a file with project goals, key steps and timelines.

■ Follow up by operating a bring forward system to remind you what you have agreed to do and what other people have agreed to do.

Polish your people skills

No one can accomplish much without working with others. The skills of working effectively with others are critical to just about everyone's career success. We look at this in detail in Chapter 2.

Are you a team player? Do you sort out your differences and work cooperatively with others in your team and with your colleagues? Do you support people without being asked, pass on information and ideas and work to the best of your ability, not for your own glory but for the benefit of the team? Do you respect other team members' different working styles and needs? Do you find out what information is important to others, what they're thinking about, what information they need from you and how and when it should be presented? Developing this kind of understanding helps you get things done and make things happen. Do you need to do any of these more than you already are?

BUILDING BENEFICIAL NETWORKS

We know that managers who are promoted often **network** more than twice as much as those promoted at 'average' rates. Networking is not just about seeing and being seen or petty politicking. A network is an informal web of relationships inside and outside your organisation you can call on for help, information, advice and support and extend the same to others in your network. It is a way of expanding your sphere of influence and increasing your sources of information. The more people you know and come together with, the more information you will have access to and the more 'behind the scenes' influence you will gradually come to hold.

Here's how ...

... to breed loyalty

- Communicate clearly and honestly.

- Be fair, tell the truth, and keep your promises.

- Be considerate, empathic and sincere.

- Remember that politeness is contagious.

- Deliver what you promise and honour your commitments.

- Remember the little things.

- Clarify expectations.

- Give lots of honest and helpful feedback.

- Build people's sense of self-esteem, dignity and self-worth, and let them know their value to the organisation.

- Respect and value differences in working styles and life experiences.

- Be a great listener.

- Accommodate people's personal needs whenever possible to encourage work–life balance.

- Let people do some personal 'stuff' at work once in a while.

- Reward talent.

- Show confidence in employees' abilities.

- Create a working environment that people find comfortable and energising.

- Praise more than you criticise so people don't think only mistakes get them noticed.

- Be loyal.

- Be willing to protect and save face for people. Be discrete and maintain confidences.

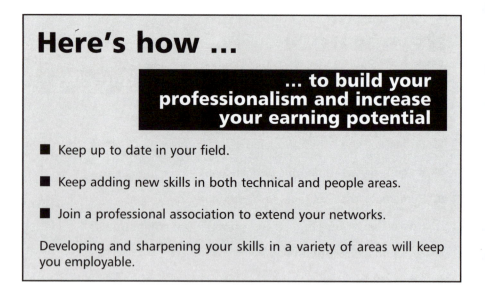

Interacting formally and informally with people inside and outside your organisation is part of networking. Being active in service clubs, social clubs, industry groups and other special-interest groups related to your work and interests are important channels of networking. Attending seminars and conferences and generally getting out and about and putting yourself, your industry and your organisation forward in a good light is also part of networking.

Find a mentor

Wouldn't it be nice to have a knowledgeable and experienced person 'show you the ropes', teach you, encourage you, help you learn from your mistakes, advise you on career options and fill you in on office politics? People who do this are called **mentors**. They are usually older, more experienced people higher up in the organisation who take an interest in you and your career. Although they are often in the same organisation, they are not necessarily your direct manager or even from your department. Wherever they are and whoever they are, they can provide help, advice and support as you travel along your career path.

Mentors usually choose the people they will guide, so if you notice a more senior manager spending time with you and offering advice, listen carefully!

Did you know ...

In *The Odyssey*, Homer tells us about Odysseus, who was leaving for the siege of Troy in 1194 BC. He wanted to make sure his son, Telemachus, would be well looked after, so he asked a friend to care for the boy and teach him, advise him and be his friend. The name of Telemachus's guide was Mentor.

SURVIVING ORGANISATIONAL POLITICS

Wherever people come together, politics will occur as individuals jostle for their place in the pecking order, for influence and for respect. In most organisations, politics affect just about everyone. In some organisations people politic so much there isn't a lot of time left for work!

Managers at every level probably need to participate in organisation politics to some degree. Those who overdo it, though, usually lose out eventually. Politicking, without the underlying management and technical skills, abilities and values to support it, is not enough in most modern organisations.

While you don't want to 'play politics' so much that it becomes counterproductive, you do need to 'play' a little. Manage your image in a positive way, blend in with and contribute to the organisation's culture, recognise who has formal and informal power and influence and network with them. Manage your boss and find out who to 'stay away from' and whose opinions you should listen to most carefully.

Fit in

People's beliefs, values, ways of working and assumptions about their industry, marketplace and customers make up an organisation's **culture** and **norms** (see Chapter 8 for more information on culture and norms). These are the unwritten, unstated codes of behaviour and attitudes that prescribe the 'rules' of 'how we do things around here' and what things mean. They have a strong influence on the way organisations operate as well as on their morale and effectiveness. If you ignore them, you will be 'punished' and pressured to conform.

If you want to be seen to 'fit in' and operate effectively, know the rules and taboos of your organisation's walk, talk, dress and manner, and observe them.

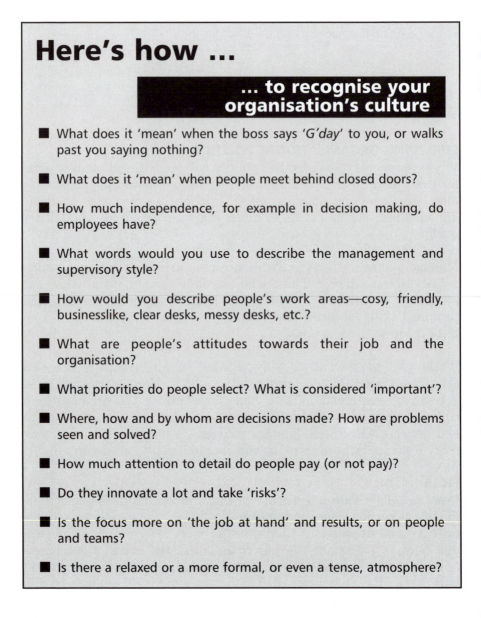

Here's how ...

... to recognise your organisation's culture

- What does it 'mean' when the boss says *'G'day'* to you, or walks past you saying nothing?

- What does it 'mean' when people meet behind closed doors?

- How much independence, for example in decision making, do employees have?

- What words would you use to describe the management and supervisory style?

- How would you describe people's work areas—cosy, friendly, businesslike, clear desks, messy desks, etc.?

- What are people's attitudes towards their job and the organisation?

- What priorities do people select? What is considered 'important'?

- Where, how and by whom are decisions made? How are problems seen and solved?

- How much attention to detail do people pay (or not pay)?

- Do they innovate a lot and take 'risks'?

- Is the focus more on 'the job at hand' and results, or on people and teams?

- Is there a relaxed or a more formal, or even a tense, atmosphere?

Here's how ...

... to recognise your organisation's norms

- What behaviours are rewarded and respected? Which are disapproved of?

- How do people treat external customers? Internal customers? Each other?

- What is the work ethic? For example, is it a 'She'll be right!' or a 'Get it right' approach? How hard do people work?

- How much fun do people have while they're working?

- Do they socialise at all? What do people do at breaks and for lunch?

- What time do people arrive for and leave work?

- How formally or informally do they dress?

- What style of language do they use?

- Do people take 'sickies'?

- What are the attitudes and practices regarding health, safety, equal opportunity and social responsibility?

Know the subcultures

Just as your entire organisation has norms, so each department has its own variation on these norms, making each one that little bit different from the others. These are the common language, dress, rituals, 'hangouts' and performance expectations of a work team. Make sure your work team develops norms that support, not sabotage, your department's performance. Your team members will take their cue from you, their leader.

Get to know the norms of the departments you work a lot with too: which departments are the most and least influential, who is in the 'inner circle' and who is excluded from it, their pace of work and so on. Observe and find out what makes one group different from another so you can overcome any barriers you might find when trying to deal with different work groups. The more you know about how the different departments in your organisation operate, the more effectively you will be able to work with them.

Building a power base

You've seen an organisation chart—those boxes showing who does what and reports to whom. That's the formal organisation. The 'real' organisation may be similar, or very different. This is the informal organisation, or power and influence hierarchy.

Power gives you some control over the behaviour of others. It can 'get you what you want'. **Influence** is another matter. The boss's secretary may have little formal power but tremendous influence (or *informal power*). You might have influence because of your expertise in certain key areas or your dynamic, articulate personality.

Are you politically astute enough to know who holds influence and power in your organisation? Do you include them in your networks? To find out who actually has power and influence, you need to read between the lines of your formal organisation chart. Who generates ideas? Who can convince others when no one else can? Whose opinion counts? Who are the informal, unofficial leaders who mould people's opinions and set the pace and the trends? What are the important networks and cliques? Who socialises with whom? Who recruited whom? Who trained whom?

Career tip

Follow the **boomerang principle.**
Showing respect (not fawning or crawling) to others will encourage them to respect you in return.

Here's how ...

... to identify power

■ *Formal power* Based on the organisation chart. When you feel you 'should' do something because 'the boss says so', you are responding to formal power.

■ *Reward power* Based on a person's ability to distribute something of value: pay increases, promotion, positive performance appraisals, overtime, interesting work assignments, friendliness, acceptance, praise and so on. When you do something, whether it's for your manager, another supervisor or an employee, in the hope of gaining something in return, you are responding to reward power.

■ *Coercive power* Based on fear and someone's ability to punish. If you do something in order to avoid an unpleasant outcome—for example, withholding of overtime, termination of employment, or criticism—you are responding to coercive power. Again, the source of the unpleasant outcome may be your manager, another supervisor or an employee.

■ *Expert power* Based on someone's special skills and knowledge, usually gained through study and experience and their 'track record'. When you do something because you assume the other person—a manager, another supervisor or an employee—'knows best', expert power is influencing you.

■ *Referent power* Based on the goodwill, liking and respect that someone has earned due to their personal traits—that special something in our personality that attracts followers. When you do something because you want to be supportive or cooperative towards someone you like, whether this is a manager, another supervisor or an employee, their referent power is influencing you.

■ *Proximity power* Based on the interesting information and knowledge a person has access to and can share with others. When you do something for someone, a manager, another supervisor or an employee, who has relatives, friends or associates 'in high places' and you hope it will get back to them, you are responding to their proximity power.

Extend your personal power

Without power and influence, you will be outmanoeuvred, overlooked and overridden. Where will it come from? From the formal power of your position—your spot in the organisation chart? Not likely. Today's employees aren't as willing as earlier generations of employees to grant automatic respect and obedience to a person simply because of their job title.

Your ability to get things done—your power and influence—is far more likely to come from within yourself. People will give you respect because of what you know, who you are and, to some extent, who you know.

Your position as a supervisor does, of course, include formal power and, with it, some coercive and reward power. In most organisations, people listen when their supervisor speaks and comply with their requests.

Influence, however, is the more important and reliable power base. It rests on the personal qualities, attributes and knowledge that people respect you for having. Qualities such as self-respect and respect for others, integrity, honesty, trustworthiness and strength of personal vision and values are particularly important in building your personal power.

Expertise attracts both admiration and respect. Much of your authority will come from job knowledge. You should ideally have some expertise in the technology and work of your group. You need to understand the organisation as a whole and how it operates. Knowing what needs to be done and where, when, why and how it should be done will earn you a great deal of personal respect. Build your expert power through training and experience.

Part of your referent power comes from your ability to build cooperative and supportive working relationships. Taking the time and trouble to develop sound relationships with others will increase your power base. Rapport, good working relationships, mutual respect, friendship and admiration all play a part. So do integrity and trust-worthiness. Acting consistently to a clear set of standards and personal guidelines that fit in with and support the organisation's standards, and not deviating from them, is very powerful and attractive to others.

Here's how ...

... to build your personal power

Sixty successful first-line supervisors from a variety of industries all over Australia and New Zealand were asked how they built their personal power. Here's what they said:

- Ask rather than tell.
- Show respect for your staff: treat each of them as a VIP.
- Walk your talk—practise what you preach.
- Be informed and share your information with your staff.
- Be approachable.
- Be 'fair dinkum'—know that loyalty is a two-way street.
- Be honest and sincere in your feedback.
- Make it happen!
- Acknowledge good effort and praise good work.
- Build and be part of high-performing teams.
- Acknowledge and assist the achievement of both personal and team goals.
- Demonstrate trust in your staff.
- Delegate increasingly larger responsibilities.
- Show empathy with your staff's personal problems.
- Hire good people.
- Give adequate training.
- Remember the social side of work—have some fun!
- Keep equipment up to scratch.
- Make sure staff uniforms look good, so that people feel good.
- Maintain adequate staffing levels.
- Know your staff's strengths and weaknesses, likes and dislikes.
- Respect yourself and others.

Proximity to powerful people also increases your power base. Have you included influential people in your organisation and industry association in your networks? Do you pass on reasons behind a decision or inside information about 'behind the scenes' goings-on to your work team (providing this doesn't breach any confidences)? Who you know can also extend your power base.

CHAPTER TWO

WORK WITH OTHERS TO ENSURE SUCCESS
Developing effective working relationships

Supervisors who don't work well with others don't go far. More than ever before, the ability to engage the commitment and co-operation of colleagues is vital to our effectiveness and success. In fact, it could be our most important asset.

To work effectively with others we need a basic understanding of 'what makes people tick'. But before we can understand others we need to understand ourselves. Knowing our values, strengths and limitations is the foundation of our ability to understand others and develop satisfying relationships with them.

WHAT DRIVES YOU?

What do you believe is important and worthwhile? What are you willing to stand up for and strive for? Knowing and acting on your values and making decisions based on them builds your integrity and self-respect. It helps you to act consistently and earns the respect of others.

Do you walk your talk?

Have you ever known anyone who says one thing and does another? A supervisor might say: *'I believe in participation and I really value the contributions of my work team'*. If this same supervisor fails to listen to team members' ideas or suggestions, their behaviour indicates a belief more like: *'People don't have any ideas worth listening to or valuable contributions to make'*. Or a supervisor might say: *'My team is great; I've taught them all they know'*, yet constantly check up on them and avoid delegating work. Their actions say they really believe: *'I can't really trust my people and need to keep an eye on them'*.

Here's how ...

... to find out what you value

Look at the values below. Circle those you believe are most important. From these, select the most important 10. Then select the most important five.

Being accepted	Looking good	Having security
Giving and receiving affection	Behaving in a professional manner	Winning
	Having lots of material 'things'	Being polite
Helping others	Being responsible for others	Loyalty
Being knowledgeable	Learning new skills	Having fun
Physical fitness	Peaceful relationships with others	Justice
Having lots of friends	Being generous	Being honest
Being in control	Feeling important	Being alone
Working hard	Following a religion	Being respected
Following tradition	Being relaxed and informal	Being on time
Saying what we think	Standing up for what we	Cooperation
Feeling fulfilled	believe in	Commitment
Showing compassion	Taking risks	Participating
Conserving resources	Being logical	Humour
Being enterprising	Dignity	Competition
Health	Excellence	Duty
Truth	Integrity	Initiative
Trust	Courage	Harmony
Quality	Beauty	Tenacity
Wealth	Perfection	Efficiency
Consideration	Optimism	Enterprise
Intelligence	Reliability	Creativity
Tolerance	Discipline	Having authority
Doing our duty	Having freedom of action	Talent

These are the top five values by which you live your life. They describe what you hold to be important, true and worthwhile. They silently steer your actions and choices and shape your beliefs. The next time you have a tough decision to make, use your top five values to guide you.

Are these supervisors hypocrites? Possibly. More often, a conflict between what people say and what they do is due to one of three other reasons. They may really value participation and *want* to believe that people are reliable, but their core beliefs, on which they base their day-to-day behaviour, haven't caught up with their values yet. Or these values might be part of their organisation's values and culture but not their own, and they feel pressured to claim they believe in these things when they really don't. A third possibility is that another, stronger, value overrides the value in question; for example, a supervisor in an organisation that punishes mistakes might value participation but values staying out of trouble more, and doesn't want to take the risk of involving the team. Either way, what they say and what they actually do don't match. They don't 'walk their talk'.

When people say one thing and do another they are difficult to work with. Do you walk your talk? If you don't, you'll lose credibility with your work group and colleagues and you'll fail to develop effective working relationships.

People are happiest and work best when their own values and the values of the organisation they work for match. That way, it's easy to practise what you preach. A strong sense of your own values and your organisation's values will help you act with integrity and consistency and earn the respect and confidence of others. This is central to working well with others.

HOW DO YOU WORK BEST?
If you understand your working style, you will be able to select working situations where you can use your strengths, avoid those that will highlight your weaknesses and choose others to build areas you need to strengthen. You will also know how to request information from others (e.g. verbally or in writing, with or without a lot of supporting detail). Here are some questions about your own working style you should know the answers to. (We'll look at working styles again later in this chapter.)

■ Do you prefer to work with people or do you work best with things or perhaps ideas? If you like working with people, is it in a team situation or as a leader, a colleague or follower? Do you prefer to be mutually interdependent or to work independently but with people nearby?

■ How do you best grasp information—when you read it or when someone tells you about it? How do you learn and clarify your thoughts best—by listening, doing, thinking about it or talking things through out loud?

■ What kind of environment do you perform best in—a highly structured and predictable one or a hectic and unpredictable one? Do you work best in a large or a small organisation? Are you more comfortable in hierarchies or in informal, relaxed structures?

■ What skills do you need to improve? What skills do you need to acquire or strengthen? Where do you have no strengths, talents or skills? These are areas to stay away from! Don't waste time developing these, as you'll have little chance of becoming even mediocre.

Career tip

Work to your strengths.

WHY DO PEOPLE BEHAVE AS THEY DO?

Have you ever been puzzled or annoyed by another person's behaviour? Understanding where people are 'coming from' and why they do the things they do makes it easier to develop effective working relationships.

Here are four reasons people behave as they do:

1. It serves some purpose for them.

2. They don't know any other way.

3. Maybe they don't.

4. That's the way they're wired.

Let's look at each of them in turn.

To achieve a goal

As we see in Chapter 7, much of our behaviour is driven by *needs*—for power, friendship, security or a sense of achievement, for example. Think of a need as a craving that we long to satisfy. We'll do whatever we think will satisfy it.

For example, if we're hungry we are motivated to eat. We might go out to buy some food for a quick snack, cook a big meal or even steal some food. We will take the action that seems most likely to achieve our goal (food) with the most positive, or fewest negative, consequences. Similarly, if we crave the respect of others, many of our actions will be designed to win this respect; for example, we might help out a workmate, teach someone how to do something or offer what we believe is useful advice.

Sometimes this is a conscious process, although more often it is completely unconscious. People do things to achieve goals that even they are often unaware of.

It's a habit

We do a lot of things through habit. If a behaviour seems to get the result we're after, we keep it. If we repeatedly do the same thing many times, eventually we do it automatically and without even realising we're doing it. We have developed a habit. If circumstances change, it may well be that other behaviours would work better, yet we stick to the 'tried and true' one that has always worked in the past.

Have you ever known someone continually to do something, even when it is obvious to those around them that it isn't working and it would be more effective to do something else? This person is the victim of their habits. When we cling to our habits we never learn better ways to achieve our goals. Do you do anything out of habit when there might be better ways to achieve your goals? Have your habits prevented you from trying out other, possibly better, ways?

It's really a mirror

We often see others through our own eyes. In other words, we interpret other people's behaviour in light of our own. This says more about us than the other person.

Listen to Joe, a retail supervisor from Fremantle:

I have an employee who is driving me nuts! He insists on taking his mid-morning break, no matter how busy things are. That's nothing but selfish, and if there's one thing I can't abide, it's selfishness.

How is this employee's timekeeping?

Great—in fact, he always gets in first, opens up, and puts the kettle on.

How is he at his other duties?

First class—I trained him myself!

What about his other breaks?

He usually works straight through. It's just that he's so selfish about his mid-morning break. I'm going to have to speak to him about it.

Fortunately for Joe, he saw the mirror in time.

I realised it's actually me who is being selfish in denying a top employee the one break of the day he really values.

Like many mothers, Joe's mother taught him not to be selfish. This made it hard for him to concede that he might be being selfish. When we have a characteristic we'd rather not own up to it's much easier to 'point the finger' at others.

Have you ever been incensed by another person's actions? Or have you ever been really drawn to someone? This is a sign that your psychic mirror was operating. You may have been seeing negative or positive qualities in someone else that you posses yourself but are reluctant to acknowledge. The next time someone really repels you or attracts you, look in the mirror first!

It's their character
The final reason people behave the way they do is simply because that's the way they are. What they do reflects their personality and working style.

We're not all alike. Everyone has different ways of operating and different inclinations, aptitudes and personalities. Are they bred (hard-wired) into us, trained into us (socialisation) or a bit of both? Fortunately, this elusive answer is more important to psychologists and brain scientists than to supervisors, so we'll move on!

If we can identify what these different ways of working and relating to others are, we can modify our approach to blend with theirs. This will reduce irritation and aggravation, help us handle people with sensitivity and help our teams thrive. In short, it will help us work successfully with others.

IDENTIFYING, APPRECIATING AND WORKING WITH
DIFFERENT WORKING STYLES

Knowing your own working style is important. Knowing the preferred working style of others is important too. If you know that, you can adapt your approach to others to make it easier to work with them.

Dealing with information

How do you prefer to receive information? Perhaps you prefer it in writing? Certainly, this is convenient and you can refer to it later, but what if your boss or employees prefer to listen or discuss, not read?

As we've seen, people tend to prefer to receive information either in writing or by talking it through. Some people want to talk it through first and have it backed up in writing to study later. Sticking rigidly to the medium *you* prefer will work well with some people but not those whose preferences are different.

Similarly, once we have information we deal with it in characteristic ways. Here are the four ways of taking information on board and dealing with it, along with some ideas on what type of work each lends itself to. This will help you present information and assign work to people in the most effective way.

Some people are *thinkers*: they need time to mull things over and come to grips with them. If you want them to take new information on board easily, present it to them clearly and logically and explain the overall concept. Assign them tasks involving facts and figures, research and analysis and try not to give them responsibility for implementing solutions.

Other people are *feelers* who see things and make decisions based on their personal values. When explaining things to them, make your values explicit so they can get a 'feel' for where you're coming from. Take care to make them feel supported and accepted and assign them tasks that allow them to work with people, organising them, harnessing their enthusiasm and building teams.

Using our intuition is the third way to work with information. *Intuitors* are good at using their imagination to come up with ideas. They enjoy playing around with concepts and theories; they see the 'big picture' easily but often miss the details. Their hunches are often correct. When introducing information to them, give them an idea of where you're headed, of your ultimate goal and vision. Assign them creative work and work involving long-term planning.

The final way of dealing with information is through our senses. *Sensors* are down-to-earth, energetic and hard-working, preferring action to words or ideas. They are practical people with a lot of common sense and are the first to 'roll up their sleeves' and 'get on with it' (often before thinking it through). Don't go into too much detail or 'fancy theory' when presenting information to them; be clear and to the point and focus on practicalities and results. Give them projects to 'get off the ground'; let them set things up, negotiate, troubleshoot and convert ideas into action.

Be flexible enough to offer information in other people's preferred mode. Find out how the people you work with want to receive and process information and, as much as you can, choose the method that suits each person best.

When's the best time?

When is the best time of day to communicate with you? Do you take information on board more readily in the mornings or later in the day? How about your boss, the members of your work group, your clients and the other supervisors you work with—when are the best times for them? To communicate for maximum effectiveness don't force your preferences on others: find out when they prefer to communicate.

Why do you do things?

Why do you exercise? Why do you work? What do you look for in a job?

Some people exercise to avoid getting fat, others so that they'll look terrific. Some people work to avoid the poorhouse, others to earn money to buy the things they want. Some people look for a job where they won't be bothered by rules and regulations, while others look for a job where their skills will be best used, where they will be working with people they like or where they'll learn a lot. In short, some people do things to *avoid* something unpleasant, others to *gain* something agreeable.

If you know whether people are *avoiders* of unpleasantness or *seekers* of pleasantness, you can fine-tune your messages and word your appeals for maximum persuasiveness.

What does it take to convince you?

Where does your proof come from? How do you know when something is 'right'—do you 'just know inside' or do you want to hear what others think?

If you're supervising people whose proof comes from inside, your compliments are largely redundant. Conversely, if they need other's opinions and you fail to compliment them, they won't be able to work at their best. Similarly, if you're trying to persuade people, you can appeal to their inner sense of rightness or show them how everyone else is 'coming on board', depending on how they're convinced.

Similarities or differences?

What do you see first—differences or similarities? How about those around you? If your boss or colleagues are *mismatchers*, don't go pointing out the similarities—highlight the differences if you want to get on the same wavelength. Don't be worried if they gloss over good points in a proposal and find the faults instead.

By the same token, when you're working with *matchers*, appreciate their positive approach and beware of their lack of skill in finding weak points and downsides.

Naturally, none of these working styles is 'either/or'. They are preferences, or inclinations. Think of them as two ends of a spectrum. Most people fall towards one end or towards the other. Know which end you gravitate towards and which end those you work with favour. Then tune your style to blend in with theirs to encourage good working relationships.

IDENTIFYING, APPRECIATING AND WORKING WITH DIFFERENT PERSONALITY STYLES

In your dealings with others, take their personality style into account too. Without wishing to 'pigeonhole' people, here are four main personality styles you can use to identify how people want to be treated. The more you meet their needs, the more willing they'll be to meet yours.

Task or people?

As we've seen, people can have primarily a *task* focus or a *people* focus. Some people just naturally attend to the job at hand as a priority, while others put people first.

Which do you focus on first—people or the task at hand? If your boss or colleagues are more task focused, get straight down to business; small talk will only irritate them. On the other hand, if they are 'people people' they will welcome a quick chat about families or the weekend before getting down to business.

Extroverts or introverts?

Similarly, some people focus their attention outwards, on the environment and people around them; they are *extroverts*, although they're not all outgoing. Others focus their attention inwards, on their own thoughts and feelings; they are *introverts*, although they're not all shy.

Four styles of personality

Figure 2.1 shows four key groupings of personality styles based on these two dimensions. Knowing people's basic personality styles makes it easier to work comfortably and effectively with them. As you read through Figure 2.1, think about who you know who fits these descriptions. (Most people won't fit perfectly but they'll fit one description better than others.) Which are you? Which is your boss? Which is each of your work group members? How about the other supervisors you work with?

Here are some hints on how to approach these four basic personality styles.

Dominant directors

- Give them all the respect they know they deserve!

- Be brief, efficient and to the point.

- Don't ramble.

- Not too many details—stick to 'the bottom line'.

- Provide recommendations or options for them to choose from.

- Update with brief status reports.

- Don't bluff.

Interacting socialisers

- Begin with 'How are you?'

- Explain the 'big picture'.

- Keep a fast pace.

- Don't bore them with detail.

Figure 2.1 Four personality styles

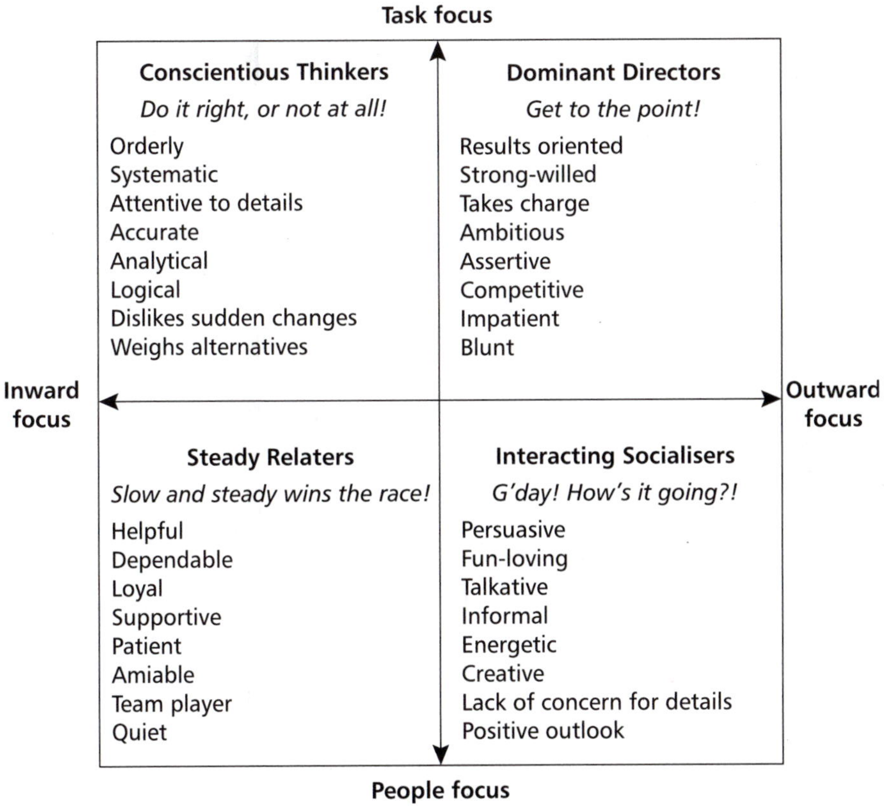

Task focus

Conscientious Thinkers	Dominant Directors
Do it right, or not at all!	*Get to the point!*
Orderly	Results oriented
Systematic	Strong-willed
Attentive to details	Takes charge
Accurate	Ambitious
Analytical	Assertive
Logical	Competitive
Dislikes sudden changes	Impatient
Weighs alternatives	Blunt

Inward focus ←——————————————→ Outward focus

Steady Relaters	Interacting Socialisers
Slow and steady wins the race!	*G'day! How's it going?!*
Helpful	Persuasive
Dependable	Fun-loving
Loyal	Talkative
Supportive	Informal
Patient	Energetic
Amiable	Creative
Team player	Lack of concern for details
Quiet	Positive outlook

People focus

- If they are a team member encourage them to plan and follow through.

- If they are your manager be enthusiastic about their ideas!

Steady relaters
- Focus on getting acquainted and building trust.

- Present information slowly and softly.

- Suggest rather than insist.

- Find ideas of common interest.

- Invite their opinion.

- Communicate progress often.

- Don't be pushy or abrupt.

35

Conscientious thinkers

- Be prepared and organised.

- Pause often to let them think through what you've said.

- Be professional and courteous.

- Don't get too personal.

- Have the facts at your fingertips to back up what you've said.

- Quote precedents and research.

- Follow procedure.

Checklist for success

☐ Know your values and stick to them.

☐ Understand what motivates you so you don't surprise yourself or others.

☐ Work to understand yourself so that you can understand others better.

☐ Work to your strengths and develop your other skill areas to increase your value to employers.

☐ Make the most of people's abilities and build cooperation by identifying and working with people's working styles.

☐ Are you accepting and tolerant of others? Don't play 'amateur psychologist'. Accept people for what they are and learn to work effectively with them.

☐ Know that people do the best they can with the skills they've got.

☐ Whenever someone really bugs you, take a good look in your 'psychic mirror'.

☐ Identify and work with people's basic personalities to maximise your effectiveness.

☐ Become familiar with the four personality styles so you can recognise them easily and work with people in the ways that will make them most appreciative of and cooperative towards you.

None of these personality styles or working styles is better or worse than the other. Each has its good points and pitfalls. Each contributes in important ways.

People's differences keep life interesting and help get things done.

Here's how ...

... to read the signs

The sign	What it says
Nodding the head	This woman is listening to me. This man agrees with me.
Scratching the neck or rubbing eyes and looking at the ceiling (if a woman) or floor (if a man)	This person may not be telling the truth.
Clenched hands	This person seems frustrated. (The higher the hands, the higher their frustration.)
Hand on cheek	This person seems interested in what I'm saying and is thinking it through.
Hand on cheek with thumb under chin	This person seems interested but has some doubts.
Picking off imaginary lint	This person may disagree with or disapprove of what I've said but doesn't want to say so.
Crossed arms and legs	This person seems to be tuning me out or filtering what I'm saying.

MANAGING YOUR BODY LANGUAGE
Body language may be silent, but it speaks volumes. If our words and our body language disagree, we lose credibility. In fact, if they're not in accord, people usually believe our body language over our words.

According to author and professor Ray Birdwhistell at Temple University in the USA, between 65% and 90% of every conversation is interpreted according to a person's body language. If you want to develop effective working relationships you need to be in charge of your body's signals so that they send the messages you intend. You need to talk your walk as well as walk your talk!

Stand for cooperation

When communicating with someone face to face, the way you sit or stand can open up or obstruct communication. There are three things to remember. First, to encourage cooperation, sit or stand at right angles or even side-by-side. This is less confrontational than facing someone directly. Second, it can be threatening when someone towers over you. So, as far as possible, sit or stand at the same level as others. This reduces possible sources of intimidation or discomfort and makes people more relaxed and responsive. Third, remember personal space: keep a businesslike distance between yourself and the other person. In a business setting, being closer than 'arm's length' makes most people feel uncomfortable and invaded.

Open up

Consider two people: one standing with their arms comfortably at their sides, facing towards you and looking at you; the other with crossed arms and legs, hunched shoulders, feet pointing away from you and chin down. Who looks more professional? Who would you rather talk to? Who would you open up to more?

The first person has open body language. It signals 'I am confident and I want to hear what you have to say'. The second person has closed body language that implies 'I'm nervous and uncertain and I'm closed to you, your information and your ideas.' When our bodies close up, our minds do too. Whether we're giving or gathering information, open body language makes us think better and look more credible.

Centre your attention

Face the person you're speaking to and listen with 'focused concentration'. Put your pen down and make the speaker and topic the centre of your attention. Put other things, including what you will say in reply and what you were doing, out of your mind and listen with your eyes as well as your ears. This builds bridges and presents a professional image. It helps the speaker get their point across and helps us hear it.

Lean slightly forward

This shows interest and involvement in the conversation. Don't lean too far forward though, or you'll find yourself invading the other person's space. Don't lean too far back either, because this is 'read' as being lacklustre and disinterested. What's the worst thing you can do? Lean far back in your chair, stretch your legs out and clasp your fingers behind your head; this sends messages of superiority, arrogance and egotism.

Make eye contact

Tune in to the amount of eye contact the other person uses and try to follow their lead. In European cultures eye contact is a sign of honesty and trustworthiness. It signals 'I'm listening, I'm interested and you can trust me' while looking away signals 'I'm hiding something'. Asian cultures place less importance on eye contact and in traditional Aboriginal culture, direct eye contact is considered disrespectful.

In any culture, too much eye contact can cause embarrassment and can be seen as an invasion of personal space. Even among high-eye-contact Europeans, making eye contact more than half the time makes people slightly uncomfortable. Nevertheless, don't underestimate the importance of eye contact in building trust and establishing effective working relationships.

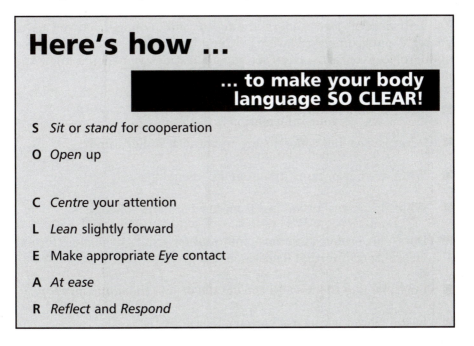

Here's how ...

... to make your body language SO CLEAR!

S *Sit* or *stand* for cooperation

O *Open* up

C *Centre* your attention

L *Lean* slightly forward

E Make appropriate *Eye* contact

A *At ease*

R *Reflect* and *Respond*

At ease

Are you a fidgeter? You'll look better if you're at ease. This means relaxed (comfortably still, not stiff) and balanced (not leaning at any extreme or awkward angles). Sit up straight and do not jiggle, tap feet or pencils or adjust clothing or hair. You'll look more professional, self-possessed and self-confident this way. It also improves communication and it's actually healthier.

Reflect and respond

Saying something that is unrelated or contradictory to what the speaker has been talking about can bring a discussion to a rapid and resentful halt. Appropriate responses, particularly building on and extending what the speaker has said, and **reflective listening** responses, show that we're following the other person's points (see below). This encourages them to continue and adds to our professionalism.

WORKING EFFECTIVELY WITH YOUR MANAGER

Do you think your boss is responsible for establishing and maintaining a good working relationship with you? Think again—the responsibility goes both ways. Managing your relationship with your boss is part of your job too. While it can take time and energy, it can increase your effectiveness in your job and save a lot of problems.

You will need a good understanding of your manager as well as of yourself, particularly regarding strengths, weaknesses, work styles and foremost concerns. Here are some questions you should know the answers to:

■ What is in her 'world'?

■ What issues and concerns are uppermost in her mind?

■ What are her organisational and personal goals?

■ What pressures are on her from her boss and colleagues?

■ Does she prefer to receive information through memos, formal meetings or informal discussions?

■ Does she like to know all the details or just the end result?

■ Is she more task focused or people oriented?

Knowing these things will help you fit in with your manager's working style and support him better. If you don't know the answers to these questions, you are flying blind and major misunderstandings are inevitable.

Find out about your boss's goals, problems and pressures. Try to put yourself in his shoes and pay attention to clues. Question him to find out what he expects from you; find ways to let him know what your own needs and expectations are. If your boss doesn't accept one of your recommendations or ideas, try to look at the situation from his point of view.

Meet regularly to keep your boss in the picture. Review progress since the last meeting, your team's results (using hard numbers and verifiable facts), problems you're working on, recommendations and actions that you think will enhance future results.

See yourself as your boss's partner in achieving results and meeting priorities. Just as you are dependent on your manager for help, guidance, resources and information, so your manager depends on you for help and cooperation. Accept her decisions and ideas and work to make them succeed.

Do what you're asked to do. If you disagree, explain why and offer an alternative. Before you do that check you've understood your boss's viewpoint by summarising it and highlight areas of agreement.

Don't expect your boss to be perfect—no one is. If you're unhappy with your boss's management style, suggest ways you could work better together. Don't focus on personal shortcomings but on specific behaviours. Describe them in objective not judgemental or critical terms. Say what you *do* want, not what you *don't* want and focus on the future and what you'd like to happen.

Use the information in the section above on identifying and appreciating working and personality styles to fit in with your boss's working styles and work in harmony with them. Observe her, see how she does things, notice what you do that goes down well and poorly.

Here are five other things bosses need from us:

1. Understanding of their jobs so we can help them achieve their goals.

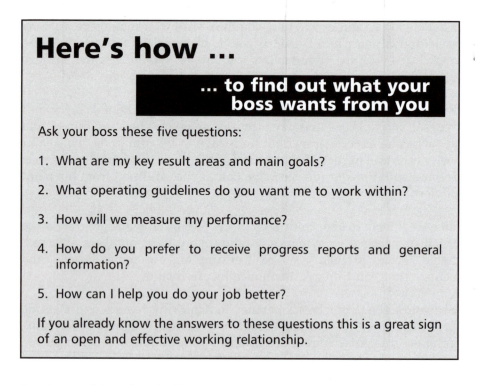

Here's how ...

... to find out what your boss wants from you

Ask your boss these five questions:

1. What are my key result areas and main goals?

2. What operating guidelines do you want me to work within?

3. How will we measure my performance?

4. How do you prefer to receive progress reports and general information?

5. How can I help you do your job better?

If you already know the answers to these questions this is a great sign of an open and effective working relationship.

2. Recognition that feedback is two-way. Give positive feedback, not insincere flattery, when they do something that warrants it. What's the difference between flattery and feedback? Feedback concerns things that are within a person's control and is usually about something they've done; flattery is about things people have little or no control over.

3. Mistakes are inevitable. When you make one, fix it. If it's serious and your boss needs to know, tell him. Take the facts with you and say what you've done or plan to do to put things right, or have one or two solutions ready to propose.

4. Take the initiative. Don't wait to be asked, or told, what to do.

5. Listen to any tips your manager passes on about how you can do your job better and put them into practice.

Ask for feedback
It's important to lubricate the communication channels, particularly when you're new in a job. If you don't know what you're doing well, it's hard to know what to keep repeating. Similarly, if you don't know

where you're falling short, it's hard to know where to focus your improvement efforts.

When you turn in work, check that it's what your manager wanted or expected and whether you could be doing anything differently. Ask; don't wait to be told. What am I doing well? What can I do to improve? What am I doing that I shouldn't be? What aren't I doing that I should be?

If there is room for improvement

Remember that when bosses criticise it's not easy for them either. Open your mind. Ask questions to find out how you can improve. Listen to the answer using the SO CLEAR body language described above and following the EARS formula. (See also Chapter 16.)

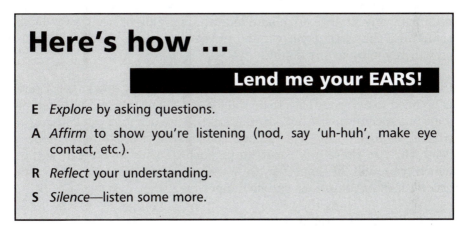

Here's how ...

Lend me your EARS!

E *Explore* by asking questions.

A *Affirm* to show you're listening (nod, say 'uh-huh', make eye contact, etc.).

R *Reflect* your understanding.

S *Silence*—listen some more.

Show that you've understood with **reflective listening**. This means repeating, in your own words, your understanding of what the other person has said or how they are feeling. If you don't understand fully, ask probing and clarifying questions and ask for examples. Keep your voice neutral and words and manner objective. Summarise the main points so that if you've misunderstood, your manager can clarify.

If you've been caught off-guard by unexpected criticism or you want to do some fact-finding, ask for time to consider the feedback and arrange to meet later. Once you have taken the feedback on board, you can assess what you need to do.

Explain yourself if appropriate, but don't make excuses, blame someone else or deny there is a problem. Take responsibility for doing something about it. Rather than lamely saying 'It won't happen again', explain what you'll do to prevent it or how you'll handle similar problems, and what you've learned from this. Say you appreciate the feedback.

Respect the chain of command

Most organisations have a *chain of command*, where one person reports to another person, who in turn reports to another. This is to prevent people from having more than one boss and from having to take directions from more than one person. This means that if your boss's boss, or anyone other than your direct supervisor, asks you to do a job, make sure you let your manager know. (See also Chapter 11.)

Receiving assignments

When you are on the receiving end of a work assignment, make sure you thoroughly understand what needs to be done. Ask questions to minimise any chance of misunderstanding and prevent you doing something that was never wanted in the first place. Clarify all areas on which you have any doubt.

Confirm your guidelines on timing, quality, quantity and so on. There is no need to ask your boss to do the job for you or to explain it step by step, but specific operating parameters will ensure that you both know what is required. How will you and your manager know you've done a good job? Are there any constraints, such as time or budget, within which you will be expected to work? Check these out and plan accordingly. Assumptions can be dangerous.

Have all the relevant people been made aware that you have been asked to carry out these instructions? Will you need to enlist the cooperation of others or temporarily acquire any special authority?

Be positive in your attitude and show, through your words as well as your actions, that you are willing to carry out the instruction.

GETTING YOUR IDEAS IMPLEMENTED

It goes without saying that your ideas need to be well thought out, practical and cost effective! But that isn't the end of the story. You can do a number of things to increase the odds that they will be accepted.

First, test them on a few people. This will help you gauge likely responses, concerns and questions, and allow you to prepare more thoroughly for your final proposal. You might also be able to incorporate others' ideas, allowing them to feel some ownership of it and respond more positively to it. Running your ideas by people first also provides a 'comfort level' with a proposal from having heard it before. Get your manager's input too.

Build support among people whose opinion is respected. Who will support you and who should you get on-side before formally putting forward your recommendations? In what order should you approach them to enlist their support? Who should you speak to face to face and who would prefer a memo? Who will want all the details and who will you interest by painting the 'big picture'?

Take into account how your ideas will be evaluated and who the decision makers will consult. A direct, formal approach to your immediate manager may not always be the best strategy. Perhaps it would be better to float the idea informally, over a coffee, say, with your manager or with someone else who has power and influence.

Prepare for opposition, too—sometimes we are so positive about our own ideas, we don't see potential opposition. Who is likely to oppose your ideas? In your previews with others, ask: If someone were to object to this idea, what do you think the objection might be?

Keep your eyes open to see how others in your organisation go about getting their ideas accepted and follow their example. Get any expertise you need, for instance help with costing your idea or developing marketing ideas.

When it's time to present your ideas, do so effectively:

- Explain your suggestion clearly; don't rush, waffle, stammer or weaken your ideas (It's *only* a thought, but ...; I *just* think ...).

- Write your proposal down clearly and persuasively and set it out well.

- Focus on what is important to the decision makers (bottom line, effect on morale or public image and so on) to encourage a positive response.

- If your boss is a slow or reluctant decision maker, try asking for a series of small decisions rather than one big one; for example, request to test the idea first.

45

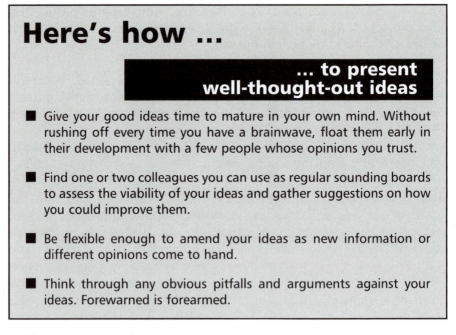

Here's how ...

... to present well-thought-out ideas

- Give your good ideas time to mature in your own mind. Without rushing off every time you have a brainwave, float them early in their development with a few people whose opinions you trust.

- Find one or two colleagues you can use as regular sounding boards to assess the viability of your ideas and gather suggestions on how you could improve them.

- Be flexible enough to amend your ideas as new information or different opinions come to hand.

- Think through any obvious pitfalls and arguments against your ideas. Forewarned is forearmed.

Sell your suggestions softly

Don't force your ideas on people. *'What if we did it this way?'*, *'Have you thought of this?'* Show how your idea supports the organisation's strategy or how your department or the company will benefit more than your idea will cost. Acknowledge any risks that are involved and demonstrate how they will be worth it.

Checklist for success

☐ Look and sound relaxed, confident and in control.

☐ Use body language that supports your verbal messages.

☐ Genuinely listen, never just fake it.

☐ Know your manager's preferred working style.

☐ Fit in with your manager's personality as much as you can.

☐ Let your boss know that you want to and can help her achieve her goals.

☐ Stay in tune with your boss's problems, pressures and foibles.

☐ Take the initiative in getting feedback; you have too much to lose if you don't and a lot to gain if you do.

☐ Learn to accept feedback without defending or excusing yourself or proving it wrong.

☐ 'Take charge' when receiving instructions to make sure you've 'got it'.

CHAPTER THREE

MANAGE YOUR TIME AND
REDUCE YOUR STRESS
Making the most of the time available

Have you ever noticed that some people get tremendous amounts done in a seemingly effortless way? They make it look easy. Others buzz around like flies in a bottle, busy, busy, busy, but actually achieve very little. A key difference between these types of people is the way they manage their time.

Time is a gauge by which we structure and calibrate our lives. We each have 86 400 seconds per day to squander or to spend wisely. Although these seconds have no substance, there is no doubt that some people do more with them than others. One of your most challenging tasks is to make the best use of the time available.

If you don't, harassment and stress will be your constant companions. You'll dash around, often trying to do several things at once, but accomplish little. When someone asks 'What did you do today?' you'll be stumped for an answer. You'll worry—usually about all the things you have left undone. Your job will control you instead of the other way around. You may work hard, but you won't achieve much.

Working hard and being effective are two entirely different things. Results, not busy-ness, are what count.

THE KEY TO EFFECTIVE TIME MANAGEMENT
To get results we need to focus our efforts, attention and energy on things that will help us reach our goals—important things. To recognise these, we first need to identify our **key result areas** (KRAs).

Key result areas
KRAs provide a framework for managing our time and efforts. They describe our main areas of accountability and responsibility. You

should be able to group your tasks into six to eight KRAs fairly easily.

For example, an assembly line supervisor might have the following KRAs:

- Output: quality, quantity, cost, timeliness
- Machine utilisation
- Staffing
- Leadership
- Health and safety
- Industrial relations
- Continuous improvement
- Administration

A retail store supervisor might have the following KRAs:

- Housekeeping
- Stock
- Customer relations
- Leadership
- Continuous improvement
- Sales budgets
- Administration

The KRAs of an office supervisor might be:

- Document preparation
- Document storage and retrieval
- Data entry management
- Liaison with internal clients on their needs
- Equipment maintenance and upgrades
- Leadership
- Continuous improvement

Notice that each KRA is written using one to five words and contains no verbs. This is because they name *areas* of accountability, not tasks. There is no 'pecking order'—each KRA is as important as every other KRA. If you fail to achieve results in any one key area, your entire job suffers.

What are your KRAs? Knowing them will help you distinguish what's important from what's unimportant, what's vital and what's super-fluous, so that you can prioritise tasks and concentrate on the activities that will contribute *directly* to your job goals.

49

The busier you are, the more good time management boils down to choice. You can consciously choose to do the most important things. You can decide what you will do *now*, what you will do *later*, what you will *delegate* and what you will only do *if time permits* based on what's important, what will contribute most to results in your KRAs.

Don't simply attend to whatever crops up, whatever is at the top of your in-tray or whatever makes the loudest or strongest attempt to gain your attention. If you do, you'll only end up 'spinning your wheels'.

Measures of success

Now it's time to set targets, or **measures of success**. These tell us whether we're achieving what we've set out to do. In fine-tuning what we should focus on, they help us manage our time. They also help us monitor our performance and boost our productivity.

Each KRA could have many targets, but aim for two or three that measure its most important or critical aspects and contribute to the overall goals of your department in some way.

Use the STAR criteria to develop objectives that will shine:

S Make sure they are *specific*. This means measurable or quantifiable in some other way. This avoids confusion and disagreements about whether a job was done correctly.

T Specify *timelines*. Knowing how long something should take, how quickly a task should be accomplished or how often it should be done gives us something to aim for and makes it easier to complete in time.

A Make sure you can quickly, easily and inexpensively *assemble* the monitoring information. If it's too time consuming, too difficult or too costly to keep an eye on your agreed success measures, you won't bother. This means you won't know how you're doing until it's too late; you could end up shutting the proverbial door after the horse has bolted.

R Make sure they are *realistic*. There is no point in agreeing to strive for a target you can't possibly reach. Realistic measures avoid disappointment and demoralisation.

Ask yourself: What do I need to achieve in this KRA in order to succeed? Some targets will be obvious. For others you'll need to think carefully. For example, 'leadership' can be difficult to specify and measure. Depending on what is important in your job, you might choose to monitor such factors as how well you are developing a successor, how well and how quickly you induct and train new employees or how well your group works as a team.

Because we tend to get what we focus on, write your measures of success in positive terms. For example, don't go for a 10% labour turnover in your department—aim for a 90% retention rate. (More about how to set STAR targets in Chapter 6.)

Knowing your KRAs and targets is the first step in managing your time well. If you know what you want to achieve, you can make time to do the right things, not fritter it away on meaningless activities. You can distinguish between the genuinely important and the merely urgent.

Important or just urgent?

Have you ever become caught in the trap of dealing with one urgent matter after another or lurching from crisis to crisis? Perhaps you have even realised that by not attending to important matters before they became urgent, you created some of the crises yourself!

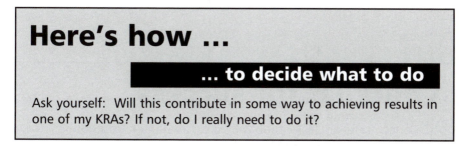

Here's how ...

... to decide what to do

Ask yourself: Will this contribute in some way to achieving results in one of my KRAs? If not, do I really need to do it?

Important tasks are the ones that net results in your Key Result Areas (KRAs). Urgent tasks often have a short-term flavour and are not necessarily important. We can often delegate them. Figure 3.1 shows how to deal with urgent and important matters.

Of course, we can't do only important things and nothing else. Sometimes we'll do an unimportant, non-urgent task just for a break. Sometimes, we'll need to deal with something that crops up that isn't strictly speaking going to move us any closer to reaching our targets. There are also things that need to be done, such as routine administration, to 'keep the system working'. Find the balance that will allow you to achieve the best you can.

Figure 3.1 Urgent or important?

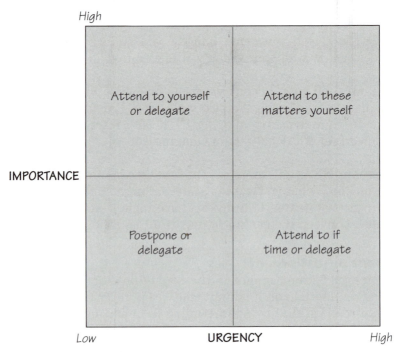

Checklist for success

- [ ] Concentrate on tasks that will make maximum contribution to achieving results in your KRAs. Set priorities accordingly.

- [ ] Don't let urgent, unimportant matters get in the way of non-urgent but important tasks.

- [ ] Set stretching yet realistic STAR targets and deadlines.

- [ ] Delegate work that you can safely delegate so you can concentrate on the most important aspects of your job (and upskill your team members as a bonus).

- [ ] Delegate, delay or dump anything that doesn't directly contribute to achieving goals in a KRA.

The 80:20 principle

A late 19th century Italian mathematical economist and sociologist named Vilfredo Pareto developed the 80:20 principle. Sometimes called the **Pareto principle**, it states that a small proportion of people, effort or time (20%) accounts for a large proportion of the results (80%). For example, 20% of salespeople in a sales team account for 80% of sales; 20% of customers yield 80% of the profits; 20% of the employees cause 80% of the problems. This is illustrated in Figure 3.2.

Do 20% of your efforts yield 80% of your good results? Do 20% of your interruptions account for 80% of your wasted time? What are your critical '20 per centers'? What four or five things do you do that add the most value (or if you don't do them there will be a price to pay)? If you find this difficult to answer, it may be because you don't have a clear idea of your KRAs and measures of success. You may not know what you're supposed to do. Better find out!

TIME MANAGEMENT TIPS

When you work on activities that will reap results in your KRAs, you'll be focusing your efforts and energy on what matters most. You'll be ready to apply the time management tips in this section to work smarter, not harder. This will make you efficient as well as effective.

Plan your work and work your plan

No matter how good your memory is, you are probably far too busy to be able to remember everything you need to do. *To Do* lists are indispensable to keep your focus on what you need to do to achieve your goals, no matter how hectic things get. They save you from the tyranny of the urgent—attending to whatever floats across your field of vision, seems the most urgent or 'makes the most noise'. Here are some specific things you should be using them for:

Figure 3.2 The Pareto principle

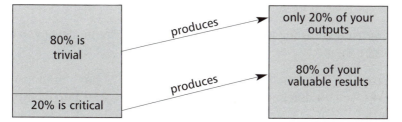

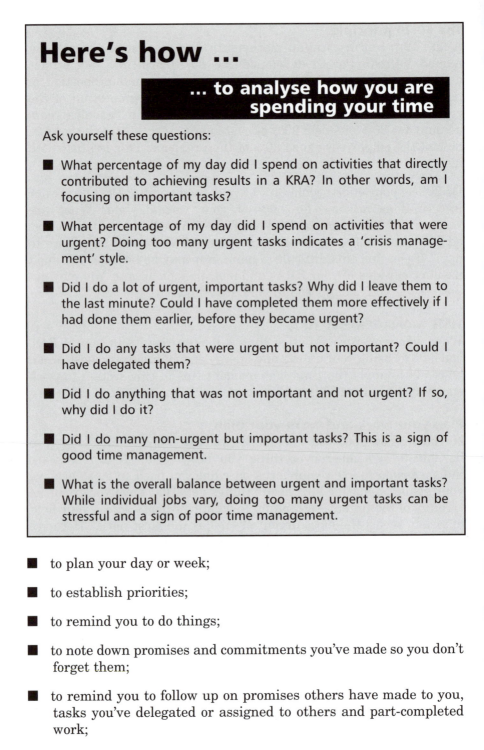

Here's how ...

... to analyse how you are spending your time

Ask yourself these questions:

■ What percentage of my day did I spend on activities that directly contributed to achieving results in a KRA? In other words, am I focusing on important tasks?

■ What percentage of my day did I spend on activities that were urgent? Doing too many urgent tasks indicates a 'crisis management' style.

■ Did I do a lot of urgent, important tasks? Why did I leave them to the last minute? Could I have completed them more effectively if I had done them earlier, before they became urgent?

■ Did I do any tasks that were urgent but not important? Could I have delegated them?

■ Did I do anything that was not important and not urgent? If so, why did I do it?

■ Did I do many non-urgent but important tasks? This is a sign of good time management.

■ What is the overall balance between urgent and important tasks? While individual jobs vary, doing too many urgent tasks can be stressful and a sign of poor time management.

■ to plan your day or week;

■ to establish priorities;

■ to remind you to do things;

■ to note down promises and commitments you've made so you don't forget them;

■ to remind you to follow up on promises others have made to you, tasks you've delegated or assigned to others and part-completed work;

■ to group like tasks together, and do them together, in blocks of time.

Figure 3.3 on page 57 shows a paper-based *To Do* list, using a simple A4-size spiral notebook. You might prefer to use an electronic palm computer or PC diary. Try several options and stick to the one you feel most comfortable with.

Select four or five categories that represent major tasks groups and enter the things you need to do. Add new tasks as they arise and cross tasks off as you complete them. If you're using a paper-based *To Do* list, turn the page and begin afresh when your *To Do* list gets too messy. Transfer undone tasks to the new page and put the date at the top for future reference. (You'll find this date can be a sanity saver!)

If you find yourself transferring a task three or more times, ask yourself why this is happening. Are you procrastinating? If so, *there's no time like the present*, as the saying goes—do it now and get it over with! Perhaps it's a low-priority task after all and you can drop it from your list. Perhaps it's something you can delegate. Perhaps it's a big job that you should divide into smaller parts and make a start. Whatever the reason, you have a clear warning signal and a decision to make.

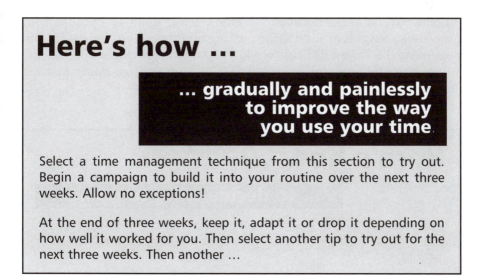

Here's how ...

... gradually and painlessly to improve the way you use your time.

Select a time management technique from this section to try out. Begin a campaign to build it into your routine over the next three weeks. Allow no exceptions!

At the end of three weeks, keep it, adapt it or drop it depending on how well it worked for you. Then select another tip to try out for the next three weeks. Then another ...

Set priorities

If you have a lot to do, use the ABC method to set priorities. Look at your tasks. Which ones most directly contribute to achieving results in your KRAs? Assign them an A, 'must do', priority. Which contribute least and can wait if you don't have enough time to do them? Assign them a C, 'could do', priority. The rest are B, 'should do', priorities.

Try and get through as much of your *To Do* list each day as you can, focusing on your A priorities. That way, if you don't get everything done, it will be less important things that are left. Don't ignore the Bs and Cs though; many of them will become urgent if you don't get on with them!

Evaluate 'urgent' matters

What happens when you are confronted with something that must be done *now*? Many tasks that we think are urgent really aren't. How often have you jumped to answer a ringing telephone only to find it was a wrong number, a call you didn't really want or a relatively trivial matter that took you away from a more important task?

Before you rush into doing it, evaluate the 'urgent' matter in terms of its urgency *and* its importance. How will doing it help you make progress in your KRAs? This will tell you whether you should do it, delegate it, delay it or dump it.

Don't kid yourself with 'busy work'

Many tasks are marginally worth doing but are neither important nor urgent. We do them because we enjoy doing them or because they provide a convenient excuse for putting off other, more important but less enjoyable, more difficult work. They might provide a false feeling of activity and accomplishment, but they stop us from doing tasks of greater benefit.

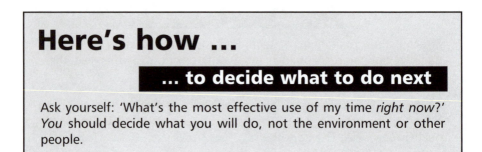

Here's how ...

... to decide what to do next

Ask yourself: 'What's the most effective use of my time *right now*?' *You* should decide what you will do, not the environment or other people.

Figure 3.3 To do list

21/7/02		Projects & On-going	
	Meetings	A	Make graphs for invoicing project
A	Bob – review Angus Corp contract	A	Prepare for presentation to
B	Linda – Performance Appraisal		management
A	Tina – go over salary package	B	Month end stats. for Vic's report
A	Vic – my performance appraisal	C	Check maintenance progress
A	HR – Brief on vacancy	B	Sam – progress on Tower order
		A	Check shipping schedules
	Telephone		
C	Sally – Xmas hampers		
B	Anne – go-ahead on Crompton?		
	Follow-up		Misc
B	Brad – results of meeting with	B	Speak to IT re software
	finance		changeover plans
B	Emily – wedding gift list	B	Check possible venues for team-
A	Angus Corp – reissued invoice?		building workshop
A	Michael – sent shipping	C	Prepare SOP for revised work
	documents?		flow
B	Bill – team BBQ?	B	Organise 'celebration' for Emily
C	Ted – car park?		– delegate to Jim?
		A	Exit interview Albert
		A	Update Albert's job spec
		A	Review training program – Liz

Tame the telephone

Does your telephone ring constantly? For many of us, telephones can waste as much time as they save by interrupting our flow of thoughts and distracting us from more important work.

Don't be tempted to control incoming calls by leaving your voicemail constantly switched on. That's disrespectful to other people and wastes their time. Use voicemail when you're in a meeting or when you need some uninterrupted working or thinking time. Leave a message saying when you will be available to take calls and invite callers to leave their details. Resist the temptation to listen in each time the voicemail picks up. Make sure you return the calls so you don't get a reputation for being rude, unreliable or disorganised. You could also route your calls to the switchboard or a team member to give you blocks of uninterrupted time.

Career Tip

Focus on what you want to achieve and make time to do things that will move you towards your goals.

To discourage lengthy calls, stand up. Your voice will take on a more 'urgent' tone and encourage callers to be more 'to the point'. Standing will also boost your circulation and reduce fatigue from sitting too long.

If someone calls you at a bad time, say so and arrange a time when it will be convenient for you both to talk, agreeing who will phone whom. This is especially useful to discourage known 'talkers'. Explain that you're in the middle of something right now and offer to phone them back. Do so 15 minutes or so before the end of their day, or when you know they'll need to leave for a meeting soon.

Make several outgoing calls together and have a note of what you want to discuss. Respect people's time by asking if they are free to talk.

Make telephone or meeting summaries

Use the other side of the *To Do* list shown in Figure 3.3 as a *Telephone Record* sheet. When you're speaking to someone on the telephone, turn the pad over and note the date, who you are speaking to, and what is agreed. Transfer anything to follow up or do to your *To Do* list on the other side.

If you have more informal meetings than telephone conversations, use the reverse side of your *To Do* list as a *Meeting Memo* sheet instead. If you're using an electronic *To Do* list, have a pad by your telephone to summarise phone conversations or meetings. Good summary notes mean you won't forget anything and will help you organise what you need to do.

Keep a list of telephone messages you leave for others and a note of what you want to speak to them about. Cross their names out when they return your call. Follow up anyone who doesn't get back to you.

Learn to say 'No' nicely

Henry Mintzberg of McGill University says that too many of us have too many *monkeys*: tasks passed on to us by our own staff. Has one of your employees ever presented you with a problem relating to their own job? If you said *'Leave it with me and I'll see what I can do'* when you could have said *'That's a tricky problem. What do you plan to do about it?'*, you accepted a monkey!

Perhaps some of your staff are unclear about your role and ask you to do things that relate to their KRAs rather than yours. These monkeys can be a great waste of time and would be better, and more properly, done by the people who 'own' them. If you suffer from management monkeys, try the above approach to keep monkeys off your back.

Make a start

Supervisor's lives are filled with interruptions. It isn't often that we can spend more than 10 or 15 minutes on a task before the telephone rings, someone needs to see us or it's time to pack up and go to a meeting. There's nothing wrong with that, except most things take considerably longer than 10 or 15 minutes to complete.

'I won't be able to finish this, so I'll do it later' is a guarantee that we'll never get anything done. Instead, work on big tasks between interruptions, in 10 or 15 minute blocks of time. Break them down into smaller tasks and make a start. You will probably find that, after your series of smaller 'attacks', all you need is one final 'assault' to pull everything together. This will make sure you attend to time-consuming but important matters.

Work on like activities together

Group related activities, such as telephone calls, reading memos and incoming mail, writing memos and letters and preparing documents, together and work on them in groups. This helps give a flow to your work and means you won't have to stop and mentally readjust as you would if you hopped from one type of activity to another.

Keep a clear desk

Do you spend time looking for things that you know are *right here, somewhere*? If so, you may need to clear your desk and tidy your drawers.

There should only be four things on your desk: your telephone, your computer, your *To Do* list and *Meeting Memo* or *Telephone Record* sheet and the job you are currently working on. Your in-tray can go on top of a filing cabinet to help you resist the temptation to look at what's just been popped into it, which breaks your train of thought and distracts you from your current work. Nothing is so important it can't wait for a few minutes.

After all, your desk is not intended as storage space. If your desk is clear, you won't have several things vying for your attention and breaking your concentration. To banish clutter, establish a sensible filing system and a place for everything. Put things away when you aren't using them. The few minutes you spend doing this will make it quicker and easier to retrieve that memo or file you're looking for.

Make the best use of your prime time

We each have our own unique 'energy cycle'—periods when we are full of bounce and energy, periods when we are a bit flat and periods in between. Use your peak energy periods for activities requiring careful thought and effort. Try to avoid interruptions during this time.

Manage your in-tray and e-mails

Set aside one or two periods during the day for looking through your in-tray and checking e-mails rather than dealing with each one as it arrives. To avoid temptation, you may want to move your in-tray away from your desk and switch off from the Internet or intranet or disable the sound function that announces the arrival of mail.

When you do deal with them, don't waste time sorting through them. Take some action on each one in turn: deal with it; delegate it; file it to bring forward at an appropriate date; throw it away or delete it (you can always get another copy later if you find you need it).

Do it right first time

Just as a stitch in time saves nine, doing something right first time saves you having to do it again. It saves you time by preventing you from wasting it. As the saying goes: If you don't have time to do it over, do it right first time.

60

Checklist for success

☐ Work at your own personal 'cutting edge' where your skills are challenged and stretched. Think about what you're doing and enjoy doing it.

☐ Avoid responding to whatever comes your way. Immediate reaction to a crisis often makes a problem worse anyway. Think first, then act.

☐ Remove anything you are not working on from your immediate vision. Have a place for everything and keep everything in its place.

☐ Set up a reliable filing system and use it.

☐ Nibble away on large tasks one bite at a time.

☐ Keep a daily or weekly *To Do* list showing priorities. You may not always be able to complete everything on it, but the sense of order and peace of mind it creates will more than compensate for the time you take to write it. Crossing items off as you complete them gives a sense of accomplishment.

☐ Keep your *To Do* list realistic and don't schedule every minute of the day.

☐ Clean out your electronic files as you go.

☐ Whenever possible, finish tasks that you begin. If you can't, make a note of where you were up to and what to do next.

☐ Take a load off your brain by writing down good ideas the moment they occur to you.

☐ Plan your telephone calls. Make a brief note of what you want to say or find out.

Delegate

Whenever possible, delegate recurring duties and pieces of larger jobs to staff members. For example, you might draft a report and ask a team member to polish it up for you, or delegate the research for a project to one or two team members (more about delegation in Chapter 11).

Don't procrastinate

If something needs to be done, do it. Putting it off won't make it go away or make it any easier. Make *Do it now!* your motto.

Set yourself targets and deadlines to work towards. If your procrastination is chronic, try setting *start* dates rather than finish dates.

Regularly ask yourself: *'What's the best use of my time right now?'*

When several things are demanding your attention at the same time, this simple question can be a great help in establishing priorities.

SURVIVING STRESS

Stress is a natural occurrence and a daily event, from the low-key choice of what clothes to wear to the high-key stress of starting a new job. Stress becomes a problem when we cannot control a stressful situation or our response to it.

The problem with stress

There are two types of stress: **eustress**, or the stress that makes us feel motivated and alive, and **distress**, which worries us and undermines our ability to cope, both physically and mentally. According to the Australian Chamber of Commerce and industry, distress ranks in the top 10 categories of workplace injury, in both self-reports and compensation claims.

Eustress and distress are different for everyone. What is challenging eustress for one person may be threatening distress for another and irrelevant to a third—just another thing to deal with and take in their stride.

Eustress helps us by providing a drive to succeed. Distress, on the other hand, drains us. It causes absenteeism, accidents, industrial disputes and labour turnover. It can lower our quality and quantity of work, creativity and job satisfaction. It can make us physically ill. The problem with stress, then, is distress. We should recognise and deal with it before these costly effects occur.

Causes of distress

Whenever the constraints, demands or pressures made on us (by ourselves, our society, our home or work lives) outweigh our ability to respond to them, become too much to cope with or threaten to become too much, we experience distress. Both *external events* (such as other people's behaviour, time pressure or social situations) and *internal events* (such as our own feelings, behaviour or thoughts) can trigger distress.

We might, for instance, feel constrained from doing something we want to do, or feel pressured to do something we feel unable to do. Equally, distress can result from a *lack* of demand, when our capabilities are under-used. Repetitive, monotonous work, for example, is a source of distress for many people.

Sources of distress are called **stressors**. Are you familiar with any of the following common on-the-job stressors?

- conflict with the boss or colleagues or within the work team
- promotion (or lack of promotion)
- not enough skills, time or equipment to do the work
- technological change
- organisation change
- retrenchments and restructuring

- change in working hours or conditions
- unclear goals and objectives
- inconsistent or insufficient recognition of effort
- little opportunity to learn from the job
- time pressures and other deadlines
- monotonous work

Are you stress-prone?

The ability to face life's demands varies greatly between people. Our genes, life experiences, backgrounds and capabilities combine to make our capacity to tolerate stress different from everyone else's.

Are you a type A person?

Evidence indicates that there is such a thing as a stress-prone person, called a *Type A* person. Do you talk, move and eat quickly? Are you very competitive, always in a hurry, easily angered and impatient (e.g. hate waiting in queues)? If so, you may be a Type A person. Trying to do several things at once and having few interests outside work also characterise Type A people. So does a higher than average number of car accidents!

If you think you might be a stress-prone Type A, pay close attention to the stress management ideas discussed below.

63

Are you a type B person?

Perhaps you are relaxed and easy-going in your pursuit of life and daily goals, casual about appointments and seldom feel rushed, even when under pressure. If so, and you have a variety of interests, yet do one thing at a time, you may be a *Type B* person. While Type As often bottle up their stress and try to cope with it alone, Type Bs tend to talk it out with others.

Many psychologists see Type A and Type B behaviour as opposite ends of a continuum. A few people are completely Type A or Type B but most of us fall somewhere between the two extremes.

Type As and Type Bs perceive their environment differently. The way we perceive our environment will, in part, determine the degree of distress we experience. For example, we have all seen drivers in a traffic jam, clenching the steering wheel with white-knuckled fists, eyes bulging, shouting at other drivers, fuming at traffic lights ... For these Type A drivers, the traffic jam is a distressing experience and will cause a variety of short-term physical responses. If they are frequently caught up in traffic jams and respond like this, we would expect to see some longer-term physical responses too.

Type B drivers are more philosophical in heavy traffic. They use time to clean their fingernails, listen to music, make plans for the coming day or muse over the day's happenings. Stress is really a matter of our perception of a situation.

Stressful situations are often more complex than a traffic jam, but the same principles apply: on the one hand, we have a stressor—a traffic jam; on the other, we have our perceptions of it—'*It's going to make me late*' (fume!) or '*Traffic should flow smoothly*' (seethe!) versus '*Heavy traffic again today*' (unruffled). The way we see a situation and the messages we give ourselves about help determine how distressing it is for us. This, combined with our skills at coping with life's situations and at relaxing, largely determine our stress level.

Other short-term factors, such as fatigue and how much we have 'on our plate' also affect our ability to deal with a stressor. In addition, sometimes we find demands on us motivating and inspirational while at other times they become the 'back-breaking straw'. At some point, 'gearing up' for an activity or event may stop being eustress, which energises us, and become distress, which wears us down.

So we don't all react to stress in the same way, nor do individuals always react in the same way to a particular stressor. Some handle stress poorly compared with others, while some actively seek stress. The question is not how you can avoid stress, but how we can best cope with it to avoid its harmful consequences.

What happens when we become stressed?

Whatever its source, stress produces very real physical, emotional and behavioural responses. It doesn't really matter whether an event is eustress or distress: going on holiday can be just as stressful as having an argument with the boss.

Each stressful event affects our body by demanding an immediate readjustment or adaptation of our natural defence mechanisms. Both the *intensity* and *number* of stressful events are important because stress accumulates. If we don't take steps to reduce its negative effects, our overall stress level will rise, putting our physical and mental wellbeing at risk.

As stress accumulates, a variety of *physical responses* usually occurs. For instance, our artery walls constrict, which increases blood pressure, heart rate and muscle tension (this is the ancient 'fight/flight' response). We can see the signs of this: sweating, flushing, grinding teeth, clenched fists. Less observable signs include nausea, loss of appetite and disorientation. Because they take place subconsciously, our body's reactions can be difficult to relate directly to a stressor.

What parts of your body tense up when you are under stress? Tension is a common physical sign of stress. Other physical symptoms include skin eruptions, headaches, an upset stomach, sweaty palms, increased heart rate, loss of sex drive, uneven or rapid breathing, diarrhoea and a generally lowered resistance to infections such as colds and influenza.

Did you know ...

The peak period for heart attacks is Monday mornings.

Over 70% of workplace absenteeism is due to stress or stress-related illness.

More than 25% of Australian workers took stress leave in 1999.

The cost of stress to the country is more than $60 million a year.

60% to 80% of industrial accidents are due to stressed workers.

65

Dr Hans Serle first identified **burnout** in the 1950s. In June 1983 it made the cover of *Time* magazine as 'the disease of the decade'; in July 1998 it made the cover of *The Bulletin* as the 'stress epidemic: the disease of the nineties'. In 1999 stress again made the cover of both *Newsweek* and *The Bulletin*.

Burnout is a common result of the physical responses to an accumulation of stressors. If we fail to recognise these symptoms and deal with the stressors in our lives, we may experience longer-term physical stress-related disorders. These include elevated blood pressure, headaches and migraines, ulcers, heart attacks, kidney disorders, some cancers, some skin allergies and a generally lowered resistance to disease.

If stress continues to build, we can expect a variety of *emotional responses* such as depression, apathy, tension, resignation, anxiety, negativism, mood swings, a sense of helplessness, dissatisfaction, low self-esteem, rigidity of views and uncertainty about who we can trust. In the longer term, various types of psychological disturbances may occur.

Eventually, our *behaviour* will change. We may become short-tempered, irritable and easily upset over trifles. We may procrastinate or have difficulty in concentrating, in organising ourselves or in making decisions. We may develop a loss of appetite or a sudden change in habits, for example in smoking or the use of drugs or alcohol. We may experience troubled sleeping patterns, sensitivity, forgetfulness and difficulty in dealing with new situations, notice a gain or loss of weight or other change in appearance or become easily fatigued. Again, if we don't deal with the source of our stress and manage our responses to it, they will become more severe.

FOUR STEPS TO MANAGING STRESS

Here are the four steps to managing stress:

1. *Learn to recognise your own physical, emotional and behavioural responses to stress.* These will alert you to the presence of a stressor you may be unaware of. If you know about your own body's stress signals, you will be able to recognise and deal with a stressor more quickly.

2. *Identify the events, or stressors, that are causing the stress.* The more sources of stress you have in your life, the more important it becomes to take action to manage your stress levels.

3. *Take steps to reduce or eliminate stressful situations, or deal with them differently.* Since prevention is always better than cure, it may be possible to modify some environmental factors. If you cannot do this, try changing the way you view them.

4. If you still experience distress, *act to reduce the stressor's negative effects.* Try some form of *stress management* (meditation, yoga, relaxation training, exercise, self-talk, etc.). Your family doctor can put you in touch with specially trained people who work in the area of stress management and a variety of evening classes in the various stress management techniques are available in most cities and towns.

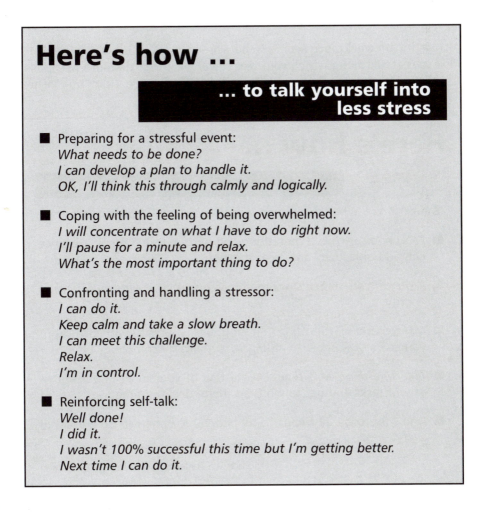

Here's how ...

... to talk yourself into less stress

■ Preparing for a stressful event:
What needs to be done?
I can develop a plan to handle it.
OK, I'll think this through calmly and logically.

■ Coping with the feeling of being overwhelmed:
I will concentrate on what I have to do right now.
I'll pause for a minute and relax.
What's the most important thing to do?

■ Confronting and handling a stressor:
I can do it.
Keep calm and take a slow breath.
I can meet this challenge.
Relax.
I'm in control.

■ Reinforcing self-talk:
Well done!
I did it.
I wasn't 100% successful this time but I'm getting better.
Next time I can do it.

Turning to alcohol, drugs, food, cigarettes or other short-term coping mechanisms may provide some temporary relief, but in the long run they are worse than doing nothing; they merely cover up the distress and fail to deal with its source or your responses to it. Medication is another short-term 'holding' strategy, providing a pause during which you can learn longer-term, safer stress management techniques.

Helping your staff overcome stress

Researchers have explored the relationship between job content and stress in white- and blue-collar settings in both the public and private sectors. They have found that stress is not restricted to managers and supervisors; it is also a problem on the shop floor, in the office and when dealing with the public. The potential cost of distress to employees, organisations and society is significant, so be alert to possible stress signals of your team members.

Stress in the workplace seems to be worsening because of *job overload* due to restructuring which requires fewer people to do more with less. In the past decade, Australia has downsized more than any other

---

Here's how ...

... to relieve stress

- *Talk it out*. When something worries you, don't bottle it up.

- *Escape for a while*. When things go wrong, take a break. Distance can add objectivity and clear thinking.

- *Work off your anger*. Do something constructive with your pent-up energy.

- *Do something for others*. If you feel yourself worrying about yourself all the time, try doing something for somebody else.

- *Take one thing at a time*. Take a few of your most important or urgent tasks and get to work on them, one at a time.

- *Don't try to be all things to all people*. No one can be perfect in everything.

Source: US National Mental Health Association

OECD country. In 1995 the Department of Industrial Relations surveyed 19 000 Australians and found a dramatic rise in stress levels. Of those employees surveyed, 57% said their job stress was up while only 4% said it was down; the other 39% reported no change in their stress levels. Clearly, a growing number of employees are unhappy and dissatisfied at work.

Poor **job design** can cause *job underload* or *job overload*. A repetitive job, having too little to do and/or a lack of control over your work or pace of work can be just as distressing as having too much to do and too many pressures. Poor supervision (e.g. under- or over-supervision or conflict with the supervisor), dissension in the work team and unclear or conflicting goals and objectives are common causes of stress at work.

Stressed people are not only less effective and productive at work, but also grumpy and hard to live with. The flow-on effects include frayed tempers, harassment and bullying. In Chapter 6 we examine how to design jobs and manage people to increase their productivity and reduce the potential for stress.

Checklist for success

- ☐ Know yourself and make sure your work allows you to use your strengths and concentrate on your talents.

- ☐ Set goals. Know where you are headed and what your objectives are.

- ☐ Review your work and personal priorities regularly and delegate wherever possible.

- ☐ If you are not succeeding with one approach, don't try harder— think of a better way.

- ☐ Say 'I could' or 'I want to' instead of 'I should' or 'I have to'.

- ☐ Give yourself time to yourself.

- ☐ Compete with yourself, not against others.

☐ Accept that you cannot do everything. Apply principles of time management.

☐ List your outside activities and interests and plan them into your diary. Don't be a 'workaholic'.

☐ Determine your optimum weight and maintain it with health-giving foods.

☐ Exercise regularly. Regular physical exercise is one of the best and healthiest ways to reduce tension in your life.

☐ Decide your minimum sleep requirement and ensure that you get it.

☐ Ask yourself whether you are having fun. If the answer over a long period is 'no', try to work out why.

☐ Identify things that are causing you to feel stress. At work, you may need to alter your job or work habits. At home, stress arises from the conflict of unsolved problems; discuss them openly with your partner and work out solutions together.

☐ Examine your self-talk and the way you think about stressors. Perhaps you can look at the situation differently and give yourself more positive messages.

PART TWO

MANAGING PEOPLE

People are a paradox. They will be the most frustrating—and rewarding—part of your job. They will be unpredictable and puzzling. They will touch your heart and fill you with pride, pleasure and admiration. The ability to identify and bring out the best in people will expand your earning potential and your job satisfaction.

CHAPTER FOUR

FIND AND FOSTER WINNERS
Recruiting, selecting and inducting

I f you are ever tempted to accept 'the best of a bad bunch' to fill a job vacancy, don't do it! Taking the time to select the right person for the job will save you a lot of heartache, wasted administration costs, lowered productivity and unhappy employees.

THINK IT THROUGH FIRST
Before you can recruit anyone you need to know precisely what you want them to do. Successful recruitment begins with a careful examination of the job.

Examine the vacancy
When someone leaves or transfers out of your department, don't just assume you need to fill their job as it currently exists. Examine it to see if it has changed. Perhaps it's a good time to change some job duties or assign them to other staff. This may mean you don't recruit anyone; or it may mean that the position you are recruiting for changes substantially from the original vacancy. It can even mean that you recruit for a different position entirely.

Similarly, although a job might have been full time, you may decide to change it to a part-time, contract, casual, project-based or temporary position. Perhaps you could make an office-based position partially or wholly home based? Think about the pool of people you will be selecting from in your area, and stay flexible and open to ideas.

Now run through a few questions to make sure you will be able to accommodate the job holder. Do you have the physical resources (e.g. furniture, space and equipment) to accommodate the person? Do you have the budget to pay them in a suitable salary range?

Make a case

Do you need to get approval for hiring from a senior manager? You'll need to be able to explain your reason for recruiting someone and how it will benefit the business. You may need to provide the job description, award rate, salary range or job level, information on the impacts of the appointment (e.g. if you are amalgamating two positions, how the rest of the group will be affected) and a workflow analysis (see **flow charts** in Chapters 11 and 15). Think this through carefully so that you can present a clear and convincing case.

Describe the job

Write or update the job description so it clearly describes the job you want done. What is its function? What will the job holder be responsible for doing and achieving? Who will they be working and liaising with? What is the work environment like?

Describe the person

Now describe the person best suited to doing this job. This is your *personnel specification* and *selection criteria*. Give it careful thought because it will help you spot the most suitable candidate.

Do you think a candidate with experience in a similar industry or job will make the best recruit? These *job skills* are certainly important. Of at least equal importance, though, are a person's *personal skills and behaviour*—their characteristics, or attributes. Such attributes could include:

Figure 4.1 So you have a vacancy?

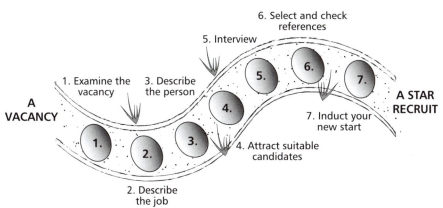

6. Select and check references

5. Interview

1. Examine the vacancy

3. Describe the person

A VACANCY

A STAR RECRUIT

7. Induct your new start

4. Attract suitable candidates

2. Describe the job

- Friendly, cheerful and helpful attitude to team mates and clients

- Efficiency orientation

- Numerate

- Well organised and tidy

- Logical thinker

- 'Do it right first time' approach (not 'Close enough is good enough')

Things like these make the difference between a good *job fit*, that is, a good match between a person and their job, and a poor one.

In fact, the main reason new recruits don't work out is poor job fit. Think back about the employees who have given you the biggest headaches. Chances are, there was a poor match between their attributes and those needed to do the job well.

Here's how ...

... to develop a clear idea of what you are looking for

Ask yourself:

- What must the person *know*? (knowledge)

- What must they be able to *do*? (skills)

- How must they *behave*? (personal characteristics)

The easiest way to do this is to imagine the ideal job holder—someone who would enjoy this job and do it really well. Then think about what they would be like as a person (the attributes or personal skills that would help them do their job well), what they would be able to do and what they would know and understand (their job skills).

Take this opportunity to build a strong team by bringing in skills it lacks. Try to avoid unnecessary overlap or imbalance when developing the personnel specification. For example, go for a balance between the personality styles, quiet and outgoing people, task-focused and people-focused people. Build missing personality styles and characteristics into your selection criteria. (See Chapter 2.)

ATTRACT SUITABLE PEOPLE

Do you want to appoint someone from inside the organisation, from outside the organisation or explore both possibilities?

Think about transferring someone in from another area, moving someone from your own area to take up the vacancy or offering the position to a temporary or casual employee who has been working with you. This is a good way to recruit because you have a good idea of the person's skills, knowledge and attributes, which reduces the risks in appointing them.

If you need to source externally, you could advertise the vacancy, although this can be expensive and is not always necessary. Local employment agencies are another source of candidates; they may have suitable people registered with them, which saves the need to advertise.

Using employment agencies

Good recruitment consultants spend time (often around an hour) taking a full brief. They want to be clear not just about the job but also about the skills, knowledge and attributes you are looking for and the environment the person will be working in.

They normally charge a percentage of the first year's annual salary, with some sort of guarantee that if the person doesn't work out they will replace them at no charge or at reduced fees. Most offer a range of services, from arranging the advertising of the vacancy and passing on all the applications to you, to interviewing suitable candidates and providing a shortlist of the three or four candidates to interview and make your final selection from.

Advertising the job

A job ad is also an ad for your organisation.

An employment agency will write the job ad for you to approve and place it in appropriate newspapers and on their website. If you are preparing the ad yourself, make sure it carries an attention-grabbing heading that will attract readers to look more closely.

The body of the ad normally has three paragraphs. The first identifies your industry sector or employer type and describes the organisation; write this to attract applicants and for general public relations. The second describes the position, including an accurate job title and a

Here's how ...

... to obtain temporary staff

To test out the feasibility of new working arrangements or fill a short-term vacancy (e.g. there may be a period of extra high workloads or a key employee may go on leave), you could employ someone temporarily.

You can use temporary staff agencies and employment agencies for this. They pay the temporary employees directly and invoice you. Because temporary staff don't receive sick pay, holiday pay and so on, there is always a 'loading' on their salaries to compensate, making them slightly more expensive than other categories of employee, which makes it uneconomical to employ them for more than 12 months. Good agencies will often put in a higher level of person than the job demands so they 'hit the ground running' and you don't lose time (and money) training them.

The procedure for obtaining temporary staff is basically the same as the procedure for recruiting through employment agencies. Explain carefully the duties the person will perform, the skills and knowledge you require and details such as hours of work.

summary of your main selection criteria; this is to attract people to apply. The third paragraph describes the ideal person for the role: the background required (education, experience) and the necessary attributes; this is to encourage applicants to screen themselves out so that only the most suitable apply.

The final two or three sentences are a 'call to action' detailing how to apply, the closing date and reference number of the vacancy (e.g. 'If you want to join a dynamic organisation, then apply in writing to … by …, quoting Reference Number …). You could also include your organisation's website address for candidates to obtain further information about your organisation.

INTERVIEW AND SELECT THE BEST PERSON FOR THE JOB
Hopefully your internal and/or external advertising has netted some (but not too many!) suitable candidates. Keep track of applications on a control sheet (see Figure 4.2). If the recruitment process is likely to be drawn out, acknowledge receipt of applications, explaining when

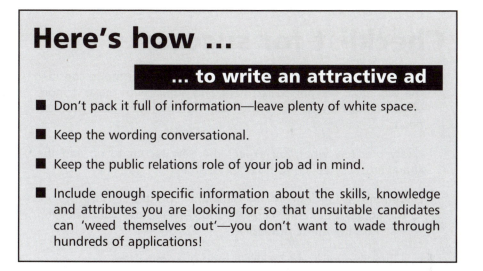

Here's how ...

... to write an attractive ad

■ Don't pack it full of information—leave plenty of white space.

■ Keep the wording conversational.

■ Keep the public relations role of your job ad in mind.

■ Include enough specific information about the skills, knowledge and attributes you are looking for so that unsuitable candidates can 'weed themselves out'—you don't want to wade through hundreds of applications!

the applicant can expect to hear further from you. Otherwise, the usual invitation for an interview or a 'thanks but no thanks' letter, described below, will suffice.

Shortlisting

If you are using an agency, they will handle the process of acknowledging applications, sending 'thanks but no thanks' letters,

Figure 4.2 Control sheet for applications received

Vacancy: Administrative Assistant, November 2002					
		ACTION			
Applicant's Name	Date received	Invite for interview	Hold	No	Outcome/comments
Bergman, Rachael	10/11	25/11			Has computer skills needed
Jones, Bethany	10/11			25/11	Poorly presented application
Chin, Jocelyn	10/11		25/11		No experience, could possibly train if necessary
McBean, Alfred	12/11	25/11			Relevant experience

Checklist for success

☐ Use the opportunity of someone leaving or transferring to consider the workflow of your department and adjust it to make it more efficient and better suit the remaining employees and business needs.

☐ Know precisely what you expect the new recruit to do and the characteristics needed to do it successfully.

☐ Everything you include on the personnel specification *must* relate to the actual requirements of the job. This ensures your selection is based on the **merit principle**.

☐ Use unambiguous and inclusive (non-discriminatory) language in the job description and personnel specification.

☐ Check any assumptions you are making about the ideal job holder or the vacancy to ensure you don't unwittingly and unnecessarily exclude potentially suitable candidates.

organising interviews and so on. If there are a lot of applicants for a position, this saves time-consuming work and frees you to carry on with other matters.

If you are preparing your own shortlist, compare each applicant's suitability for the position with your selection criteria and shortlist only those who seem to meet your needs best. This ensures that you interview only the most suitable candidates.

If you have a large number of applications, divide them into 'Yes', 'No' and 'Maybe' piles. You may want to prepare a matrix of your selection criteria and place a tick (meets criterion), cross (does not meet criterion) or question mark (not known if meets criterion) against each item for each candidate, using the information presented in their written application. This should help you to remain fair and objective and 'prompt' you at the interview to follow up the question marks. Interview applicants from the 'Yes' pile first and move on to the 'Maybes' if you need to.

If you're following best practice, politely write to unsuccessful applicants explaining that you will not be proceeding with their applications and thanking them for their interest. If you have a lot of vacancies, this is not a cheap exercise and takes time; however, if you don't respond to all applicants you risk giving a very poor impression of your organisation. If you don't let applicants know what's happening, be prepared for them to telephone you to ask.

Arrange the interview schedule

It's a big mistake to interview one candidate after another—they will all blur into each other! When you set up the meetings to interview your shortlisted candidates leave plenty of time between interviews for four things:

- to complete your notes on the interview to jog your memory later;

- to consider the evidence you obtained and think about how the candidate does and does not meet your selection criteria, and perhaps complete a *candidate ranking form*;

- to attend to any matters that have arisen while you have been interviewing;

- to ensure candidates do not meet each other in the corridor or waiting room.

In your phone call or letter inviting candidates to an interview, tell them where to come (e.g. to the front reception desk), who to ask for and where to park, as well as the day and time of the proposed interview. Also thank them for their application and interest in working in your organisation and inform them of any interview requirements, for example whether they will be taking any skill or aptitude tests.

Career tip

Spend time at the front end to save time at the back end. Avoid future problems by never settling for 'second best'.

Behavioural interviewing

If you want to know whether candidates can keyboard accurately at 100 words a minute, give them a skills test. If you want to know whether they know how to troubleshoot, ask them to describe the process they use. Skills and knowledge are easy to assess. Attributes can be more difficult.

How can you find out whether someone is polite, cheerful and helpful, even to the most demanding customer? How can you find out whether they're a willing, cooperative worker? Or a tidy worker who looks after the details? Or is able to think for themselves?

If you ask them outright, only the dimmest of candidates would admit to being rude, surly, uncooperative, unwilling or untidy! A better way to find out is through **behavioural interviewing**. In a behavioural interview, we ask candidates to give us specific examples of what they have done in the past and use this information to predict what they will do in the future. Questions revolve around our selection criteria, so we can make job-relevant assessments of a candidate's suitability for the vacancy.

During the course of an interview, you will build up a clear picture of the candidate's work preferences, working style and attributes on which to make a selection decision you can feel confident in.

Remember: you can train someone to keyboard. You can train someone to troubleshoot. But you can't train attitudes. That's why behavioural interviewing works so well.

Ask the right questions
Asking good questions is the key to good interviewing. With the right questions you can help candidates bring out their relevant attributes, skills and experience. You can find out the specific ways that candidates are suited, and not suited, to your vacancy.

Asking good questions comes with preparation and practice. Formulate yours with thought. First decide which aspect of the personnel specification you want to target; then ask a question aimed at drawing out relevant information.

Once you have opened a topic listen carefully, follow the candidate's train of thought and ask follow-up (*clarifying* or *probing*) questions as necessary so that you draw out all the details and information you need.

Your best guide to the next question to ask is to follow up something the candidate has just said. You will need to listen carefully. Don't

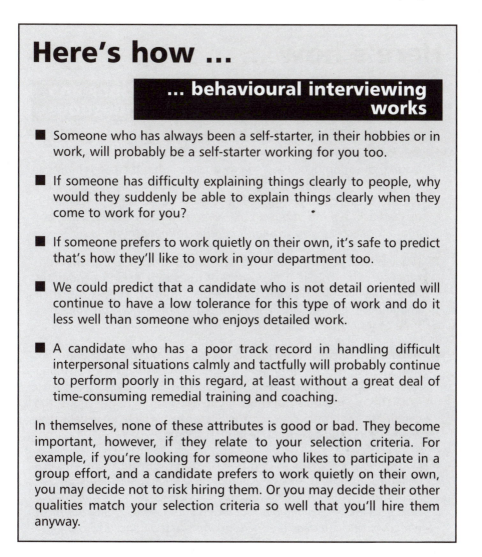

Here's how ...

... behavioural interviewing works

- Someone who has always been a self-starter, in their hobbies or in work, will probably be a self-starter working for you too.

- If someone has difficulty explaining things clearly to people, why would they suddenly be able to explain things clearly when they come to work for you?

- If someone prefers to work quietly on their own, it's safe to predict that's how they'll like to work in your department too.

- We could predict that a candidate who is not detail oriented will continue to have a low tolerance for this type of work and do it less well than someone who enjoys detailed work.

- A candidate who has a poor track record in handling difficult interpersonal situations calmly and tactfully will probably continue to perform poorly in this regard, at least without a great deal of time-consuming remedial training and coaching.

In themselves, none of these attributes is good or bad. They become important, however, if they relate to your selection criteria. For example, if you're looking for someone who likes to participate in a group effort, and a candidate prefers to work quietly on their own, you may decide not to risk hiring them. Or you may decide their other qualities match your selection criteria so well that you'll hire them anyway.

make the mistake of getting the candidate talking and then thinking about what your next question will be, rather than listening to their answer. This results in a choppy interview and unearthing little information.

The recruitment interview

Here is where the 'rubber meets the road'. If you don't know how to follow a plan and ask good questions, conducting 1000 interviews won't make you a good interviewer. Nevertheless, you can only sharpen your interviewing skills through practice.

Here's how ...

... *not* to ask questions and how to ask questions

■ *What would you do if you had two important jobs that needed to be done and it meant staying late to finish them off?* This is a *leading* question because it's fairly obvious what the correct answer is ('Oh, well naturally I'd stay late. I will always do what's necessary to get the job done right—I'm a very conscientious worker!'). Instead ask: *Tell me about a time when you had deadlines to meet and it looked like you wouldn't be able to meet them.*

■ *What would you do if a manager from another department were rude to you?* This is a *hypothetical* question. Asking candidates how they would handle a made-up situation only tests their imagination. Instead ask: *Tell me about a time when someone was rude to you. How did you handle it?*

■ *What was your favourite job and what did you like best about it? And can you tell me a bit about your manager and your working relationship? And the people you worked with—what were they like?* This is a *multiple* question. If you ask a string of questions, the candidate will only answer the last one, which is usually the weakest. Instead ask one question at a time.

■ *Do you prefer to work as part of a group or on your own?* This is a *limiting* question: it asks the candidate to choose from an either–or response, neither of which may be the correct or most informative one. Instead ask: *Thinking about when you have been at your most effective, can you describe the working situation and environment?*

■ *Do you think you have the aptitude to pick up this sort of work?* This is another *leading* question because it indicates the answer you are looking for. Work out the answer to this yourself, based on the behavioural evidence you build up during the course of the interview.

■ *Why do you job-hop so much?* This is a *value-laden* question; questions that give away your own feelings, especially negative ones, are apt to influence the candidate's reply. Instead ask: *What led to your decision to leave your last job? ... How about the job before that?*

Here's how ...

... to find out valuable information

- What responsibilities do you have in your current/last job?

- What do you like most about your job? What do you like least about it?

- Describe the most frustrating/enjoyable part of your current/last job.

- Describe a difficult client (or workmate) you have encountered and how you handled them.

- Tell me about a recent typical day and how you planned it.

- Describe a time in your job when you needed to work without supervision.

- Tell me about a time when you had to make an important point by explaining it well.

- Of the jobs you have had, which did you enjoy the most? Why? Give me an example of that.

- Describe a difficult problem you have confronted and how you handled it.

- Describe a time when you felt particularly effective in your job.

- Tell me about ...

- What did you do then?

- Exactly what happened?

- Give me an example ...

Prepare for the interview

You'll need an *interview plan*. Just as a meeting is in danger of rambling aimlessly without an agenda, so you'll have difficulty keeping your interview under control without an interview plan. This

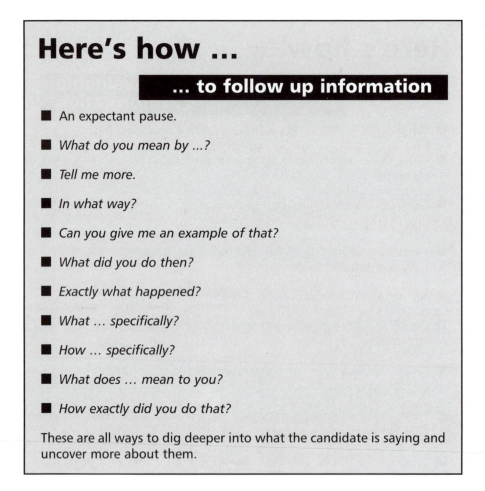

Here's how ...

... to follow up information

- An expectant pause.

- *What do you mean by ...?*

- *Tell me more.*

- *In what way?*

- *Can you give me an example of that?*

- *What did you do then?*

- *Exactly what happened?*

- *What ... specifically?*

- *How ... specifically?*

- *What does ... mean to you?*

- *How exactly did you do that?*

These are all ways to dig deeper into what the candidate is saying and uncover more about them.

also helps you ask the same basic questions of each candidate, which can be important for legal and ethical reasons.

Plan the flow of the interview (what you will cover and in what order), your opening questions and a few key questions carefully. Have an additional list of behavioural, job-related questions to refer to if you need them.

Think about how you will describe the vacancy and your organisation. Where will the candidates wait? Who will greet them when they arrive? Will you need to book any selection tests? Will you interview the candidates in your office or will you need to book an interview or conference room? Make sure you have a quiet place, free from interruptions.

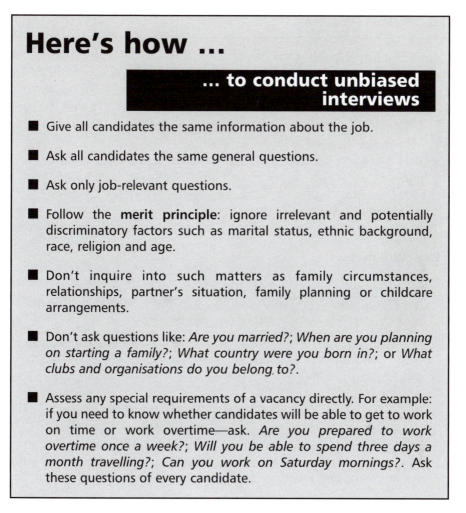

Here's how ...

... to conduct unbiased interviews

- Give all candidates the same information about the job.

- Ask all candidates the same general questions.

- Ask only job-relevant questions.

- Follow the **merit principle**: ignore irrelevant and potentially discriminatory factors such as marital status, ethnic background, race, religion and age.

- Don't inquire into such matters as family circumstances, relationships, partner's situation, family planning or childcare arrangements.

- Don't ask questions like: *Are you married?*; *When are you planning on starting a family?*; *What country were you born in?*; or *What clubs and organisations do you belong to?*.

- Assess any special requirements of a vacancy directly. For example: if you need to know whether candidates will be able to get to work on time or work overtime—ask. *Are you prepared to work overtime once a week?*; *Will you be able to spend three days a month travelling?*; *Can you work on Saturday mornings?*. Ask these questions of every candidate.

Carry out the interview

Think of the interview in the three stages shown in Box 4.1.

Opening the interview lasts up to 10 minutes. Then the 'real' interview begins. Find out as much as you can about each candidate, exploring their past performance and experience as they relate to the requirements of the job. Aim to make an accurate assessment of how well they match your selection criteria.

Don't fall into the trap of hearing all about the candidate's current or last employer, what their systems and policies were, how their workplace was organised and who else worked there. Keep looking for behavioural examples of what the candidate did or does. Only these

Box 4.1 Interview outline

Open the interview

1. Welcome candidate.
2. Invite the candidate to sit down—indicate where.
3. Thank the candidate for coming.
4. Outline the purpose and format of the interview.
5. Give a *brief* description of job duties and organisation.
6. Put the candidate at ease.

Body of interview
(Note: Change this order according to the applicant's background.)

1. *Work history*
   Key tasks
   Assess match/mismatch with personnel specification.
   Get behavioural examples—what did/does the candidate do that may show match/mismatch to selection criteria?

2. *Relevant educational and/or technical qualifications and experiences*
   (Note: Educational experiences may not be relevant with older candidates.)

3. *Special requirements*
   Ability to travel interstate; driver's licence; ability to work shifts/overtime/weekends if required, etc. Naturally, these should not be probed unless they are clearly relevant to the job requirements. Childcare arrangements, for example, are unlikely to be relevant to job requirements and therefore should not be asked about.

4. You may need to discuss how much *notice* (advice of resignation) the candidate would need to give and an expected starting date. You may also need to at least open discussions on salary.

Close the interview

1. Any questions?
2. Still interested?
3. Clearly advise next step.
4. Get names and telephone numbers of two referees, preferably previous employers/supervisors.
5. Thank the candidate.
6. End firmly (e.g. stand up, shake candidate's hand).

---

give a reliable indication of whether or not the candidate meets your selection criteria.

Maintain rapport and show you are listening by leaning forward slightly and making eye contact and periodic summaries. Whether you agree or disagree with what the candidate is saying, remain neutral.

Take brief notes during the interview to jog your memory. Don't write down everything candidates say, though. This is off-putting to candidates and if you go overboard on taking notes you'll miss a lot: while you're writing you're not listening or observing.

Make it clear when the interview is over. Stand up, shake the candidate's hand and thank them for their time.

Did you know ...

The *halo–horns effect* can trap you into a poor selection decision. It happens when you make up your mind in the first few minutes of the interview and spend the rest of it seeking evidence to confirm your initial impression.

Don't let one or two positive (or negative) qualities of a candidate colour your judgement on all their other qualities. A well-groomed person is not necessarily a reliable worker any more than a good tennis player is necessarily a cooperative and friendly worker. Treat each skill, area of knowledge and attribute separately.

After the interview
Pause and consider the evidence you have gathered. Which aspects of your selection criteria does the candidate meet and not meet? Make a few notes to refer to. Don't rely on your memory because after a few interviews you'll forget who said what.

If you are interviewing several candidates, or if they all seem similar, develop a *candidate ranking form*. List items from your selection criteria along one axis and each candidate you are interviewing along the other and allocate each candidate points out of 5 or 10 for each item, based on the evidence you have obtained. (See Figure 4.3.)

Figure 4.3 Candidate ranking form

Criteria / Candidate	McBeal, J	Tan, K	Idnani, R	Johnson, L
Able to work unsupervised to set procedures	7	5	9	2
Works confidently in a team environment	3	4	9	2
Helpful approach to customers	6	4	7	9
Desk top publishing familiarity	2	9	9	9
Reliable, follows through	8	7	8	3
Takes directions willingly	4	8	3	8
Total	58	74	84	62

Ranking: 1 – poor   5 – acceptable   10 – excellent

Interviewer: B Paul, Date: 11 November 2002, Position: Clerical Officer, Grade 3, Location: Central Admin.

Decide

Every selection decision is to some extent a compromise: your personnel specification describes the ideal candidate and it is unlikely you will find someone who matches it exactly. You are looking for the *best possible match*. After you have completed all your interviews, make a preliminary decision about which candidate best matches your selection criteria.

Check the references of this candidate (discussed below) and make the job offer. You will normally telephone first to make the job offer and follow up the candidate's verbal acceptance with an *offer of employment* letter and a contract stating the hours of work, job role and duties, rate of pay, date at which the job commences, when the offer expires and so on.

When the candidate has accepted your offer of employment, inform the unsuccessful candidates by letter or telephone. Why wait to notify the other candidates? If for some reason your job offer is not accepted, you can still move to your second choice if that person meets your selection criteria well enough.

When you let each of the other candidates you have interviewed know they have been unsuccessful, thank them for their time and interest. Everyone you have interviewed deserves to hear from you.

Check references
In order to protect your organisation's interests, carry out at least two reference checks on your chosen candidate prior to making the final decision and job offer. If you are working with a recruitment consultant, they can do this for you. Ask to see their written notes of the reference discussion.

The purpose of checking references is to validate your selection decision by further probing key aspects of your selection criteria and obtaining further information on how the candidate specifically meets or fails to meet them. Reference checks can also confirm information given by the candidate, such as dates of employment, main duties and salary. Box 4.2 shows some typical questions for reference checks; use this to develop your own questions.

When checking references try to speak to people who have supervised the candidate. If the candidate has not had a full-time job, they may have had a part-time job. Failing this, speak to their teachers or tutors.

These discussions can take 20 to 30 minutes and sometimes more. Because they are time consuming for both parties, carry out reference checks only on the candidate to whom you intend to offer the job.

How much weight should you give written references? People don't write poor ones, they write nice ones as truthfully as they can, leaving out any negative information. This means they're not of much value in making a selection decision.

Box 4.2 Sample questions for telephone reference checks

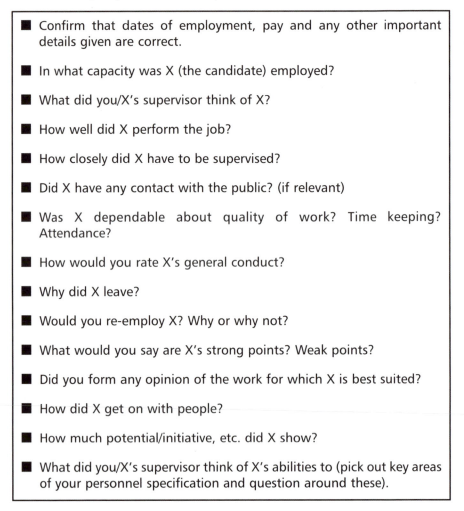

- Confirm that dates of employment, pay and any other important details given are correct.

- In what capacity was X (the candidate) employed?

- What did you/X's supervisor think of X?

- How well did X perform the job?

- How closely did X have to be supervised?

- Did X have any contact with the public? (if relevant)

- Was X dependable about quality of work? Time keeping? Attendance?

- How would you rate X's general conduct?

- Why did X leave?

- Would you re-employ X? Why or why not?

- What would you say are X's strong points? Weak points?

- Did you form any opinion of the work for which X is best suited?

- How did X get on with people?

- How much potential/initiative, etc. did X show?

- What did you/X's supervisor think of X's abilities to (pick out key areas of your personnel specification and question around these).

What if a reference is poor?

If the references 'check out', that's great. If they do not, continue checking with other referees. Some employers may feel resentful about someone leaving their employment and give a harsh reference. If your candidate's references continue not to check out well, you may want to consider whether you have made the best decision or whether to move on to your second-choice candidate. However, if only one reference is poor you may decide to ignore it, or discuss it with the candidate before making your final decision.

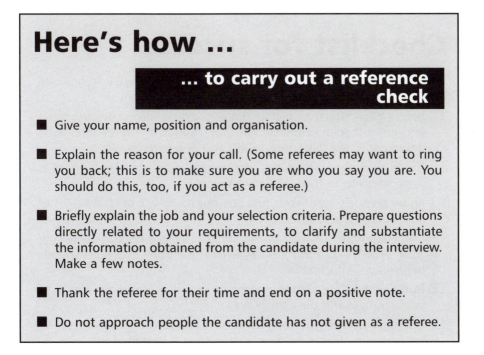

Here's how ...

... to carry out a reference check

- Give your name, position and organisation.

- Explain the reason for your call. (Some referees may want to ring you back; this is to make sure you are who you say you are. You should do this, too, if you act as a referee.)

- Briefly explain the job and your selection criteria. Prepare questions directly related to your requirements, to clarify and substantiate the information obtained from the candidate during the interview. Make a few notes.

- Thank the referee for their time and end on a positive note.

- Do not approach people the candidate has not given as a referee.

THE FIRST FEW DAYS

People's first few weeks in a new job are critical. For better or worse, they develop lasting impressions and attitudes. How quickly and comfortably they settle in determines how quickly they become effective members of the group. A large part of this is the induction you provide.

Welcome to our enterprise

Induction can generally be split into two distinct parts. The first is *induction to the organisation*, which the human resources (HR) department often carries out. This part of the induction program covers general items such as pay arrangements and employee benefits and activities, and deals with the organisation as a whole: how it is structured, where the new recruit will fit in, the organisation's history and its products, services and customers.

HR departments of large organisations sometimes have induction videos or provide this information on its intranet and/or in booklets. If your organisation doesn't provide organisation induction, develop a checklist based on Box 4.3 for inducting new employees to your organisation.

Checklist for success

☐ Respect the privacy of applicants' details. Store applications and your notes in a secure place and don't discuss them.

☐ Before each interview review the application form, covering letter and any other information you have about the candidate. Note down additional questions to ask and points to cover.

☐ Don't read the candidate's information back to them off their application form. They already know it.

☐ Know precisely what your first few questions will be. Have a list of other questions to refer to.

☐ Don't ask 'cute' or trick questions like *'Tell me about yourself'* or *'Why should I give this job to you?'*. These don't draw out specific behavioural information.

☐ Don't unduly pressure interviewees or put them under contrived stress to measure their tolerance.

☐ Be friendly when you interview and observe the usual courtesies, for example: *'Please come in'* rather than *'Come in'*.

☐ Aim for a conversational flavour to the interview, not a rigid question-and-answer session.

☐ Give your full attention to candidates and get them talking. You won't learn anything about them while you're talking!

☐ Question with a purpose and ask one question at a time. Don't waffle!

☐ Seek behavioural examples and build up a list of past behaviours to predict the candidate's ability (or lack of it) to meet your criteria.

☐ Find out whether the candidates *want* to do the job as well as whether they *can* do it.

☐ Hone in on personal skills that will help or prevent applicants from doing the job well.

☐ When you ask a question give the candidate time to think. Don't let a thoughtful silence worry you.

☐ Probe carefully and take nothing at face value. Be careful not to draw a conclusion without concrete behavioural evidence to support it.

☐ Avoid giving non-verbal or verbal messages that convey agreement or disagreement.

☐ Be aware of the image you are projecting of yourself and your organisation. Candidates should leave the interview feeling they have been fairly treated and with a positive picture of the company.

Here's how ...

... to save your department money

A poor job match or poor induction cause many new employees to quit during their first three months. This means all the time you spent processing candidates, interviewing and preparing for the interview, reference checking and inducting and training the new employee has been wasted.

Between your wasted time and wasted administration and advertising costs, lowered productivity of the employee while they were learning the job, possible negative effects on other group members and a host of lost opportunities and hidden costs, it is estimated the cost to your department will be between one and three times the departing employee's annual salary.

Box 4.3 What to include in enterprise induction

- History, background
- Nature of activities (the products or services provided, who its customers are, locations of various operations, etc.)
- Who's who in the organisation (show the organisation chart and explain key roles and functions)
- Introduction to key staff members from other departments and the management group
- Organisation vision and values
- A tour of the organisation's main functional areas
- Key policies (e.g. EEO, health, safety and welfare, smoking) and sources of advice and assistance within the organisation
- Benefits (e.g. superannuation, credit union facilities, employee purchase schemes)
- Details of relevant awards, enterprise agreements, pay arrangements
- The performance appraisal system
- How wages are calculated and paid
- What training is available in the company

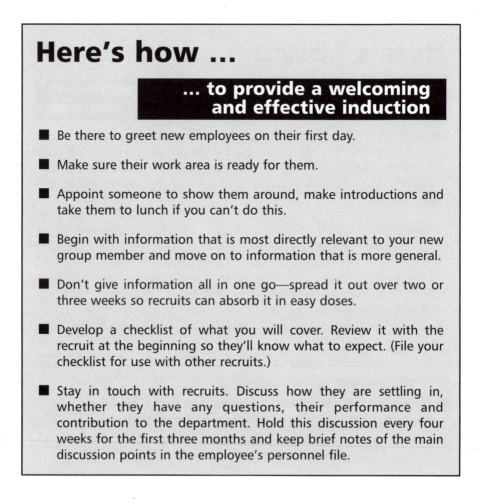

Here's how ...

... to provide a welcoming and effective induction

■ Be there to greet new employees on their first day.

■ Make sure their work area is ready for them.

■ Appoint someone to show them around, make introductions and take them to lunch if you can't do this.

■ Begin with information that is most directly relevant to your new group member and move on to information that is more general.

■ Don't give information all in one go—spread it out over two or three weeks so recruits can absorb it in easy doses.

■ Develop a checklist of what you will cover. Review it with the recruit at the beginning so they'll know what to expect. (File your checklist for use with other recruits.)

■ Stay in touch with recruits. Discuss how they are settling in, whether they have any questions, their performance and contribution to the department. Hold this discussion every four weeks for the first three months and keep brief notes of the main discussion points in the employee's personnel file.

Welcome to our department

Do you need to induct someone who transfers to your group from another area in the organisation? Absolutely. They won't need company induction but they will need departmental induction.

Does the induction you currently provide make new employees feel welcome? Does it help them fit into their new workplace? Does it explain their job in relation to others in the department and organisation?

Supervisors usually induct recruits to their new department, although they may delegate some aspects to senior group members. The more quickly you can help new employees fit in and contribute to their workplace, the happier and more productive they, and the whole work group, will be.

Discuss any special duties and responsibilities involved in the job. Show them where to put their personal items, give them their own workspace or workstation and show them where to obtain the supplies they'll need. Show them how the telephone system works and outline the procedures for answering each other's telephones and taking messages. Tell them a little bit about the surrounding area: nice places to go for a walk, nearby shopping and so on.

Spell out rules and regulations to minimise future misunderstandings. Describe how you expect the group to operate together and what to do if they don't understand something, if they run into problems or if they have an idea to improve something. Review the health and safety requirements of the job and where to find further information. Explain your housekeeping policy.

Box 4.4 shows some other things to include in your departmental induction.

Box 4.4 What to include in departmental induction

- Introductions to workmates and worker representatives (e.g. health and safety representative, union representative) and others they will be working with or 'seeing around'

- The role of their new department in the organisation

- Department tour: location of fire escapes, equipment

- Review job description, rules and regulations, any special duties and responsibilities, how their job fits into the work of the department and the organisation as a whole

- Outline of the job training you will provide

- Everything about the job—what tools, equipment and supplies the recruit will be using and how to obtain them, safety requirements, housekeeping, your expectations of them, what others expect of them and so on

- Hours of work, breaks, start and finishing times, holiday arrangements

- What to do if they're late or ill

- Location of amenities: toilets, washroom, kitchen facilities, canteen, café bar, car park, etc.

- General familiarisation with equipment and its operation

- Security and emergency systems: fire drills, fire warden, location of fire extinguishers, warning signals, what to do in case of an accident

---

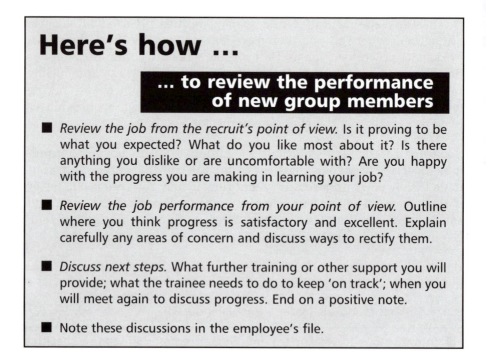

Here's how ...

... to review the performance of new group members

■ *Review the job from the recruit's point of view.* Is it proving to be what you expected? What do you like most about it? Is there anything you dislike or are uncomfortable with? Are you happy with the progress you are making in learning your job?

■ *Review the job performance from your point of view.* Outline where you think progress is satisfactory and excellent. Explain carefully any areas of concern and discuss ways to rectify them.

■ *Discuss next steps.* What further training or other support you will provide; what the trainee needs to do to keep 'on track'; when you will meet again to discuss progress. End on a positive note.

■ Note these discussions in the employee's file.

This is the perfect opportunity to outline clearly the type of attitudes to safety and care of equipment you expect, the importance of following procedures and the general performance standards and work behaviours you require. Make your expectations for the new employee's work behaviour and contributions to the department clear so everyone will start off on the 'right foot'.

Remember ...

... to induct contractors and temporary staff!

They may not need the full induction but should receive a shortened form of it, concentrating on departmental induction.

CHAPTER FIVE

DEVELOP WINNERS
Improving results through training

ever cut corners when training employees. Yes, training costs time, effort and money. But think how much time, effort and money *not* training would cost!

Good training builds employees' confidence and increases their value to the organisation. It saves you the time and irritation of fixing 'mistakes', repeating earlier training and correcting bad habits. The systematic approach described in this chapter will help you decide who needs training in what, and when and how to provide it. It will reduce the time you spend training and increase efficiency, productivity, quality of work and morale.

IDENTIFYING TRAINING NEEDS
Do you recognise any of these common indicators of possible training needs?

- High error rate
- Slow work speeds
- Some tasks are avoided
- High levels of complaints
- Jobs being done a second or third time due to errors
- Measures of success not achieved (speed, quantity, quality, cost)
- Too many accidents and near misses
- Last-minute 'panics' to meet deadlines
- Conflict or poor working relationships within the department or with customers
- People working overtime
- Excessive absenteeism
- Excessive labour turnover
- Changing customer needs or expectations
- Organisational changes
- Staff changes
- Technology changes

Is training really the answer?

Of course, some of these warnings could be caused by other factors too, such as poor supervision, poor teamwork, poor work systems and procedures, faulty or inadequate equipment or being understaffed. Before launching into any training program, make sure training is what you really need by discussing it with the job holders, assessing group members' current competency or skill levels under normal job conditions and observing the way the work is being carried out. Use the Five Building Blocks (see Chapter 6) or *Ask Why Five Times* technique (see Chapter 15) to make sure training really is the answer.

If you decide training is the answer, think about what type of training would be best: on-the-job training, off-the-job training, coaching, self-study, etc.

Know why you're training

Whether it's to upgrade existing skills, build new ones or correct a performance problem, know what you expect the training to do. What outcomes or results are you looking for? What new behaviours or skills

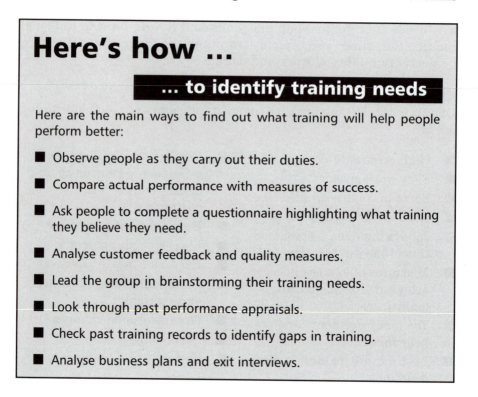

Here's how ...

... to identify training needs

Here are the main ways to find out what training will help people perform better:

- Observe people as they carry out their duties.

- Compare actual performance with measures of success.

- Ask people to complete a questionnaire highlighting what training they believe they need.

- Analyse customer feedback and quality measures.

- Lead the group in brainstorming their training needs.

- Look through past performance appraisals.

- Check past training records to identify gaps in training.

- Analyse business plans and exit interviews.

do you want to see used? How will you recognise them? Use the STAR **measures of success** to set clear training targets (see Chapter 3).

Involve employees
If you're not sure whether training is the answer, discussing the issue with your group can point to the best course of action. It provides some 'ownership' in and commitment to the decision and builds interest and enthusiasm for training. Involvement also helps people accept responsibility for learning new skills and building their knowledge base.

Here's how ...
... to stay ahead of the trend

Not so long ago organisations used to manage people's careers. Today, it's more a case of 'Me Pty Ltd'. Individual employees are taking more and more responsibility for managing their own careers. This means deciding on the training they need and making sure they get it, through self-managed study, their employers or a combination of both.

Encourage your group members to take responsibility for and manage their own learning.

DEVELOPING A TRAINING PLAN
Because they keep track of who needs training in what and by when, training plans help make sure the training in your department is up to date.

Individual training plans
Make a training plan for everyone who joins your department. If you plan to delegate some of the training to experienced workers or use off-the-job training programs, the training plan should also indicate who will be carrying out the training. It might look something like the partial plan shown in Figure 5.1.

You'll probably agree upon training needs with other employees during their performance appraisals. If anyone needs training before the official performance appraisal, though, don't wait—see to it now.

Figure 5.1 Training plan for a new group member

Job title:	Administrative assistant			
Job duties	Measures of success	Training to commence	Trainer	Training completed
General filing	Filing to be completed daily to 100 per cent accuracy.	1/6/03	Marion	8/6/03
Telephone answering	Telephone answering support for managers to be provided as requested. Telephones to be answered as shown and within 4 rings. Messages to be taken accurately.	18/5/03	Supervisor	26/5/03
Storage of material for field staff	Orderly and tidy storage of all materials used by field staff to enable rapid and easy retrieval.	15/6/03	Brendon	

Departmental training plans

Here's how to prepare a training plan quickly and easily for your whole department. First, list all the jobs or tasks carried out in the department and indicate the ideal number of people who should be able to do each (taking into account holiday periods, absenteeism, busy periods, etc.). Then list staff and note who can do which tasks, who needs training, when the training should take place and so on.

Plans like these are great because they give an overview of your department, clearly indicating where job coverage is excessive or inadequate, which staff members are the most and least skilled and who needs further training. They also help you set priorities for training. To turn the skills audit into a training plan as shown in Figure 5.2, simply add dates showing when you plan to begin training.

Figure 5.2 Training plan for a milk bar

Employee \ Task	Stock shelves	Price goods	Order goods	Take inventory	Make change	Operate cash register	Deal with customers	Record GST payments
Jean	✓	✓	✗	✗	✓	✓	✗ 1/7	O
Yunhua	– 15/6	O	✓	✓	✓	✓	✓	✓
Alf	✗ Review 15/6	✓	O	✗ 30/6	✗	✗ Review 15/6	– 1/7	O
Morgan	✓	✓	✓	✓	✓	✓	✓	✓
Terry	✓	✗	✗	✗ 30/6	✓	✗ Review 4/6	✗	O
Ideal number to perform task	5	3	2	3	4	4	5	2
Actual number able to perform task	3	3	2	2	4	3	2	2

Key: ✓ Can do well
 ✗ Can do but needs more experience or training
 O Cannot do and does not need to do
 – Cannot do and should be trained to do

Prepared by: J. McTavish
Date: June 2003

101

Funding training

Training is often a separate budget item. If you don't have a specific training budget, set out a clear business case for spending money on training. What benefits do you expect to gain as a result? Can you quantify how much these benefits will save your department in terms

Here's how ...

... to identify training needs and develop training plans

Stages	Key points
1. Identify training needs	Staff changes Performance standards Forward planning of work Cover key tasks for emergencies Increase job interest Cross-skill or multiskill
2. Develop a training plan	Select people to be trained Decide training method Fix date for start/completion of training Make best use of each person's abilities Keep plan up to date
On-the-job training	
3. Make instruction plan	Aim of session Skills required Measures of success Method of instruction
4. Prepare job breakdown	Do task Divide into stages Select key points Safety factors always key points
5. Arrange everything for training	Lay out the work area Put materials in order Ready any equipment Gather any instruction aids Prevent interruptions

Stages	Key points
Off-the-job training	
3. Select training provider	Internal training program External (public) training program In-house training by external provider Videos, e-training, self-paced study, etc.
4. Arrange training	Ensure within budget Obtain necessary approvals
5. Reinforce training	Discuss training objectives prior to training with trainee Discuss learnings and applications after training with trainee

of money or time, how much they will improve productivity or service levels or how they will equip your department to meet the future needs of the business better?

Whatever you are quoted as the cost of training (and venue hire if you decide to hold the training off-site), your organisation can claim the GST back, making the actual cost 10% less than the figure(s) you are quoted.

ARRANGING TRAINING
What kind of training do you need?

1. Technical skills (e.g. answering customer queries, working with spreadsheets, setting up equipment).

2. Personal skills (e.g. time management, conflict management, introducing change, planning, solving problems and decision making).

3. Interpersonal skills training (e.g. communication, teambuilding and team skills).

4. Training on specific topics (e.g. client service, managing projects, health and safety).

The first category of training is usually catered for on the job, while, depending on the numbers of people being trained and your specific needs, the last three tend to be run off the job, either through public programs or programs run solely for your own employees. Some topics in the first, second and final categories of training are also suitable for self-study and **e-training**.

On-the-job training

Do your training needs revolve around specific job skills? This lends itself more to on-the-job training, usually one-on-one or in small groups of up to four or five people.

This can take several forms: working beside a more senior or experienced employee, rotating duties with other employees, 'shadowing' or assisting other employees or more formal training that you or a nominated experienced worker provides.

Coaching

Coaching is a way of developing skills and knowledge in an informal or semi-formal way, often through conversations or having someone work alongside you to 'learn the ropes'. You can pass on your own skills and knowledge and suggest books, periodicals or trade publications to read, networks to join and websites and other sources of information to help employees build their skills. You can ask a more experienced employee or employees with specialist skills to coach team members, and build skills through special assignments, attending meetings and visiting other plants or parts of the organisation.

Off-the-job training

If the training needs are for other than specific, technical job skills, you will probably opt for off-the-job training. Your own corporate trainers or outside training consultants can design and run workshops for your employees to meet the training objectives you identify. They can be run on your own premises (in-house training) or you can take people off-site, away from the work environment; this helps them concentrate fully on the training and signals its importance.

Other alternatives are for a few of your group to join a public program (e.g. through universities, colleges or private providers) or to use self-paced learning, self-study or e-learning.

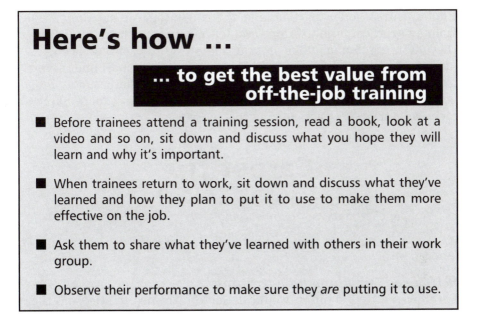

Here's how ...

... to get the best value from off-the-job training

■ Before trainees attend a training session, read a book, look at a video and so on, sit down and discuss what you hope they will learn and why it's important.

■ When trainees return to work, sit down and discuss what they've learned and how they plan to put it to use to make them more effective on the job.

■ Ask them to share what they've learned with others in their work group.

■ Observe their performance to make sure they *are* putting it to use.

In-house courses

If you have more than six or eight people to train, consider running a workshop solely for them, either in-house (in a training or conference room) or off-site at a local hotel or training facility. This is usually more economical than public courses because you will be charged per day rather than per person. It has the added advantage that the training will be specifically designed to meet your needs and that it allows your whole team to hear 'the same message'. As an added bonus, in-house training often builds team spirit.

Speak to several potential trainers or training organisations to get a feel for what they offer and how they work. If you are considering using a large training organisation, ask to speak to the people who would actually be conducting the training, not just their salespeople. Brief them clearly on your training needs, agree the objectives or outcomes you want the training to meet and get their commitment that training will be customised to meed your specific needs.

Public courses

If you have fewer than six people to train, it may be more economical to send them on a public course. Many TAFE colleges, Employers' Chambers and large training organisations publish an annual calendar of training programs. They charge per person and run these programs on their own premises or at city venues.

Public courses offer participants the advantage of meeting people from a variety of organisations and learning about the different ways they do things. Some public programs allow 50, 100, or more, people to attend, which makes the training very impersonal and trainer focused; other organisations limit numbers so that there is more interaction between participants and the trainer, making it more likely to meet your trainee's particular needs.

Career tip

Don't wait for your employer to manage your career: take charge of your own learning and development needs.

Self-paced learning and e-training
Perhaps the best solution would be for the trainee to study on their own. There are lots of varieties of self-study, too: books, the Internet, e-learning, joining professional associations, videos, attending evening classes and so on. This takes more effort and a greater time commitment on the trainee's part and for this reason the results are sometimes disappointing.

PROVIDING TRAINING
When you train people on job skills, should you just sit them down, quickly run through what they need to know and leave them to it? That was a leading question because the answer is obvious—*No!* Put in a bit of preparation and thought beforehand and follow a systematic training process, even if you know the task you intend to teach someone really well.

Did you know ...

Systematic job training was first introduced during World War II when large numbers of new factory workers needed to be trained to replace the experienced tradespeople who had gone off to war. Systematic training, based on job descriptions and the four-step training method explained below, helped factories reduce the length of the training period from four years to 12–18 months without any loss to quality or speed.

Use a job breakdown

Giving information in a series of logical steps makes it easier to learn. A **job breakdown** helps you do this in two ways. It details the clear, correct and safe work procedure that you want followed. Exactly *how* do you want the job done? What should be done first, second, third and so on? It also reminds you to tell trainees the most important information, or *key points*, that will help them do the job correctly.

Box 5.1 shows how to make a job breakdown. Notice that it contains phrases only. Because you will be using the job breakdown as a memory jogger while you train, there is no need to write long sentences and paragraphs. The acid test of a good job breakdown is being able to do the job using only the stages you have written.

Box 5.1 A job breakdown of making a job breakdown

Stages	Key points
Go through the task. Select suitable portions for the trainee to master.	Anything which might affect *safety*, *quality*, *speed*, or *accuracy*. Tricks of the trade to make learning easier.
1. Examine job.	Do it yourself. Ensure safe and efficient method.
2. Select stages.	Do the job again. Maintain sequence and select units of instruction. Not too big or too small. Maximum of seven stages per job breakdown.
3. Record stages.	Use actions—verbs. Be brief.
4. Select key points.	Do the job again. Look for: Safety—Quality—Accuracy, special movements, essential information, Positive not negative.
5. Record key points.	Be brief. Essential points only. Maximum of four per stage (usually).

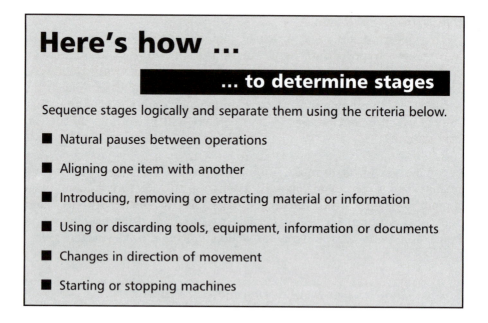

Here's how ...

... to determine stages

Sequence stages logically and separate them using the criteria below.

- Natural pauses between operations

- Aligning one item with another

- Introducing, removing or extracting material or information

- Using or discarding tools, equipment, information or documents

- Changes in direction of movement

- Starting or stopping machines

Too many stages confuse and frustrate the trainee, resulting in a longer training time. So if a job or task requires more than seven stages, break it in half and teach each half as a separate unit; for even longer jobs conduct several training sessions. Go for a few small, readily remembered chunks for each training session.

Because our brains tend to skip over negatives, use positive, not negative language. For example, *'Never leave the door open'* is negative and, because we might focus on the *'leave the door open'* part of the message, it can easily lead to the door actually being left open. *'Always close the door'* is positive and more easily and correctly remembered, and therefore more likely to be followed correctly.

There are usually three or four key points per stage, with one or two words per key point. If there are more than six key points in a stage, consider splitting that stage into two stages.

Follow the four steps to first-rate instruction

It's easy to fall into poor training habits when you have a lot of other demands on your time.

To train correctly and avoid the mistakes described above, work through the following four systematic steps summarised in Box 5.2.

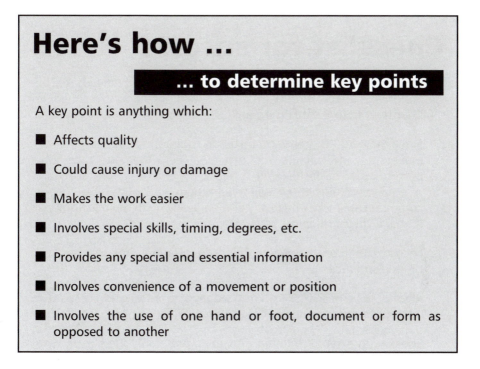

Here's how ...

... to determine key points

A key point is anything which:

- Affects quality

- Could cause injury or damage

- Makes the work easier

- Involves special skills, timing, degrees, etc.

- Provides any special and essential information

- Involves convenience of a movement or position

- Involves the use of one hand or foot, document or form as opposed to another

This will keep the time you spend training down to a minimum and dramatically increase its effectiveness.

Some general points

We know that two things in particular help people learn: providing small amounts of information at a time, and offering plenty of positive feedback and encouragement as they progress. So take it slowly and provide a positive, supportive learning climate and help when it is needed. Give trainees frequent feedback on their progress. People take time to build up their skills and confidence and they need to know someone is there to notice and appreciate their efforts.

Have a simple and workable method for checking the trainee's progress and use it consistently. Trainees may do the job slowly at first, which is to be expected. However, never accept poor quality work—set high standards right from the start. And make sure the trainee knows precisely what those standards are and why they're important.

Have you ever trained someone and been surprised when they seemed to stop learning? Or perhaps you've been learning something and you've 'hit the wall'. Most of us have periods when our performance

Checklist for success

☐ Training is not always the answer if productivity needs to be improved. Check through the Five Building Blocks described in Chapter 6 before settling on a course of action.

☐ Since most adults aren't interested in 'training for training's sake', make sure any training you offer will help them do their jobs better, easier or faster. Will it allow them to use new software or equipment efficiently? Will it help them work better together or communicate more effectively and enjoyably with their customers? Manage their time more efficiently and effectively?

☐ Focus training on the needs of the organisation, on outcomes and on performance.

☐ Identify your needs (skills, knowledge, attributes) and compare it with current performance. Then plan to fill any gaps.

☐ Speak with external training providers, preferably the person who will be carrying out the training, to make sure they can meet your objectives and expectations.

☐ Support off-the-job training and make it clear you expect trainees to apply what they've learned and share it with colleagues.

☐ Establish clear measures of learning success and share these with the trainee.

☐ Make sure your job breakdowns contain only *essential* information.

☐ Instruct people in the attitudes you are looking for (e.g. customer service orientation, helpfulness to colleagues, friendliness, tidiness), as well as job skills.

☐ After training, give a copy of the job breakdown to the trainees to refer to until they have mastered the job.

☐ Add other information as the trainee begins to get the hang of the job.

☐ When you have finished using your job breakdown, file it to use with your next trainee.

Here's how ...

... *not* to train

■ Rush through it, to 'get it over with' and make the trainee feel unimportant.

■ Swamp trainees with a lot of irrelevant information.

■ Backtrack a lot, to bewilder the trainee.

■ Don't teach the job in a logical sequence of stages. Hop around, so trainees don't know whether they're coming or going.

■ Don't stress key points. Why make it too easy?

■ Just show and tell, without wasting time giving trainees a go to make sure they've grasped it.

■ Distract trainees by talking while they are concentrating.

■ Insult the trainee by asking *'Do you understand?'* rather than a more tactful *'Did I explain that clearly enough?'*

■ Leave trainees to practise on their own, without taking the time to check back to see how they're going.

and ability to learn slows down a bit, regardless of how much we're trying. This is called a **learning plateau**. It's as if we've become saturated with all the new information and we need a mental 'time out' to absorb it before we can move on and learn some more.

Don't let trainees become discouraged if they plateau—they should keep practising what they've learned so far and move on when they're comfortable with that.

EVALUATING TRAINING'S EFFECTIVENESS
Successful training meets its objectives. It builds the skills and knowledge it set out to build and motivates people to apply them. You'll know whether off-the-job training has achieved the desired outcomes when you discuss what the trainees have learned and watch them apply it on the job.

111

Box 5.2 The instruction sequence

1. *Motivate.*	**Prepare** Put at ease. Clearly state job or subject. Show a completed workpiece. Check existing knowledge. Create interest in learning. Ensure correct position.
2. Provide *understanding* of what is being taught.	**Present** Tell, show, illustrate, as appropriate. One stage at a time. Stress key points. Instruct clearly, completely, patiently. Give essential information at a suitable pace. Refer to job breakdown. Pause for four seconds between stages.
3. Provide *involvement* and *participation* in the learning.	**Try out** Ask trainee to do the job and explain what they're doing. Correct errors as they occur. Check understanding of key points. Keep quiet. Continue until satisfied.
4. Let trainee *apply, practise* and *develop* newly learned skills.	**Put to work** Indicate performance targets to aim for. Name person who can help if you are not available. Encourage questions. Check back as necessary.

If they don't apply it, sit down and find out why. Did the trainer fail to deliver the needed information? Is applying it 'too hard' or unrewarding in some way? For example, do existing systems and procedures make it difficult to apply the training? Is there not enough time to put it into practice? Perhaps the trainee is the only person to have learned a skill and is reluctant to try it out. Perhaps the trainee didn't realise you really do expect them to use their new skills!

Here's how ...

... to build great rapport with trainees for smoother learning

Match your voice speed and volume to theirs. For example, if they speak quickly, do the same; if they often pause thoughtfully, do the same. If they speak softly, do the same.

Checklist for success

- [ ] Plan training sessions and organise your materials ahead of time.
- [ ] Stay flexible—speed up or slow down to suit your learner.
- [ ] Set clear goals so trainees know where they're headed and can measure their progress.
- [ ] Explain why a task needs to be done, or done in a certain way, and how it fits into the 'big picture'.
- [ ] Give learners plenty of time to practise what you've shown them, not just watch what you do.
- [ ] If trainees make a mistake, resist stepping in and taking over; encourage them to work out what they've done wrong and what they should do instead.
- [ ] Ask questions to ensure learners understand.
- [ ] Praise learners as they make progress.
- [ ] Don't criticise, but do give helpful hints on how to improve their skills.
- [ ] Keep your instructions brief, clear and at a suitable pace.
- [ ] Don't try and teach more than seven stages at a time.
- [ ] Take nothing for granted. The learner doesn't have the same background knowledge and skills that you have, so explain slowly, clearly and patiently.
- [ ] Avoid using jargon and technical terms the trainee doesn't know yet.

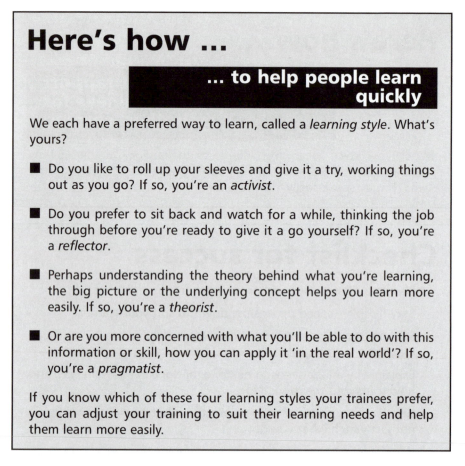

Here's how ...

... to help people learn quickly

We each have a preferred way to learn, called a *learning style*. What's yours?

■ Do you like to roll up your sleeves and give it a try, working things out as you go? If so, you're an *activist*.

■ Do you prefer to sit back and watch for a while, thinking the job through before you're ready to give it a go yourself? If so, you're a *reflector*.

■ Perhaps understanding the theory behind what you're learning, the big picture or the underlying concept helps you learn more easily. If so, you're a *theorist*.

■ Or are you more concerned with what you'll be able to do with this information or skill, how you can apply it 'in the real world'? If so, you're a *pragmatist*.

If you know which of these four learning styles your trainees prefer, you can adjust your training to suit their learning needs and help them learn more easily.

If you or one of your team members has conducted on-the-job training, you'll know whether you've succeeded because the trainee will achieve the measures of success you established at the outset. If this is not the case, find out what is happening. Do you need to explain it more clearly? Has the trainee not had enough time to build the skills needed to attain the desired level of performance? Is lack of time, poor systems or faulty equipment holding them back? Only rarely is the reason likely to be because the trainee is not motivated to apply the skills or unsuited to the work.

Because training is an investment in time and money, always make sure it is being applied on the job.

Training pays

Some companies calculate the return they get for their training dollars. Motorola, for example, calculates a return of over $50 for each dollar they spend on employee training.

A US study called the 1997 Human Performance Practices Survey found that organisations that invested an average of US$900 per employee on professional development outperformed organisations that invested an average of US$275 per employee. They achieved 57% higher sales per employee and 37% higher gross profit per employee.

According to Thomas A. Stewart in *Intellectual Capital: The New Wealth of Organisations*, a 10% increase in the educational level of the workforce increases productivity by 8.6%. Compare this with a 10% increase in plant and equipment values, which yields only a 3.4% increase in productivity. Which would you invest in?

CHAPTER SIX

BUILD PEAK PERFORMANCE AND PRODUCTIVITY
Releasing people's potential

n organisations trying to do more with less, productivity is a critical issue. You need to know what stimulates productivity and what stifles it.

Have you ever tried to do something well, but didn't succeed as well as you'd hoped? What prevented you? It probably wasn't lack of desire or lack of effort. Was it lack of time? Lack of information or experience? Lack of support from others? Did your tools or equipment let you down? Perhaps you weren't quite sure what you were supposed to do or how to go about doing it.

If you're ever tempted to blame employees for poor productivity, don't. Chances are you'd be wrong. Chances are the employees are doing their best and something is preventing them from being as productive as they would like. The Five Building Blocks to peak productivity explained in this chapter will help you find out what curbs productivity so you can fix it.

THE FIVE BUILDING BLOCKS TO PEAK PERFORMANCE AND PRODUCTIVITY

If any of the Five Building Blocks of peak performance and productivity is deficient, employees won't be able to do the best job they are capable of. The Five Building Blocks are:

1. *What to*—people need to know precisely what is expected of them.

2. *Want to*—people need to enjoy the work they are doing and know that it's both valuable and valued.

3. *How to*—people need to be trained and allowed to build up experience.

4. *Chance to*—people need to work in an environment that supports, not suppresses, their good performance.

5. *Led to*—people need to work with a fair and positive leader who appreciates their efforts and helps them reach their potential.

These are the building blocks that unlock performance, productivity and achievement. They don't happen by chance: you need to manage them. If you manage each of them well, you will release people's ability to perform well. You will increase their productivity and job satisfaction and enhance their ability to satisfy customers.

WHAT TO

Have you ever been given a task to do and you weren't sure exactly what you were supposed to do, why it needed to be done or how it fitted into the larger whole? It's difficult to get wildly enthusiastic about tasks like this.

People need to know clearly and specifically what you expect. Explicit roles and responsibilities give people something to focus on and strive towards; without them, they're working in the dark. Knowing what is expected of them encourages people to monitor their own performance and take responsibility for it.

As Figure 6.1 shows, there are three aspects of the *what to* building block: the framework, non-task goals and the **hot stove principle**.

Figure 6.1 The three aspects of the *what to* building block

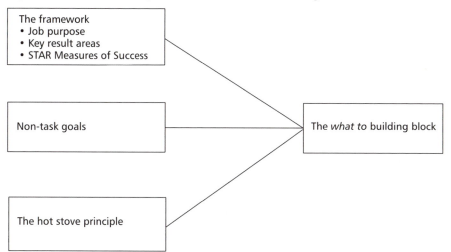

117

The framework

Always explain tasks and duties, roles and responsibilities in the context of an overall framework of **job purpose**, **key result areas**, and clear **measures of success**. This framework prevents people from seeing their jobs as just a series of tasks. It gives their role, responsibilities and duties a context and a purpose.

Job purpose

Do you remember Sisyphus? The gods condemned him to ceaseless effort rolling a rock to the top of the mountain, whence it would fall back down. They believed there is no more dreadful punishment than hopeless and futile labour.

With time at a premium in most organisations, it is more important than ever that everything we ask people to do is valuable. Job purpose statements make sure people know why their jobs are worth doing.

Box 6.1 Job purpose

Training officer	To design and deliver training products that develop and extend the skills of employees in my organisation, so that they and the organisation succeed and prosper.
Retail store supervisor	To achieve or exceed sales and other targets in a way that delights my customers, my staff and myself.
Retail sales assistant	To present myself and the store professionally and advise and interact with customers in a way that will make them want to return repeatedly to purchase from us.
Assembly line supervisor	To help my team produce quality product within time and cost budgets so that the organisation's reputation is enhanced in the marketplace both as a quality producer and a quality employer.
Assembly line operator	To work with the team to produce the best possible product within the company's cost and other requirements so that I feel proud of my contribution and customers are glad they bought from us.

They are a succinct statement of why the job exists. They are motivating and provide overall guidance in how people should approach their jobs. They act as a personal job vision or mission statement. Box 6.1 shows some typical job purpose statements.

Key result areas

As we saw in Chapter 3, key result areas (KRAs) describe the main areas of accountability and responsibility of a job. Remember to keep them short and not to use verbs. Most jobs have six to eight KRAs, each as important as the other. Make sure everyone working in your department knows clearly what their KRAs are, and review them together at least once a year. Performance appraisals are a good opportunity to do this.

Each KRA contains many individual tasks, which together contribute to achieving results. This is how KRAs put tasks into context. Each task employees do should be contributing in some way to achieving results. If it isn't, why are they doing it?

Measures of success

Performance and productivity blossom when people can monitor them themselves. The measures of success for each KRA should provide a measuring stick that lets job holders judge for themselves how good a job they are doing.

As we saw in Chapter 3, meaningful measures of success meet the STAR criteria. They are:

S   *Specific*—measurable or quantifiable in some other way

T   *Timelines* are specified

A   We can *assemble* performance information quickly and easily

R   *Realistic*, or achievable

If a task is too easy people won't put much effort into it, yet if it is too hard and they don't believe they can do it, they won't put in much effort either. Measures of success should also contribute to overall organisational, departmental or job goals. For example, a poor target would be to '*reduce defects in your work to a minimum*'. This is not clear, specific or time-framed. No one would ever know whether it had been reached; consider the following:

- An employee had 10 parts rejected because of cosmetic flaws.

- Twelve parts were rejected because they would not function properly.

- The total number of rejects was reduced from 80 to 50.

- Defects reduced by fifteen last week.

In which case did the employee reach the target? There is no way of knowing the answer because the target is not specific or measurable. It doesn't tell us what a 'minimum' number of defects is and by when this minimum number should be reached.

If instead the measure of success is for the employee to *'increase the number of parts passed for finish quality to 99% and the number of functional units produced to 92% of an average daily output of 2000 units by the end of the current quarter'*, then we will all know whether the performance target has been reached.

Targets like these are also easily tracked or monitored, which means that corrective action can be taken quickly. This is critical in today's demanding marketplace. Every task should have objectives like this so that people know what they are trying to do and can easily check how well they are doing it.

Whenever possible, establish success measures jointly with employees. Working together, identify, agree on and write down what must be accomplished, by when and to what standards. Make sure the success measures relate only to those parts of a job that are actually under the employee's control.

Some areas are harder to pin down than others. How can you measure dependability, for example? You might look at whether a person gets the facts before leaping in, whether their reports and paperwork are accurate and punctual or whether they follow up and complete outstanding items. With a bit of thought, even intangible attributes can be objectively assessed.

Targets tend to fall into five main areas:

- Cost
- Quantity
- Time
- Quality
- Safety

Here's how ...

... to write targets

Terms	Example
Percentages	x% pass rate; y% machine utilisation; X% of customers greeted within Y seconds.
Frequency of occurrence	Stocks to be checked every three months; mail to be sorted twice daily.
Averages	X per week, per day, per hour; X documents to be prepared daily; Y items to be completed hourly; X% of telephone queries to be answered successfully by first point of contact.
Time limits	All accidents or near misses to be investigated within three working days; all calls to be answered within X rings.
Absolute rule	All machinists to wear approved safety gear at all times when inside designated areas; all site personnel and visitors to wear hard hats and safety boots at all times.

Use these categories to write targets. Remember to use positive terms—focus on what you *do* want, not what you *don't* want.

A clear framework like this helps build performance and productivity because people know precisely what they need to achieve, when they need to achieve it by and why it's important. They can monitor their own performance and will be motivated to find ways to continually improve it, provided the other building blocks are in place.

Making sure each employee is aware of their job purpose, KRAs and measures of success is one of the most important things you can do to help your work group reach peak productivity.

Did you know ...

Study after study has found that goal setting increases productivity more than any other technique, including pay rises.

Non-task goals

You probably expect employees to also meet non-task goals. For example:

- Be cooperative, friendly and helpful to colleagues and customers.
- Try to finish one task before moving on to another.
- Make our customers glad they are dealing with us.
- Look for better ways of doing things.
- Keep your work space tidy.

Don't leave things like this as unspoken group **norms** and expect employees magically to 'pick them up' for themselves. Make them explicit so you can be sure people understand them and work towards achieving them.

The 'hot stove' principle

The third and final aspect of the *what to* building block is the **hot stove principle**. These are 'bottom-line' rules and regulations that apply to everyone. They often involve safety, following standard operating procedures, housekeeping standards, working with others and customer service.

If people breach important rules, procedures, standards of behaviour or expected ways of working, apply the hot stove principle. Everyone should know what you expect in these areas. If they don't meet your expectations, the penalty should be immediate, impartial and consistent.

WANT TO

There's nothing worse than a mundane, repetitive task, is there? Henry Mintzberg, a McGill University management professor, pointed out an important principle in achieving maximum productivity:

If you want someone to do a good job, give them a good job to do.

Here's how ...

... the hot stove principle works

Advance warning	Just as we can see from a distance that a stove is hot and will burn us if we touch it, so everyone should know your bottom line rules *in advance* and that they will be 'burned' if they break or bend them.
Immediate	Just as when we touch a hot stove we are burned straight away, so the consequence of breaking or bending a bottom-line rule should be *immediate*. If someone breaks a 'hot stove' rule, discuss it with them straight away (in private) to make sure it doesn't happen again.
Impartial	A hot stove is impartial: everyone who touches it is burned. Don't play 'favourites'—bottom-line rules *apply to everyone*.
Consistent	A hot stove is *consistent*. People are always burned if they touch it. The hot stove rules in your department need to apply to everyone, all the time.

In other words, we need to make sure jobs are interesting. The way we arrange jobs, or **job design**, is an important source of job satisfaction, motivation and productivity.

Job design

The 3 Es: enlarging, enriching, empowering

A 'good job' often involves the three Es: enrichment, enlargement and empowerment. **Job enlargement** means expanding a job *horizontally*: the job holder takes on more duties at the same level of responsibility. **Cross-skilling** and **multiskilling** are forms of job enlargement.

Job enrichment means expanding a job *vertically*, increasing the depth of the employee's responsibilities. If the additional duties are at a higher level of responsibility, multiskilling can enrich a job.

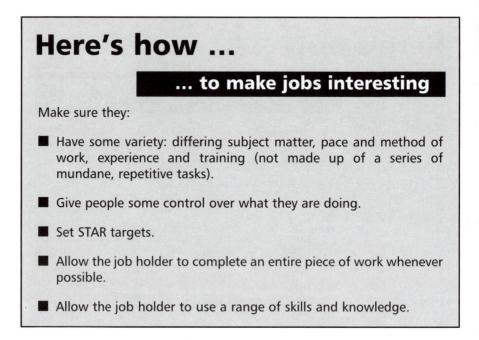

Here's how ...

... to make jobs interesting

Make sure they:

- Have some variety: differing subject matter, pace and method of work, experience and training (not made up of a series of mundane, repetitive tasks).

- Give people some control over what they are doing.

- Set STAR targets.

- Allow the job holder to complete an entire piece of work whenever possible.

- Allow the job holder to use a range of skills and knowledge.

Empowerment is an expanded form of job enrichment. Empowered employees and teams take on responsibilities previously carried out by supervisors or middle managers.

Job enlargement, enrichment and empowerment go hand in hand with training to expand people's skills. Particularly with empowerment, training must include interpersonal skills and such skills as problem solving, decision making, communication and leading and participating in meetings.

Well-designed jobs benefit your department and organisation in a number of ways. They increase motivation, performance and productivity. They can increase organisational flexibility and responsiveness, strengthen customer and supplier relationships, and even help an organisation restructure result in greater efficiency and competitiveness.

Job placement

Have you heard the sayings 'square pegs for square holes; round pegs for round holes' or 'horses for courses'? Suitable **job placement** means putting people in jobs that call for their particular skills, knowledge and attributes and that they will enjoy doing because they suit their work style preferences (see Chapters 2 and 4).

■ Who in your work group enjoys detailed work and who prefers taking a more 'broad brush' approach?

■ Who likes to work on their own, who wants to feel part of a team and who prefers to work alone but with people around them?

■ Who finds it easy and fun to work with the general public and others they've never met before and who works better with people they know quite well?

■ Who likes to move about while they work and who is happier staying in one place?

■ Who enjoys routine, predictable work and who prefers variety?

■ Who welcomes the chance to solve problems and work things out and who wants to know their job, do it well and not get 'hit' with unexpected 'hassles'?

Do you know the working preference of people in your work group? If you do, you can offer job opportunities they will appreciate, enjoy and find challenging. The satisfaction a job like this offers ensures they will try hard to do it well.

Of course, we may not like each task we need to do or even each KRA. That's okay. We all have aspects of our job that we don't like. The important thing is that they are outweighed by tasks and KRAs we enjoy.

Figure 6.2 The three aspects of the *want to* building block

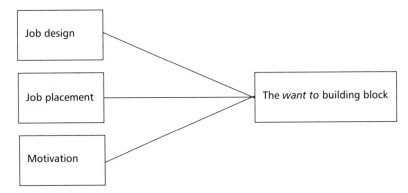

A motivating job

The final aspect of the *want to* building block is motivation. What makes you want to do a good job and willing to put in the effort required? As we see in Chapter 7, motivation results from a number of things:

- doing something we enjoy;

- knowing it's important and valued;

- feeling 'in control';

- feeling able to and responsible for achieving results;

- having clear goals to work towards; and

- being able to 'see' the results of our efforts.

These psychological rewards unlock performance and productivity.

Use the *want to* building block to motivate employees and match their attributes and abilities with job requirements.

HOW TO

Skills and experience make up the bulk of the *how to* building block. Experience reinforces training and together they boost productivity.

Figure 6.3 What motivates people?

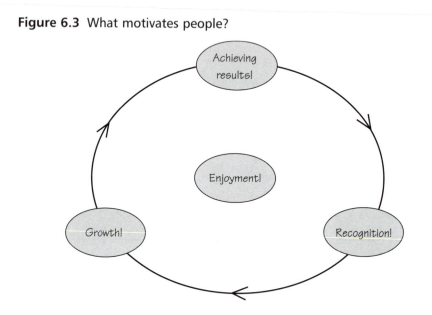

Checklist for success

☐ Is there any hopeless and futile labour in you department? What is it? How could you eliminate or improve it?

☐ Can every employee in your department state their job purpose in one clear and motivating sentence?

☐ Does everyone know precisely what you expect and can they monitor their own performance?

☐ Can they list their KRAs and measures of success?

☐ Do they know how their jobs fit into the wider scheme of things?

☐ Do people in your work group know they are doing something worthwhile? Do they have 'good jobs' to do?

☐ Are they able to feel a sense of achievement when they reach their targets?

☐ Do you let them know you appreciate their efforts?

☐ Does everyone know and understand your 'bottom-line rules'?

☐ Are people proud of their work?

☐ Are they able to use their talents?

☐ Do you think carefully about people's skills and preferences when assigning jobs?

☐ Do people treat each other with respect?

We examined how to recognise people's training needs, and offer on- and off-the-job training to meet them, in Chapter 5.

As Figure 6.4 shows, working in an environment where people want to extend their skills, share their knowledge and find better ways of doing things further enhances their ability to do a great job.

CHANCE TO

What could account for poor performance if employees know *what to do*, *how to* do it and *want to* do it well? This is where the *chance to* building block comes in. It shows where to look for the things that either sustain or smother performance.

This building block helps us ensure that work methods, systems and procedures and other elements in the job environment promote

127

Figure 6.4 The four aspects of the *how to* building block

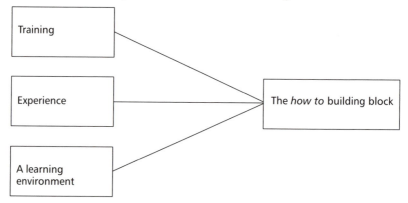

productivity. Unfortunately they often do just the opposite—they interfere with people's ability to do their job well.

Figure 6.5 shows the five aspects to the *chance to* building block.

Tools and equipment
Poor, faulty, badly designed and maintained or inadequate tools and equipment are a more common cause of poor performance than we

Figure 6.5 The five aspects of the *chance to* building block

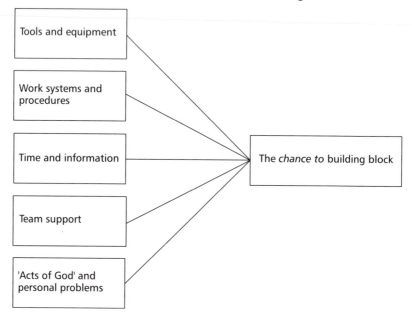

might think. Are the tools and equipment in your department well designed, properly maintained and suited to the job at hand?

Systems and procedures

Cumbersome work systems and procedures are like shackles that restrain productivity. They are discouraging and ultimately sap people's motivation. Because changes are usually made *ad hoc* and informally, unwieldy work methods mushroom, usually unnoticed. This is an all too common cause of sub-optimal performance and productivity.

Streamline and simplify the work systems and procedures in your department. Make sure each step flows smoothly, logically and easily into the next. This will make people's jobs hassle free, speed up the workflow, improve quality and reduce waste. (In Chapters 11 and 15 we look at how to use flow charts and in Chapters 14 and 15 at other techniques for analysing and improving work systems and procedures.)

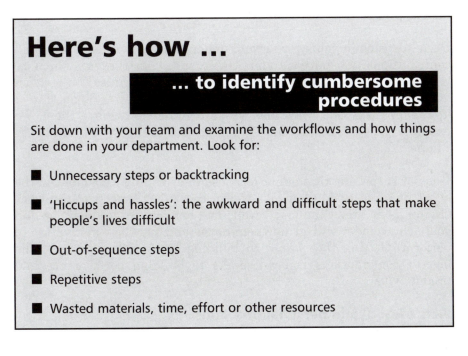

Here's how ...

... to identify cumbersome procedures

Sit down with your team and examine the workflows and how things are done in your department. Look for:

- Unnecessary steps or backtracking

- 'Hiccups and hassles': the awkward and difficult steps that make people's lives difficult

- Out-of-sequence steps

- Repetitive steps

- Wasted materials, time, effort or other resources

Time and information

Is your organisation running 'lean and mean'? While reduced staffing levels can reduce overheads, it can also mean that sometimes people just don't have the time to do a job properly or the time to pass on full information.

How much time is wasted in your department by doing a job a second or third time because someone didn't do it right the first time? Studies in Australia have shown that this can be as high as 33% of a working week. Imagine saving 13 hours per person per week by eliminating rework!

Get people into the habit of doing things 'right first time' and passing on needed information. It's largely up to you to make sure they have the right job aids, feedback on performance and the time and information they need to do their job well.

Team support
People working together can achieve far more than people working on their own. If team members don't understand what everyone is trying to achieve, share common goals and purposes and support and value each other's efforts, work becomes unnecessarily difficult. Performance, productivity and goal achievement suffer.

Does everyone in your work group understand each other's roles and contributions (job purpose and KRAs) and what they together are working towards (your department's and the organisation's vision and objectives)? This helps make sure everyone shares ownership of key team tasks and roles and works together to achieve them. We examine how to build and lead high-performing work teams in Chapter 8.

It is not surprising that employees lose their willingness to put in the effort required to do their jobs well if these four aspects of the work environment aren't managed well. The barriers to productivity and goal achievement will 'grind them down' and sap their motivation to perform. Getting the *chance to* building block right is one of the biggest contributions you can make to building performance and productivity.

'Acts of God' and personal problems
The **85:15 rule** tells us that, provided people know clearly what is expected of them, know how to do it and want to do it, 85% of causes of poor performance lie in the *chance to* building block with the four factors we've just looked at: tools and equipment, systems and procedures, time and information, and team support.

The remaining 15% of causes are split between personal factors and 'Acts of God', or things that just can't be helped. For example, if your factory or office floods or loses its electricity it would be difficult to get work out on time.

Personal factors include the occasional 'bad hair' day, domestic problems that are so pressing it is difficult to concentrate properly on work or severe personal problems such as alcohol or drug abuse. They can also be nice things. For example, people might find it hard to keep their mind fully on the job if they're getting married soon.

It makes sense to concentrate your efforts on improving productivity and performance where they are most likely to pay off—in the work environment. Instead of urging employees who aren't doing well to 'Try harder!', sit down and discuss what problems they are having in achieving their targets, what is causing these problems and how to remove them to put performance on track.

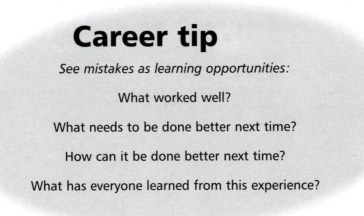

Career tip

See mistakes as learning opportunities:

What worked well?

What needs to be done better next time?

How can it be done better next time?

What has everyone learned from this experience?

LED TO

In 1847 the 12-year-old son of a handloom weaver emigrated from Scotland to the USA. He built a steel empire employing thousands of people and became one of the wealthiest and most influential people in America. His name was Andrew Carnegie and here's what he had to say about how to bring out the best in people:

Men are developed the same way gold is mined. Several tons of dirt must be moved to get one ounce of gold, but one doesn't go into the mine looking for the dirt, one goes in looking for the gold.

Are you the sort of leader who polishes people's gold?

We look further at leadership in Chapter 7. Meanwhile, here are six essential things to do to make the *led to* building block work for you. These important leadership actions link with the five mindsets for success we looked at in Chapter 1.

Build self-esteem in others

To be a great leader you need high self-esteem. The value and respect you have for yourself supplies the self-confidence you need to supervise others well and manage operations properly.

You also need to build self-esteem in others. Since only people with high self-esteem can perform their jobs with excellence, building self-esteem in others also builds performance and productivity.

Figure 6.6 The six aspects of the *led to* building block

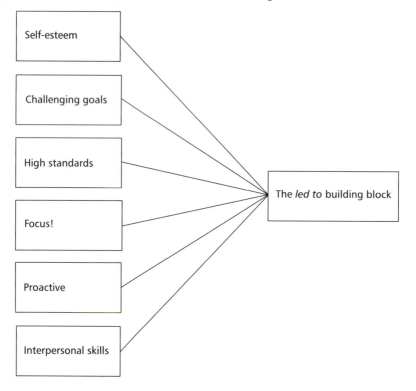

Set challenging goals
Setting challenging (yet achievable) goals raises productivity. People and teams who aim high achieve more than people and teams who aim low.

Have high standards
Never accept second best or a second-rate job from your work group. Expect the best—of yourself and others. After all:

Mediocrity is a choice.
So is excellence.

Focus!
To meet your high standards and achieve your challenging goals you need a steady focus. If you want to build productivity and performance, 'keep your eyes on the ball'. Keep your goals clearly in mind and find ways to achieve them, despite the obstacles.

Be proactive
Don't sit back and wait, blame others or find excuses for mediocre performance or not achieving goals. Take responsibility for making things happen, not making excuses. Find ways to help your team achieve their goals.

Hone your interpersonal skills
Building performance and productivity also takes strong interpersonal skills. Communicating and working effectively with others allows you to have the influence you need to encourage and guide people to lift their performance and productivity.

To maximise the productivity of your department, become expert at using the Five Building Blocks to analyse performance shortfalls and encourage peak performance. You will discover what is preventing people from doing the best job they can and find ways to help them get better results. People will be able to do the good job that most of them want to do.

Checklist for success

☐ Train employees systematically.

☐ Increase the value of off-the-job training by following up on it.

☐ Keep people interested in extending their skills and helping team-mates to extend their skills.

☐ Encourage people to share ideas about developing better ways to do things.

☐ Show people how to learn from their mistakes.

☐ If someone isn't doing their job as you expect, sit down with them to work out why, using the Five Building Blocks to structure your discussion.

☐ Set high standards and expect the best from everyone in your group.

☐ Set a compelling vision and goals for your department.

☐ Instead of complaining about all the problems and difficulties you face, see your way past problems by focusing on your goals and how to achieve them.

☐ Know the answer to this question: Why would anyone want to be led by you?

CHAPTER SEVEN

BE A GREAT LEADER
Leading and motivating others

We can hire people to turn up to work and go through the basic motions for a certain number of hours. But we can't buy their enthusiasm, their cooperation or their commitment. For this, we need leadership and motivation.

The ability to bring out the best in people is a priceless asset. Can you get work done through others and inspire them to do their best?

WHAT SORT OF PERSON IS A LEADER?
Over 2 500 years ago, the Chinese philosopher Lao-Tzu said:

> *Avoid putting yourself before others and you can become a leader among men.*

An article by Jim Collins in the January 2001 issue of *Harvard Business Review* ('Level 5 Leadership: The Triumph of Humility and Fierce Resolve') argues, based on extensive research, that to attain the pinnacle of leadership a person must be humble.

It seems obvious that someone who is arrogant, self-important or condescending can never be a good leader. Nor can someone who doesn't want to lead. In fact, according to Nigel Nicholson, professor of organisational behaviour at the London Business School, the desire to lead is 'the baseline requirement for competent leadership'. If you're a reluctant leader, you'll never be a good one.

Sir Edward 'Weary' Dunlop developed his 'empathic' approach to leadership in the Japanese POW camps during World War II. He identified 11 desirable aspects of leadership:

- Motivation
- Responsibility
- Judgement
- Courage

- Initiative
- Knowledge
- Decisiveness
- Integrity

- Ability to communicate
- Selflessness
- Loyalty

He was thinking of military leadership. Would these characteristics make you a better leader?

Here's how ...

... to develop your leadership qualities

- Take courses to improve your speaking skills.

- Learn to send powerful messages through ceremonies, celebrations, 'small touches' and symbolic gestures.

- Learn to think more critically about the *status quo* and its shortcomings.

- Do more to enthuse your team.

- Be passionate about what you do.

- Learn to become comfortable with taking risks and standing up for your convictions.

- Make your goals and future vision attractive and attainable and learn to communicate them clearly.

Source: Professor Jay Conger, London Business School

WHAT DO LEADERS DO?

Leaders have two primary areas of concern: the *task* and the *people* performing it. When you're focusing on the task, on the job at hand, you're likely to set standards, monitor results, check that people have the skills and knowledge they need, ask people how things are going and whether they're running into any difficulties, summarise progress and emphasise timelines and other **measures of success**.

When you're focusing on people, you can focus on individual contributors or the team as a whole. You'll consult people about how to do things better, coordinate team efforts, encourage and develop people's ideas and suggestions, be approachable and friendly, relax and enjoy people's company, celebrate success and learn from failures, express appreciation for people's contributions, clarify aims and goals and coach people.

Figure 7.1 shows how Professor John Adair illustrates this:

Figure 7.1 What do leaders do?

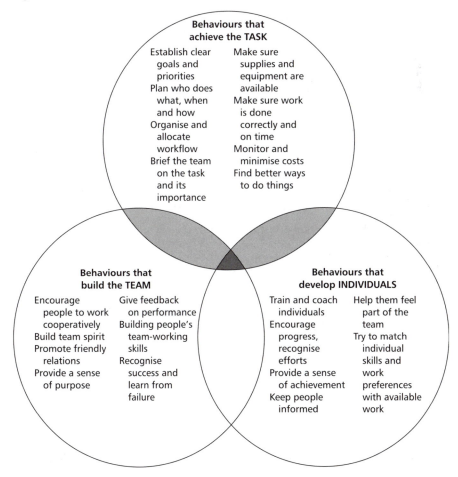

It's possible to get results in the short term by concentrating on task needs while neglecting people. But eventually people will give less than their full effort and productivity will fall behind. Similarly, concentrating only on creating team spirit while neglecting the task or individual contributors will produce a happy work atmosphere, but people will eventually lack the real sense of individual achievement that comes with task success. In the long run, focusing only on the task or only on people doesn't achieve the best results. Focus on all three areas.

Here's how ...

... to meet the task, team and individual needs of your group

Task needs

■ Be clear about your department's tasks and objectives and how they fit into the overall short-term and long-term goals of your organisation.

■ Explain this to your work group.

■ Plan how to accomplish your department's goals and brief people fully.

■ Explain each task's importance and measures of success.

■ Provide the necessary resources, including time, information and equipment.

■ Make sure people have the necessary skills and knowledge to do the job effectively.

■ Ensure the structure and systems of your department allow the job to be achieved efficiently.

■ Monitor progress and provide feedback to your work group.

Team needs

■ Set and maintain group objectives and standards.

■ Involve the group in achieving the objectives.

■ Help your work group feel like a special group.

■ Monitor and encourage friendly and supportive interactions between people.

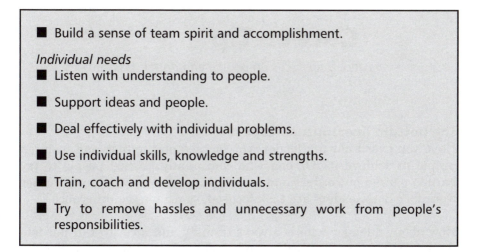

A finely tuned balance between focusing on the task, the team *and* individuals gets the best results. This is not always easy. For example, in times of extra high workload you'll need to focus on the task more than usual; when this happens, take care to emphasise team and individual needs once the work crisis has passed in order to bring things back into balance. Or if you know a particularly busy period is approaching, take some time out first to relax and have fun with your team and spend some time chatting with each group member.

Checklist for success

- ☐ Formulate goals and communicate them in a way that inspires and energises others.

- ☐ Don't kid yourself that you're better than the people you lead.

- ☐ Make sure you follow all the rules you set (dress code, timekeeping policy, etc.). Bending the rules for yourself or others sabotages your credibility.

- ☐ Treat people as individuals by celebrating their birthdays, showing interest in their leisure and family activities and discussing their hobbies with them.

- ☐ Know that you need to earn leadership.

- ☐ Look for the best in people.

- ☐ Stay calm and keep smiling.

Career Tip

Balance your focus on people and on the task.

The bottom line: mutual respect

Have you ever known a leader who focused on the task and inspired people to achieve it? Or one who continually pushed people to try harder, barked out orders and issued threats? Who would you rather work for? Both leaders are task focused, so what's the difference?

How about a leader who is always friendly and nice to staff but lets them 'get away with murder' and another leader who is a friendly coach who expects, and gets, excellent results? Who would you rather work for? Both leaders are people focused, so what's the difference?

It's the *way* a person does something that matters. Leaders who respect themselves as well as their followers are able to focus on the task when the need arises without getting people off-side. They are also able to focus on people without letting them forget who's boss and what everyone is there to achieve.

A question

How is leadership like a piece of string?

LEADERSHIP BEGINS INSIDE

Your beliefs about employees colour your behaviour as a leader. Which of the two lists below better reflects your opinions about the people in your work team?

List X

■ People are basically lazy and work only because they have to.

■ Because people dislike work, they will avoid it whenever possible and therefore need to be closely supervised, forced or threatened with 'the sack' before they will make the effort to contribute a fair day's work.

■ Employees are basically passive and would rather be told what to do than think for themselves or assume responsibility.

■ They aren't interested in or committed to the goals and vision of their organisation or department.

List Y

■ Work is as natural as rest or play.

■ Given the opportunity, employees will accept and even seek responsibility, respond to a challenge and feel satisfied when they do their jobs well.

■ Self-motivation, enjoyment, the reward of individual effort and making progress lift productivity better than force and punishment.

■ Employees would rather be committed to goals they believe are worthwhile, including organisational goals, than bored for eight hours a day, five days a week.

If the first list describes your views better than the second list, you might be what the late industrial relations pioneer, Professor Douglas McGregor, called a **Theory X** leader. If the second better expresses your views you might be what he called a **Theory Y** leader.

Our leadership style reflects our inner beliefs about people. Theory X leaders, for example, tend to trust people less and supervise their work more closely than Theory Y supervisors, who tend to give people more responsibility and involve them more.

We also know from the **self-fulfilling prophesy** that people are likely to respond to us in the manner we treat them. In short, we get what we expect, which reinforces our beliefs.

Firm but fair?
Does it strike you that Theory Y supervisors would be 'soft' and 'easy' on employees and that Theory X supervisors would be 'tough task masters', and 'take no nonsense'? Actually, some Theory X supervisors are 'tough' and others are 'soft'.

The 'tough' ones are often called *dictatorial* or *authoritarian* leaders. 'Dictators' rule through force, holding threats of punishment over people's heads to compel them to perform. This may get results in

141

some work situations but not surprisingly, the quality and quantity of results do not remain at a high level for very long. On the contrary, dictatorial leadership usually creates unrest and dissatisfaction. Sooner or later, employees 'revolt' by doing the bare minimum or transferring to another job.

Authoritarian leaders also exercise strong control. They avoid participation and withhold information, preferring to make decisions themselves. They issue orders with no questions allowed and no explanations given. This tends to make employees dependent on them for decisions and directions, and can result in the group feeling 'lost' and unable to perform in their absence.

'Soft' Theory X leaders don't fare much better. Since they regard employees as basically lazy and not very bright, they don't expect much from them. Because of this they don't set high standards of performance or treat employees with respect. They allow people to perform less well than they could and, by their behaviour towards them, 'train' them into believing poor or average productivity is okay. As a result, their working relationships with their work group are often poor.

'Soft' Theory Y leaders are often called *laissez-faire*. They don't appear to give active leadership at all. They provide the group with information and possibly some general direction and then let them get on with the job with little or no interference.

This can be effective when the work group is highly skilled and motivated and the work is complex or unstructured. This may be the case when supervising professionally qualified employees. However, when established standards and goals need to be met on a regular basis this is probably not the most suitable style of leadership.

The best Theory Y supervisors are 'hard' and 'firm but fair': they set and demand high standards of performance because they believe their staff are capable of reaching them. They provide challenging work and coach, train and develop people to reach their potential. Because they respect employees they listen to their opinions and suggestions and involve them in solving work-related problems. Because employees are well informed and used to solving problems themselves they don't need close supervision. Not surprisingly, most of these 'tough' Theory Y supervisors get the results they expect. Sadly, so do the Theory X supervisors.

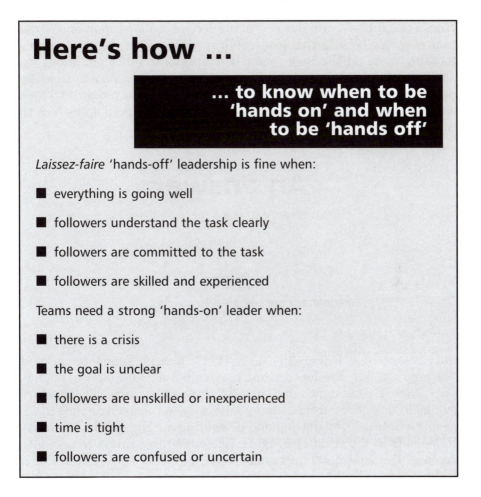

Here's how ...

... to know when to be 'hands on' and when to be 'hands off'

Laissez-faire 'hands-off' leadership is fine when:

- everything is going well
- followers understand the task clearly
- followers are committed to the task
- followers are skilled and experienced

Teams need a strong 'hands-on' leader when:

- there is a crisis
- the goal is unclear
- followers are unskilled or inexperienced
- time is tight
- followers are confused or uncertain

In an odd way, if you want to have great people working on your team, you need first to *believe* they are great. Then you will treat them as if they are great and they will to rise to your expectations. Or as the German poet Johann von Goethe put it:

> *Treat people as if they were what they ought to be and you help them to become what they are capable of being.*

Horses for courses

We can say that in most situations, with most employees, you'll get better results with a Theory Y mindset that respects people and sets high standards. We can predict that you'll be a better leader by showing more humility than narcissism. We can generalise and say you need to focus on the task at hand *and* the people working on it.

Here's the rub: we can also say that effective leadership in one situation may *not* be effective leadership in another. In some situations focusing more on the task is our best option; in other situations we should focus more on people. The trick is to know when to focus on people and when to focus on the task. Once we can recognise which situations call for us to concentrate on the task at hand and which to concentrate on people, all we need is flexibility.

An answer

How is leadership like a piece of string?

Pull the string, and it will follow.

Push it and it will go nowhere.

People are the same.

Fifty years ago, leadership researchers Robert Tannenbaum and Warren Schmidt developed what they called a *continuum of leadership styles*. This is shown in Figure 7.2. It shows a range of behaviours available to leaders, from keeping authority to themselves and *telling* people what to do, to sharing and delegating authority. Which is best? It depends on the situation. Figure 7.3 shows three things to take into account when deciding: the task at hand, your followers and your own inclinations.

1. If the *task* is highly complex or has huge ramifications if not done correctly, you can't afford to move too far to the right of the continuum; at most, you might only consult your work group. Similarly, if *time* is tight you can't afford the time to discuss at length what to do or how to do it.

2. If your *followers* are highly skilled and experienced, willing to become involved and used to participating, you can move towards the right end of the continuum. Move to the left if your work group is lacking in skills, experience or desire to participate, or if it's very large.

3. If you, *the leader*, are comfortable with involving people and confident in their abilities, and if your organisation culture

144

Figure 7.2 Continuum of leadership styles

Leader-centred
leadership

Employee-centred
leadership

Use of authority
by leader

Area of freedom
for followers

Tells	Sells	Consults	Shares	Delegates
Leader announces what is to be done	Leader explains what is to be done and why	Leader presents the required end result, invites suggestions and makes the final decision	Leader outlines the situation and decides jointly with group	Leader permits employees to function within defined limits

Figure 7.3 Selecting a leadership style

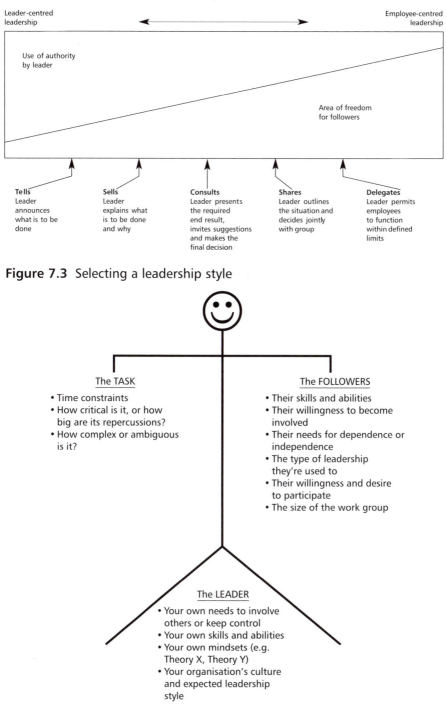

The TASK
• Time constraints
• How critical is it, or how big are its repercussions?
• How complex or ambiguous is it?

The FOLLOWERS
• Their skills and abilities
• Their willingness to become involved
• Their needs for dependence or independence
• The type of leadership they're used to
• Their willingness and desire to participate
• The size of the work group

The LEADER
• Your own needs to involve others or keep control
• Your own skills and abilities
• Your own mindsets (e.g. Theory X, Theory Y)
• Your organisation's culture and expected leadership style

145

supports participation, you can move towards the right of the continuum. Move to the left if you prefer to keep a tight rein on things, make decisions yourself, are not comfortable with people's ability or willingness to participate or if the expectations in your organisation are for authoritarian leadership.

Here's how ...

... to select the right leadership style

Tells —— Sells —— Consults —— Shares —— Delegates

One best way	Many alternatives
Critically important to the organisation	Not critically important to the organisation
High degree of risk	Low risk
Time shortage	Plenty of time available
Large numbers	Smaller numbers
Less skilled, experienced or motivated staff	Highly skilled, experienced or motivated staff
Low involvement or effect on employees	Highly involved or affected employees

WHEN ARE YOU A LEADER?
Leadership isn't a title. It's a package of mindsets, attributes, skills and knowledge.

You'll know you're a leader when people:

■ Listen to your ideas and follow your suggestions.

■ Look to you for signals or instructions on what to do.

■ Seek your opinions and advice.

■ Look to you to speak the truth.

You display your leadership by:

- Learning from your mistakes.

- Doing your 'homework' and being prepared.

- Treating everyone with respect and courtesy.

- Sharing the credit, taking the blame.

- Communicating and staying focused on a clear vision and setting energising goals.

- Surrounding yourself with competent people.

- Staying optimistic, even in challenging circumstances.

- Involving and including others.

- Thinking systematically.

- Seeking ways to improve things, do things better, easier, faster or more economically.

- Clarifying goals.

- Helping people reach their potential.

Here's what management guru Peter Drucker says about leadership:

Leadership is not magnetic personality—that can just as well be a glib tongue. It is not 'making friends and influencing people'—that is flattery. Leadership is lifting a person's performance to a higher standard, the building of a personality beyond its normal limitations.

Is that the kind of leader you are?

WHAT INSPIRES MOTIVATION?

It has been said that there are no unmotivated *people*—only unmotivated *workers*. The person who leaps out of bed at 5 a.m. to go jogging may well be the same person who merely goes through the motions all day at work and rushes off at 5 p.m. precisely.

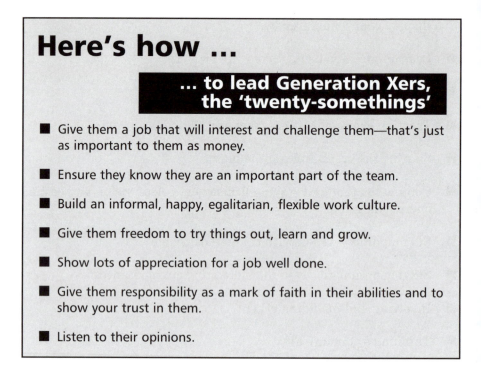

Here's how ...

... to lead Generation Xers, the 'twenty-somethings'

■ Give them a job that will interest and challenge them—that's just as important to them as money.

■ Ensure they know they are an important part of the team.

■ Build an informal, happy, egalitarian, flexible work culture.

■ Give them freedom to try things out, learn and grow.

■ Show lots of appreciation for a job well done.

■ Give them responsibility as a mark of faith in their abilities and to show your trust in them.

■ Listen to their opinions.

The fact is, most people aren't born lazy or troublesome. Your challenge is to channel people's existing energies into the good work performance that results from motivation.

What motivates you?

Stop for a moment and think of a time in your life when you have been highly motivated. What was motivating you? Take a look at Box 7.1. Is your list similar?

These are the things that motivate most people. Interestingly, you can't see or touch any of them—they're all in our heads! Motivation, like leadership, is a state of mind. Good leaders know how to create this energised state of mind by creating opportunities for people to challenge their skills, learn and do new things, feel responsible and so on. How do you create those opportunities for the people who work with you?

Does fear motivate?

Have you heard of the carrot and stick form of motivation illustrated in Figure 7.4? Sometimes we're motivated by fear of losing something or fear of negative consequences. For example, people may fear losing

Box 7.1 What motivates us?

- Challenge
- Doing something new
- Praise from the boss
- Helping/contributing to team effort
- Respect of others
- Self-respect

- Enjoy the job
- Promotion
- Opportunities ahead
- Chance to learn
- Feeling responsible
- Achieving goals
- Pride

their job if they don't perform well, or they might want to avoid harsh words from their supervisor if they clown around too much.

Fear can sometimes act as a motivator. However, it's a weak form of motivation. Usually after we have lived with a fear for a while we come to accept it and it loses its power.

Figure 7.4 The carrot and stick approach to motivation

move away from

move towards

The Push: fear of being hit—negative consequence

The Pull: desire to gain something we want—positive consequence

Think of fear as 'the stick': a mechanical, outside push that we want to move *away* from. It is weaker, and therefore less effective in the long run, than 'the carrot': an inner, magnetic pull *towards* something. Wanting to do a job well because of the rewards it brings—a sense of achievement, pride, rising up to a challenge and so on—is a stronger form of motivation.

What *really* motivates?

If you are doing a good job managing the Five Building Blocks to productivity and peak performance discussed in Chapter 6, motivation will be ready to soar. Let's examine the *want to* building block in more detail.

We know people's willingness to do a job depends largely on how much they *enjoy* doing the work and whether they *value* it as important and worthwhile. This is why it's important to place people in jobs they will enjoy and make sure they realise their value to the department and the organisation.

People also need to be *confident* in carrying out a task. This is why it's important to *train* them properly, give them time to build their skills and provide enough background *information*, adequate *tools and equipment* and organisational *support* for them to do it well.

People must also feel that doing their job well will provide something they value *in return*. What do you value from your work? What are the five most important things you need if you are to feel motivated to do a job well?

- [ ] Interesting and worthwhile work
- [ ] Achieving results
- [ ] Responsibility
- [ ] Feedback
- [ ] Appreciation
- [ ] A chance to learn and develop skills
- [ ] A friendly work atmosphere
- [ ] Working for an organisation you can be proud to be associated with
- [ ] Feeling you're making a contribution to a valuable 'something'
- [ ] Earning lots of money
- [ ] Having lots of 'perks'
- [ ] Having a fancy workstation with all the latest equipment

☐ Being kept informed and 'in on things'

☐ Working with nice people

☐ Flexibility in your working arrangements

Different people put these things in different orders of importance. Do you know what order the people in your work group would put them in? What can you do to make sure doing their jobs well rewards them in ways they appreciate? Conversely, does poor job performance make it less likely they will be rewarded?

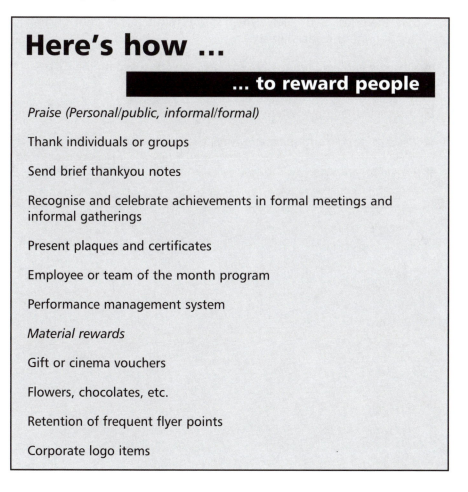

Here's how ...

... to reward people

Praise (Personal/public, informal/formal)

Thank individuals or groups

Send brief thankyou notes

Recognise and celebrate achievements in formal meetings and informal gatherings

Present plaques and certificates

Employee or team of the month program

Performance management system

Material rewards

Gift or cinema vouchers

Flowers, chocolates, etc.

Retention of frequent flyer points

Corporate logo items

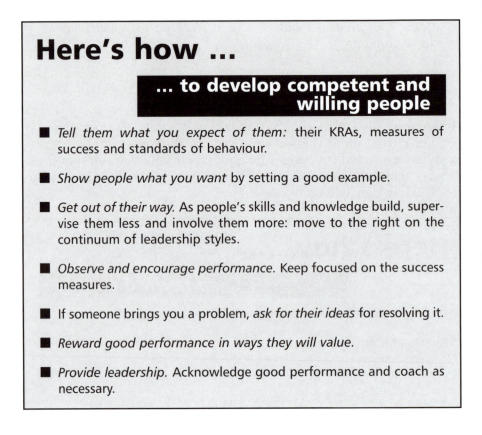

Here's how ...

... to develop competent and willing people

■ *Tell them what you expect of them:* their KRAs, measures of success and standards of behaviour.

■ *Show people what you want* by setting a good example.

■ *Get out of their way.* As people's skills and knowledge build, supervise them less and involve them more: move to the right on the continuum of leadership styles.

■ *Observe and encourage performance.* Keep focused on the success measures.

■ If someone brings you a problem, *ask for their ideas* for resolving it.

■ *Reward good performance in ways they will value.*

■ *Provide leadership.* Acknowledge good performance and coach as necessary.

Checklist for success

☐ Apart from important rules and procedures, give people as much autonomy and responsibility as possible.

☐ Don't take people for granted—say *'Thankyou!'*

☐ Ask, don't tell.

☐ Provide psychological rewards for each individual contributor and the group as a whole for achieving the goals: a sense of achievement, recognition, feeling that they are part of something worthwhile, a chance to learn and develop their skills.

☐ Create an enjoyable working environment.

☐ Be a coach not a critic.

☐ Find ways to match jobs to people's skills, abilities and interests.

☐ Try to match people with jobs that offer the greatest opportunity for satisfying their particular needs and matching their work preferences.

☐ Try to ensure that they realise how their job can meet their needs and that they will receive rewards they value by doing their job well.

☐ Always recognise their efforts.

CHAPTER EIGHT

BUILD A PRODUCTIVE TEAM
Developing a strong team that achieves results

f you're like most supervisors, managing people is your biggest challenge. Whether as individuals or in groups, people can be tricky and unpredictable.

How do you see the role of a team leader? As controller, commander, ruler and decision maker? Or as delegator, coach, champion, catalyst and guide? With the growing use of teams—work-based teams, virtual teams, merged teams, temporary project teams, problem-solving and value-adding teams—your ability to help people achieve more together than they could on their own is a valuable skill.

WHAT IS YOUR TEAM'S CULTURE?
What groups and teams do you belong to? What are their unwritten codes of behaviour, assumptions about their world and ways of doing things? How do people help and support each other? Who talks to whom? Who ignores whom? Whose lead do people follow? What are their energy levels: for example, how fast do people walk and how quickly do they get things done? What is the dress code? How much do they laugh? These are all aspects of a team's culture.

First, let's get two terms straight: *group* and *team*.

Do you have a group or a team?
Does each person in your work group rely mostly on themselves to get their own job done? If so, you may have a work group. Or does everyone pitch in together, able to contribute because of everyone else's contributions? Then you probably have a team.

Work *groups* are made up of individual contributors who don't really need each other for their own contribution to be effective. They may work in the same area and be friendly and talk to each other a lot, share ideas and even help each other occasionally, but if people basically relies on themselves to complete their job satisfactorily they are a work group. Nevertheless, they will have a culture, norms and climate just as a team does. They may even have 'team spirit' and a sense of 'us'.

In a *team*, people depend on each other: it's only through 'pulling together' that they achieve their goals. In 'real' teams, people's skills are complementary. They may or may not work in the same physical location, but they combine to achieve something together that no one could achieve on their own. People can work individually, in subgroups or as a whole team as the need arises. In effective teams, there is a feeling of 'us', an *esprit de corps*, and a 'we're all in this together' camaraderie.

Whether you are supervising a work group or a team, develop a shared vision and shared commitment to goals, a sense of team spirit and cooperation, respect and appreciation for each other's differing contributions. You will reap the benefits in increased cohesiveness, morale and productivity. For that reason, we use the terms 'group' and 'team' interchangeably in this chapter.

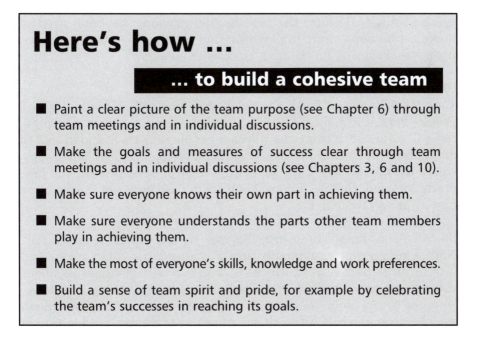

Here's how ...

... to build a cohesive team

- Paint a clear picture of the team purpose (see Chapter 6) through team meetings and in individual discussions.

- Make the goals and measures of success clear through team meetings and in individual discussions (see Chapters 3, 6 and 10).

- Make sure everyone knows their own part in achieving them.

- Make sure everyone understands the parts other team members play in achieving them.

- Make the most of everyone's skills, knowledge and work preferences.

- Build a sense of team spirit and pride, for example by celebrating the team's successes in reaching its goals.

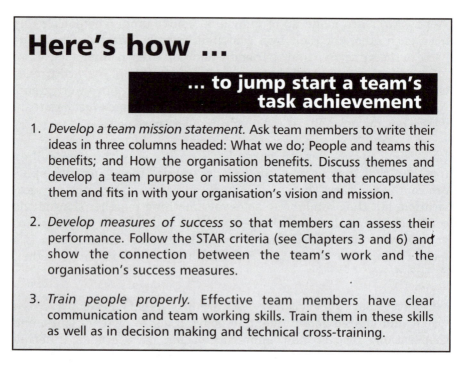

Here's how ...

... to jump start a team's task achievement

1. *Develop a team mission statement.* Ask team members to write their ideas in three columns headed: What we do; People and teams this benefits; and How the organisation benefits. Discuss themes and develop a team purpose or mission statement that encapsulates them and fits in with your organisation's vision and mission.

2. *Develop measures of success* so that members can assess their performance. Follow the STAR criteria (see Chapters 3 and 6) and show the connection between the team's work and the organisation's success measures.

3. *Train people properly.* Effective team members have clear communication and team working skills. Train them in these skills as well as in decision making and technical cross-training.

Your team's temperament

The **task** is *what* your team is trying to achieve. A large measure of their success at the task depends on their **process**, or *how* they're going about it. Because the task is more obvious, we often need to make a conscious effort to pay attention to and develop strong team processes. Focusing on the task alone isn't enough.

Shape your team's culture and norms

Your team has a **culture**: the rules and taboos that guide the way people work, their shared values, symbols, rituals, beliefs and practices. It covers such things as whether people take risks and attend to detail, how much they focus on results and keeping customers happy, where the balance lies between being people or task focused, and how much internal change occurs. Your team's culture can cultivate or constrain its productivity.

So can its **norms**. These are 'the way we do things around here'. Norms are a group's commonly accepted standards of behaviour and form a large part of its culture. Your group will have norms about things like 'how hard we work', whether it's okay to take 'sickies', whether or not to be on time for work and for meetings, how much we joke around while we work, whether or not we say 'good morning' to one another and offer to help each other out, how we dress and how loyal we are to each other, the boss, the organisation and our work. Norms have a powerful effect on performance and some researchers say their effect is at least as important a factor in a person's productivity as their motivation and ability. (See also Chapter 1.)

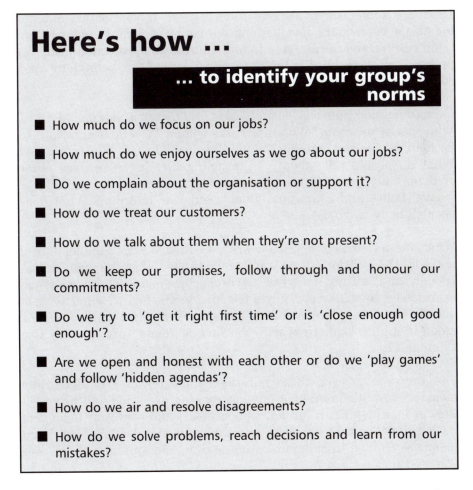

Here's how ...

... to identify your group's norms

- How much do we focus on our jobs?

- How much do we enjoy ourselves as we go about our jobs?

- Do we complain about the organisation or support it?

- How do we treat our customers?

- How do we talk about them when they're not present?

- Do we keep our promises, follow through and honour our commitments?

- Do we try to 'get it right first time' or is 'close enough good enough'?

- Are we open and honest with each other or do we 'play games' and follow 'hidden agendas'?

- How do we air and resolve disagreements?

- How do we solve problems, reach decisions and learn from our mistakes?

Norms develop over time as people work together. They partly reflect the wider organisation's culture and norms, partly your style of supervision and partly the nature of the individuals in the group.

Learn to recognise the culture and norms of your work group and address it openly. Make sure they work for you, not against you, by building and maintaining your team (see page 164).

Direct your team's dynamics

An important part of a team's culture is its **group dynamics**: the balance and type of relationships and communications between group members. **Group maintenance**—looking after group dynamics so they benefit your team—helps ensure task success, while ignoring group dynamics invites disastrous results.

Here are some things to pay attention to. If you notice a team member's behaviours and actions damaging a strong and positive team culture and norms, step in and address the problem quickly (in private, of course). Establish ground rules for behaviour and communication that build the culture you want.

Communication patterns, participation and decision making

Who speaks to whom? Who interrupts whom? Who do others turn to for help, advice and opinions? Who talks most? Least? Who is left out? What do people talk about? Do people really listen to each other or listen only for their turn to speak? Are communications clear or vague? Polite and courteous? Businesslike or informal? What does people's body language say?

What are decisions about? How are they made? For example, do you make all the decisions or do you include the team? Is the team skilled enough and willing to work towards consensus, where everyone expresses opinions, or are only a few loud voices heard? What sorts of discussions take place before a decision is reached? Are decisions made in an atmosphere of win–win and customer service? (See also Chapter 14.)

The way you answer these questions indicates how skilful group members are at communicating and making decisions and how well they use their skills. It influences how easily and well your team gets its job done as well as its satisfaction and morale. Are your team members trained in communication and decision-making skills? Are you a good role model?

Climate

What does it 'feel' like to be a member of your team? That you're respected, understood and supported? That people care about you? Or that no one cares about you or the job you're doing? Do people channel their efforts and energies towards the team's and their own goals and feel a sense of achievement when they reach them? Or do they go through the motions doing as little as possible? Is there a sense of friendship and fun in the team? A sense of who 'we' are and what makes us unique and valuable to the organisation?

A group's climate can be positive or negative. A high-stress, relentless 'we're just cogs in a wheel with our noses to the grindstone' atmosphere or one that is controlling, rigid and punishing, stifles creativity, enjoyment, satisfaction and productivity. Establish a goal- and customer-focused climate of support, cooperation, learning and trust so that your team can achieve goals easily and enjoyably.

Cohesion
Is your team a fragmented collection of individuals or does it have a solid sense of unity? Are people proud to say they're part of your team? Do they have a sense of identity that others can recognise too?

Cohesive teams tend to work better together because team members don't want to let each other down and want to support and help each other. Forge team solidarity with opportunities for team members to get to know and respect each other as individuals.

Behaviours
Box 8.1 shows some behaviours which are fairly self-explanatory. Have you seen any of them in action? Where? What was their effect on the way the group worked and achieved its goals?

These behaviours will help or hinder your team doing its job, reaching decisions and solving problems. Make sure your team members use the helpful behaviours and deal with the unhelpful ones to minimise or eliminate them.

Power and influence
Who *really* 'calls the shots' in your work group? Who do others listen to and go to for advice, assistance or just a chat? Who do they copy? Admire? Who speaks for the group? These are the informal leaders. It's important that the example they set supports your section's and organisation's goals and purpose because the 'pull' of the informal leader can be stronger than the 'pull' of either you or the organisation.

HOW WELL DEVELOPED IS YOUR TEAM?
A strong, productive team doesn't appear overnight. All teams go through five developmental steps, called *the stages of team growth*. These are shown in Figure 8.1 on page 163. The fourth stage, perform-ing, is where teams achieve synergy, the ability of the whole to achieve

Box 8.1 Helpful and unhelpful team behaviours

	Helpful behaviours	Unhelpful behaviours
Task behaviours	Seeking information Seeking opinions Analysing Giving information Giving opinions Building on other's ideas Coordinating Summarising Generating ideas Organising procedures Setting standards Initiating Clarifying Teaching, coaching Following agreeably Building consensus Mediating Getting the ball rolling Minding the details Solving problems logically	Squashing ideas Dominating Competing Being aggressive Criticising Deflating people's enthusiasm Dissenting and disagreeing Being stubborn Changing the subject Sabotaging others' efforts Manipulating people Speaking on special interests Seeking sympathy Complaining Showing off Nitpicking Finding fault
Process behaviours	Relieving tension with humour Making sure everyone has a say Seeking approval Encouraging others Compromising Keeping the peace Being a friend Being enthusiastic	Being disruptive, clowning around Domineering Withdrawing 'Yes man' Making sarcastic remarks Daydreaming Seeking recognition or status Sniping, being cynical Seeking conflict Avoiding conflict

more than its individual parts, get results and deal well with complexity. This is what to aim for.

The stage your team reaches and how quickly it reaches it has nothing to do with how long people have worked together or their age. It has to do with how skilled and willing they are to work together, how well each person is able to contribute to the whole and complement the skills of other team members and how capably you lead them.

What to do when people leave or join your team

When people leave or join a team, loyalties, communication patterns and group dynamics may shift, and people's skills may be used and appreciated differently than previously. This often causes a team to regress to an earlier stage of development. For example, a team that is *performing* will often go back to *norming* to re-establish the ways everyone works together; a team that has *normed* may regress to *storming* and argue, openly or covertly, about task or process matters. This can be a difficult time for everyone, so don't ignore the important process issues in your group when people leave or join your team.

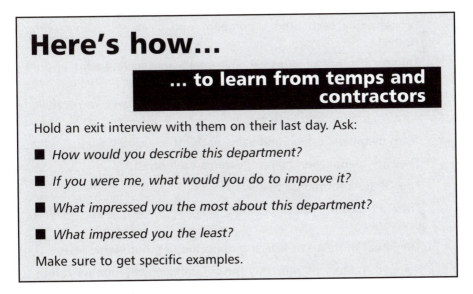

Here's how...

... to learn from temps and contractors

Hold an exit interview with them on their last day. Ask:

■ *How would you describe this department?*

■ *If you were me, what would you do to improve it?*

■ *What impressed you the most about this department?*

■ *What impressed you the least?*

Make sure to get specific examples.

While new members are struggling to understand the group's norms and culture, they can unintentionally disrupt them. This makes everyone uncomfortable and reduces the effectiveness and output of the team. Spell out important aspects of your group's norms and culture whenever you induct someone into your team so they aren't left to flounder and pick them up as they go along.

DEVELOPING COMMITMENT AND COOPERATION

What is the difference between conflict and cooperation on the one hand, and compliance and commitment on the other? Cooperative and committed work teams are generally productive and a pleasure to supervise. These things don't happen by chance—they need to be developed and nurtured.

161

Checklist for success

☐ Make sure the following describes your team:

☐ Everyone can express the essence of our organisation's vision and main goals.

☐ Everyone demonstrates an understanding of how they contribute to it.

☐ Everyone demonstrates an understanding of our organisation's performance and the issues affecting it.

☐ Everyone knows what the team is trying to achieve and does their share to achieve it.

☐ People enjoy each other's company and treat each other with respect.

☐ There is a sense of purpose, enjoyment and achievement in our team.

☐ Team members communicate openly, honestly and respectfully with each other and with me.

☐ Team members respect and value each other as individuals.

☐ They are friendly and helpful towards each other.

☐ They share information readily.

☐ They air problems and resolve them in a way that satisfies everyone.

☐ They treat mistakes as learning opportunities, not blame fests.

☐ Remove mystery as much as possible and openly discuss results with your team.

☐ Don't just speak to people when there's a problem; share the good news too.

☐ Train people in skills that will allow them to be useful members of the team.

☐ Make sure everyone knows how important their contributions are and recognise those contributions.

☐ Draw people's attention to the helpful and unhelpful things they do in the team.

Figure 8.1 Stages of team growth

STAGE 1

FORMING
Sorting out exactly why we are here and what we are supposed to be doing. People are often anxious, cautious and self-conscious. Productivity is low.

What to do
Provide clear direction by establishing the team purpose, setting goals and success measures, and so on.

STAGE 2

STORMING
On the task side, disagreements surface about goals and how to do things. On the process side, there is conflict over who plays which roles and what group dynamics will come to the fore. Productivity is low.

What to do
Provide strong, hands-on leadership to keep people talking and task focused.

STAGE 3

NORMING
Codes of behaviour become established and an identifiable group culture emerges. People begin to enjoy each other's company and appreciate each other's contributions.

What to do
If a positive culture and norms develop and if team members are skilled, begin to take a back seat while the group sorts out task issues involving who will do what, and how. Monitor, guide and confirm that things are going well as the team begins achieving good results.

STAGE 4

PERFORMING
Teams that reach this stage achieve results easily and enjoyably. People work together well and can improve systems, solve problems and provide excellent customer service. The team is productive, creative and harmonious and satisfaction, synergy and spirit are high.

What to do
Sit back and relax while keeping a watchful eye.

STAGE 5

ADJOURNING
Temporary project teams and other shortlived teams reach this stage.

What to do
Offer people an opportunity to celebrate their team's achievements and formally say their 'goodbyes'.

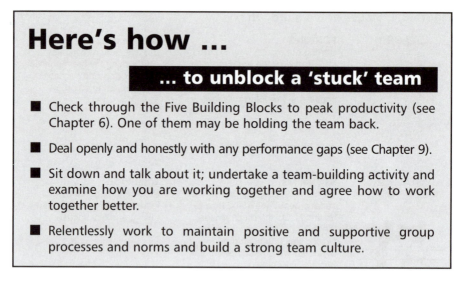

Here's how ...

... to unblock a 'stuck' team

■ Check through the Five Building Blocks to peak productivity (see Chapter 6). One of them may be holding the team back.

■ Deal openly and honestly with any performance gaps (see Chapter 9).

■ Sit down and talk about it; undertake a team-building activity and examine how you are working together and agree how to work together better.

■ Relentlessly work to maintain positive and supportive group processes and norms and build a strong team culture.

Build your team
Our tools for developing a performing team are **team building** and **team maintenance**.

Team building
Effective ways of working together generally don't emerge by themselves and team members won't necessarily focus on the task unless you make it clear and compelling. You can do this through a process called team building.

Team building is a 'time out', away from the work area, for the team to focus on what they are trying to achieve, how each team member contributes (their own **job purpose** and **key result areas**; see Chapter 6) and the ways team members work together to achieve the task (decision making, cooperation, communication and so on). At the end of the one, two or three days, the team has a clear sense of direction and plans for working more effectively together to reach its goals.

Team maintenance
Just as a car needs maintenance, so do a team's processes if they are to remain effective. You don't need to wait for an official team-building meeting to carry out a bit of 'team upkeep'. Every time your team meets is an opportunity to clarify its purpose, celebrate how well it is achieving its goals and discuss what the team could do differently to improve its results. Each time you meet is also an opportunity to build team spirit, strengthen working relationships and move the team along the growth road to the *performing* stage.

Here's how ...

... to help your team deal with a departure

■ Let the group know when some is leaving and discuss the reasons for it (a promotion, a move to another company, full-time study or part-time work).

■ Let them express their sorrow.

■ Discuss how individuals and the team as a whole might be affected and how to reduce the negative effects of the departure.

■ Flag any projects or tasks that might be especially vulnerable and discuss how to protect them.

■ Plan, together if possible, how to cover for the departing person until a replacement joins.

■ Explain how and when a replacement will be recruited.

■ Discuss whether reallocating duties or redesigning the workflow would be desirable.

■ When the new person joins, do everything you can to make them feel welcome and find their place in the team quickly. (See Chapter 4.)

Give lots of feedback

People need feedback. No matter how old they are or how long they have been in a job, people need to know that others see and appreciate their contributions. Don't assume that an employee whose work is always good doesn't need to hear it from you. Most people don't equate silence with approval.

People also need constructive feedback to help improve their performance. Unfortunately, no matter how tactfully we word it, it can still sting. Lessen the sting by making sure you don't imply you're criticising the person. Use the BAT MICE mnemonic to focus on objective behaviours, not character or abilities. Show how what you're commenting on will help the department, the team and the person to whom you're giving the feedback.

165

Figure 8.2 The BAT MICE feedback formula

B *Balanced* Be both positive and constructive. Build self-esteem. Don't criticise. Do point out what people can do to improve their performance.

A *Actionable* Make sure this is something the person can actually do something about.

T *Timely* When will be the best time to discuss this? Count to 100 and think it through.

M *Meaningful* Make your feedback about a success measure not achieved or a behaviour (something you can see or hear) that does not meet expectations. What *should* the person be saying or doing?

I *'I' language* Say 'I' more than 'you'—it comes across as less pushy, domineering and controlling and will meet with less resistance. Saying 'I need ...' not 'you must' or 'you should' also establishes you as the boss.

C *Constructive* If you're a coach not a critic, and want to help not hurt, you will be constructive.

E *Empathic* Put yourself in the other person's shoes and, unless it's praise, give feedback in private.

The more regularly you give both of these types of feedback—positive and constructive—the more effectively you will build individual performance and develop a high-performing team.

Don't store feedback up—give it often. The opportunities are endless: at meetings, during a project, by memo, e-mail or informal discussions. Post team progress on notice boards. Keep an open-door policy so people feel free to discuss things with you: an open working relationship makes it easier for employees to take your feedback on board. Devote part of every day to feedback. Even a few encouraging words are powerful.

If your feedback is positive, don't delay it! Let people know you've noticed they are meeting their goals or contributing to teamwork. Post graphs showing what the team has achieved. Mark the achievement of major milestones or goals with a celebration: bring in pizzas for lunch for everyone to share, put up balloons, send thankyou notes.

If you ignore success people will think it doesn't matter after all and stop trying.

Here's how ...

... to turn complaints into feedback

- Aim only at changes in employee behaviour that will bring a measurable difference in results both you and others can see.

- Suggest specific actions employees could take (or stop doing) to improve their performance.

- Correct *work*, not *people*.

- Do everything you can to build self-confidence and self-esteem. You can't get a winning performance out of someone who thinks they're a loser.

- Use neutral words, stay objective and keep your voice steady.

- Comment on good work too.

- Speak up when you see the need for improvement. If you let things slide, people will think all is well and what they're doing is acceptable. At the same time, don't speak in haste—think it through first.

- Let employees have their say too, without interruption.

- Before parting, summarise what you've agreed and make sure the employee understands that the purpose of the feedback is to help them do the better work you know they are capable of.

- Offer improvement suggestions.

- Help the person learn from mistakes: *'Let's see what we can learn from this'*, *'If you did this* over, *how would you do it differently?'*

- Focus on the future (*'From now on...'*, *'Next time...'*).

- Explain what you *do* want, not what you *don't* want.

If your feedback is negative, and the situation has upset you or the employee, delay it only enough to 'cool down' and be objective. (Don't wait longer than a week though.)

SUPERVISING 'INVISIBLE' EMPLOYEES
Are you supervising any 'invisible workers'—people who work out of sight, in another location? They may work from home part or all of the time, in other cities or even in other countries.

How do you know whether people are working if you can't see them? You don't. Now more than ever, we pay people for results, not time spent. Set 'out of sight' workers a goal and let them achieve it in their own way. Leave how and when they do it up to them. In a way, this makes your job easier: know what end product you're looking for, establish timelines and other constraints, agree upon milestones to monitor and let them 'go for it'.

Actually, it isn't that simple. If you focus only on task issues, you risk losing the good will, enthusiasm and commitment of the employee (or never developing it to begin with). On the process side, it's essential to keep up the communication flow, including, and perhaps especially, the friendly chats. Reverting to the 'bad old days' of treating people like cogs in a wheel would be easy, but a big mistake.

Warning: when working from home works, productivity often soars. It isn't for everyone, though, and takes getting used to. If one of your employees opts for home-based work, help them set up a viable and safe home office and learn how to 'switch off' when they 'leave work' and 'switch on' when they 'go to work'. Research how to turn the downsides of working from home into upsides and spend time making it work.

LEADING A MERGED TEAM
Mergers have become commonplace, which means you may well find yourself leading a merged work team. Aligning people to the new organisation's vision and goals and helping them deal with the changes and grow into a performing team will be a top priority.

Communication is a must. Keep the lines open between employees and yourself and act as a conduit of information from the organisation as a whole. Know what the new organisation's vision and objectives are and make them clear to everyone, over and over again. The more you communicate, the more you will defuse the rumour mill. Listen as well as talk, and deal with issues quickly. (See also Chapter 16.)

Here's how ...

... to manage off-site employees

■ Make sure they understand the workflow of your department and organisation.

■ Alter measures of success to reflect the new ways of working and make them crystal clear.

■ Be clear about the results you expect. Leave the 'how tos' and time needed to achieve them up to the employee.

■ Agree how you will monitor progress and identify difficulties.

■ Hold them accountable for results, not time spent.

■ Keep them in the 'communication loop' through regular formal and informal contact (telephone, email, etc.).

■ Create opportunities for get-togethers, both social and work related, to develop and build relationships.

■ Involve them in non-work communications and activities.

■ Include them in in-house meetings, even if it's by speakerphone.

■ Train on-site employees to work effectively with off-site employees. Keep on-site people up to date on off-site employees' contributions and activities.

■ Listen carefully when you communicate over the phone; you don't have their body language to help you 'fill in the blanks'.

■ Make sure that 'out of sight' is not 'out of mind'.

BE LIFE FRIENDLY

Would you like to save the high hidden costs of recruiting and rebuilding your team whenever someone new joins? People-friendly work practices can help you by attracting and retaining skilled and talented employees.

In the last few years work–life balance has become important in organisations interested in retaining valuable staff. These are practices that recognise that employees are people, with lives outside work.

What began as a realisation that the same 'rules' and cultural expectations and assumptions that applied to males should also apply to working mothers has extended to include everyone. Everyone has a life outside of work. Both men and women have children and ageing parents that need their attention, for example. Today, family-friendly and life-friendly organisations might be a 'luxury' pioneered by the top companies, but the standards they are setting will soon be applied to all employers.

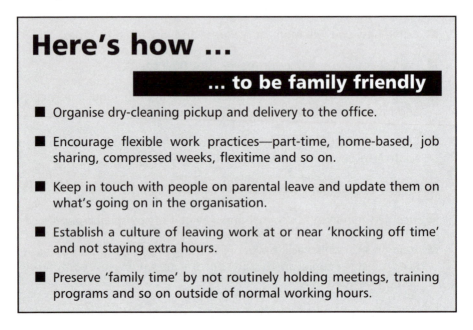

Here's how ...

... to be family friendly

- Organise dry-cleaning pickup and delivery to the office.

- Encourage flexible work practices—part-time, home-based, job sharing, compressed weeks, flexitime and so on.

- Keep in touch with people on parental leave and update them on what's going on in the organisation.

- Establish a culture of leaving work at or near 'knocking off time' and not staying extra hours.

- Preserve 'family time' by not routinely holding meetings, training programs and so on outside of normal working hours.

People want and need a life outside work. The benefits to the organisation reflect in its morale, operations and bottom line. Work practices like these can help keep good employees, reduce absenteeism and reduce work-related sickness and stress.

PUTTING TOGETHER THE PERFECT TEAM

Imagine being part of a team where everyone thought just like you, had the same basic ideas, the same type of experiences, the same outlook on life, the same skills, knowledge and attributes. Pretty boring? It would be if you believe that 'variety is the spice of life'!

Not only that, but how much innovation would occur? How quickly would the team be able to respond to changing circumstances and take advantage of unexpected opportunities? How well would everything that needed to be done actually be done? If everyone is the same, you've got a club, not a team! It might be 'comfortable' and predictable, but it wouldn't be very effective or productive. It takes all kinds of people to make a great team.

Career tip

Resist the urge to recruit people who are 'like' the other team members. You don't want to end up with too many or too few people from a particular personality type.

When you're putting a team together, include a mixture of people. Look for people with different backgrounds, different ways of doing things and different skills, abilities and work preferences. This makes for a well-rounded team. Make sure everyone appreciates each other's unique and valuable perspective and the different contributions this allows them to make. (See also Chapters 2 and 4.)

For example:

- Too many *dominant directors* will fight among themselves for control, while too few can mean a team has difficulty making decisions and lacks energy.

- Too may *interacting socialisers* can mean a team has lots of fun but achieves few results, while too few can dampen team spirit and creativity.

- Too many *steady relaters* without a leader can cause a team to stagnate and fail to improve, while too few willing hands to do the work can mean it never gets done.

- Too many *conscientious thinkers* can cause a team to suffer from paralysis by analysis, while too few can mean the important details are overlooked. (See Chapter 2.)

171

Checklist for success

☐ When new people join, make them feel welcome, give them a defined role to fill and a contribution to make and help them get to know their teammates as quickly as possible.

☐ Give new teams a 'feel' for what they are supposed to be doing and where they are headed. Set the scene for how team members should work together, how formal or informal you want them to be and how much focus there should be on the task at hand.

☐ Look after the *process* needs as well as the *task* needs of the team, for example by providing opportunities for people to come together to discuss work as well as enjoy each other's company.

☐ Make sure healthy team norms develop, such as 'We insist on high quality', 'We put the customer first', 'We listen to each other's views' and 'We turn up on time'.

☐ Discuss how your team is working together at team meetings. Bring up any deviations from the agreed ways of working together.

☐ Periodically review your team's overall purpose and success measures.

☐ Streamline workflow and organise it so it allows people to work together and everyone's contribution to show.

☐ Make members of your team feel like 'winners' and enjoy a sense of achievement and pride.

☐ Be liberal with your public praise and private constructive feedback.

☐ Make sure team members' working styles are complementary

CHAPTER NINE

DEAL WITH THE TOUGH STUFF
Managing conflict and improving and appraising performance

W ho do you know who has never had a difficult conversation with someone? No one? That's not surprising. Whether it's a discipline interview, dealing with an employee with a personal crisis or helping a wayward employee get back on the rails, handling the 'tough stuff' well takes care and skill.

Talking is like playing the harp; there is as much in laying the hand on the strings to stop their vibrations as in twanging them to bring out their music.

Oliver Wendell Holmes, Sr (1809–94)
Poet, novelist, essayist and physician

Sometimes, holding our tongue is the greatest skill of all. When we do speak, we need to be careful of the words we let out of our mouths because once they're gone, we can't get them back. The tougher the situation, the more this holds true.

RESOLVING CONFLICT
Things don't always go smoothly. Some conflicts, of course, are minor irritations that we can quickly and easily forget. Others are more serious and can do lasting damage if we don't manage them well.

When a conflict or a difference of opinion, priorities or perspectives arises in the workplace, we need to take special care to keep communication flowing. Just as a ball rolling down a hill gathers momentum, so does conflict. Ignoring it or sweeping it under the carpet leaves it unaired and unresolved, to intensify and worsen.

As a matter of fact, conflict and differences of opinion are natural and healthy. If you recognise conflict and deal with it openly and honestly, you won't end up with hard feelings, bruised egos or lingering hostilities. The time, energy and patience you invest in finding a solution that everyone can live with will be well spent.

Career tip

Think of conflict management *as* agreement management.

How do you respond to conflict?

How do you handle conflict? Do you snap into *compete* mode and force your solution on others? If so, you risk losing respect and good will. If people accept your solution, it is likely to be only half-heartedly and they may even undermine it. So unless the other person is totally unimportant to you or the issue itself is hugely important, avoid imposing your solution on people.

Perhaps you automatically give in, or *accommodate* the other person. This ultimately saps your self-esteem and self-respect. Others quickly learn they can 'walk all over you' because you let them. Unless the issue is of no importance to you, speak up for yourself.

Do you prefer to *avoid* conflict by 'letting sleeping dogs lie' or 'sweeping it under the carpet'? Sometimes it is better to diplomatically sidestep an issue or postpone a discussion until a later time. However, people who prefer 'peace at any price', even when the issue or relationship with the other party is important, often find matters worsen over time. Everyone loses.

Are you often tempted to 'split the difference' and *compromise*? As quick and easy as this is, the result is often that no one is really satisfied and the underlying conflict smoulders on. Unless you're looking for an interim solution or time is running out, you can often do better than settling for a quick fix.

Perhaps you are inclined to sit down and talk through your differences with the other person, exploring what each of you wants and discussing various ways you can both be satisfied. This *collaborating* approach takes time, but preserves relationships and solves the real issues. Do you have the willingness to try good communication and problem-solving skills and the self-confidence and patience they take?

These five conflict management styles, summarised in Figure 9.1, are based on the work of Kenneth Thomas and Ralph Kilmann. They seem to be habitual; in other words, we tend to use the same one or two styles every time we find ourselves in a conflict situation.

Figure 9.1 Five ways to handle conflict

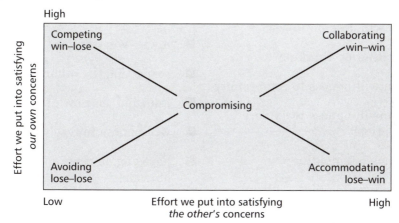

Is your usual conflict management style a helpful one? Will it help you develop effective working relationships with your colleagues, customers and work group? Will it help ensure your own needs, as well as others', are met? Do you need to improve your skills in using any of them?

Which of the following helping and hurting responses to conflict do you employ?

Hurting responses

■ avoiding it

■ personal attacks

■ getting angry

■ changing the subject

■ apologising inappropriately

Helping responses

■ trying to understand the other's point of view

■ being willing to listen

■ keeping calm

■ knowing what you want

175

Hurting responses	*Helping responses*
■ playing the martyr	■ clearly stating your position and goals
■ pretending to agree	■ isolating what you are disagreeing about
■ giving up and giving in	
■ trying to turn the conflict into a joke	■ getting a 'referee'
	■ looking for mutual goals
■ a win–lose mind-set	
■ 'either/or' thinking	■ a win–win mind-set
■ unwillingness to compromise	■ respecting the other party
■ unwillingness to explore options	■ knowing your own limits
	■ willingness to resolve
■ lack of empathy	■ agreeing on clear goals or outcomes
■ refusal to see the other's point of view	■ empathy
■ being negative	■ assertiveness
	■ mutual respect
	■ being positive

To turn conflicts into agreements, keep these questions in mind:

■ How can we move towards the same side?

■ How can we reach a joint understanding?

■ How can we prevent problems or misunderstandings from occurring again?

Four steps to reach agreement
Should you say anything or not? Think about two things:

1. The issue and your goals.

2. Your relationship with the other person.

How important to you is each one? Say something when both your goals and the relationship are important to you. Say something when the issue alone is extremely important to you. Say something when the relationship is important. Save your breath when neither is that important.

If you decide to work towards agreement, here are the four steps to follow to reach a collaborative solution.

Step 1: Open the discussion
The best way to open a discussion is with a short **framing statement** outlining the 'whats, hows and whys' of a conversation before beginning it. This 'sets the scene', explains what you want to discuss and prevents you from 'jumping in with both feet'.

Think about what a frame around a picture does: it draws our attention to it, highlights its main features and colours and separates the picture from its surroundings. A frame to a conversation does the same. It identifies what will be and what won't be discussed. It introduces the topic and often specifies how the conversation will proceed.

Developing and delivering a short framing statement will help you in three ways. It will ensure you have analysed and organised your information and thoughts. It will help clarify your purpose and the way you will go about achieving it. And it will help set the scene for a productive discussion.

Step 2: Give good information
Next, state your point of view clearly and concisely. The most effective way to do this is to explain how you or the department are affected by the concern you are raising. This makes it less likely the other person will 'counterattack' or become defensive. You might find the **'I' statement** formula shown in the box on page 179 helpful.

Or say something like: *'When you ... it's a problem because ... What I'd like from now on is ...'*

Use objective, neutral language to avoid antagonising the other person and keep your comments about factual, specific and observable matters; avoid conjectures, guesses, hearsay or speculation. Don't exaggerate and keep it brief.

Here's how ...

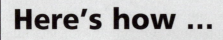

... to make a framing statement

State the problem	'We haven't seemed to blend our maintenance efforts and I think this is causing us both extra work. I'd like to see if we can find a way to work better together on this.'
Map the discussion	'Before discussing your productivity rate, I suggest we first review the required standards. Then I'd like to move on and see if we can figure out what is preventing you from meeting them consistently. How does that sound to you?'
Point to your goal	'Lee, I want you to succeed at this job and I'd like to discuss some ideas that may help you.'
Establish what will be focused on and what won't	'Today, we won't be talking about your overall job performance, which is excellent, but only about the incident with Jo last Tuesday.'
Review relevant key events	'We have spoken twice over the past month about figures from your department not reaching us on time. It happened again yesterday.'
Outline the information you want to discuss	'During this meeting I would like to review the customer survey and delivery figures and formulate an action plan for improving both of them.'

Step 3: Gather good information

You've stated your point of view. Now it's time to hear and understand the other person's. Use your empathy and the EARS formula (see

Box 9.1 'I' statement

1. **The action**	*When* (objective, non-evaluative description of the other person's behaviour or target not met)
2. **My response or why it matters**	*I get/become/feel* (a no-blame description of your own feelings or the effect of the action on you [e.g. angry, annoyed, frustrated, worried]) or describe the effects on output, quality, other staff etc.
3. **My preferred outcome**	*I'd prefer* (description of what outcome you would like without telling the other what to do).

Example:
1. *When your report is late, as it was today,*
2. *I get annoyed and frustrated because it holds up my work.*
3. *I'd like to work out a system so that this won't happen again.*

Chapters 2 and 16) to gather good information and show that you have heard it. Ask questions to clarify and explore the other person's thinking, and summarise often. Be sure you fully understand each other's position before moving onto Step 4.

> *E* Explore by asking questions.
>
> *A* Affirm to show you're listening.
>
> *R* Reflect your understanding.
>
> *S* Silence—listen some more.

Step 4: Problem solve
A problem-solving approach can help produce a solution you can both support. Develop some possible solutions.

When you have some options to select from, assess them. Look for a good, workable solution, not just any solution. Are there any flaws in any of the possible solutions? Any reasons why a solution might not work? Would it be too hard to implement or carry out, or not suit your organisation's way of doing things? Is it fair to everyone involved?

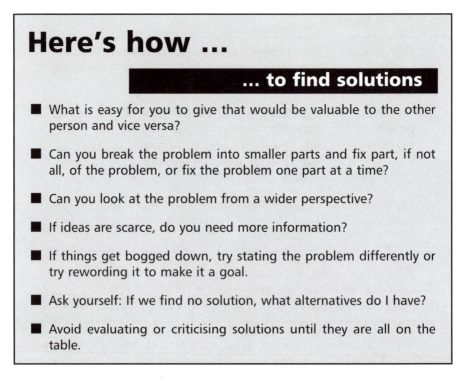

Here's how ...

... to find solutions

- What is easy for you to give that would be valuable to the other person and vice versa?

- Can you break the problem into smaller parts and fix part, if not all, of the problem, or fix the problem one part at a time?

- Can you look at the problem from a wider perspective?

- If ideas are scarce, do you need more information?

- If things get bogged down, try stating the problem differently or try rewording it to make it a goal.

- Ask yourself: If we find no solution, what alternatives do I have?

- Avoid evaluating or criticising solutions until they are all on the table.

A mutually acceptable solution is essential because you want the commitment of both parties. Once you've settled on a solution, decide how to implement it and talk about how you will follow up and evaluate how well it's working.

You'll know if you've done a good job because you'll both be satisfied with the outcome and work even better together as a result. You will be able to manage further conflicts more effectively and you'll have a deeper appreciation and understanding of each other.

After you've resolved a conflict, review it and learn from it.

- What caused it? Have you removed the cause so it won't occur again?

- What helped you reach agreement? What held you back?

- What were the signs that conflict was brewing? Would identifying and addressing it earlier have helped? What could you have done?

- What should you bear in mind for the future?

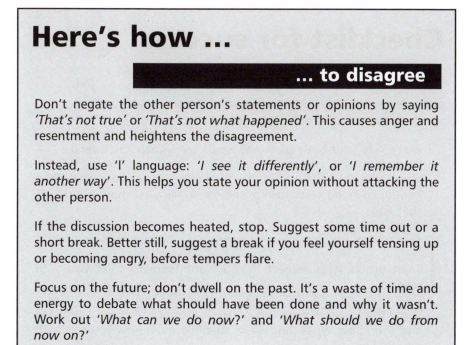

Here's how ...

... to disagree

Don't negate the other person's statements or opinions by saying *'That's not true'* or *'That's not what happened'*. This causes anger and resentment and heightens the disagreement.

Instead, use 'I' language: *'I see it differently'*, or *'I remember it another way'*. This helps you state your opinion without attacking the other person.

If the discussion becomes heated, stop. Suggest some time out or a short break. Better still, suggest a break if you feel yourself tensing up or becoming angry, before tempers flare.

Focus on the future; don't dwell on the past. It's a waste of time and energy to debate what should have been done and why it wasn't. Work out *'What can we do now?'* and *'What should we do from now on?'*

DEALING WITH POOR PERFORMANCE

If someone's performance is not reaching expectations, don't wait until appraisal time rolls around before addressing the problem. Deal with it quickly, before it deteriorates even further or becomes a hard-to-break habit, and before your temper frays and your comments are motivated more by anger than helpfulness.

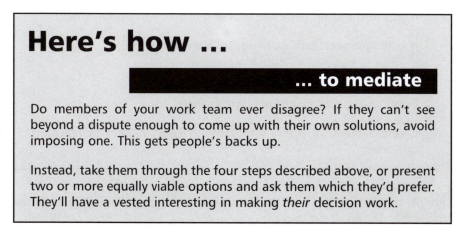

Here's how ...

... to mediate

Do members of your work team ever disagree? If they can't see beyond a dispute enough to come up with their own solutions, avoid imposing one. This gets people's backs up.

Instead, take them through the four steps described above, or present two or more equally viable options and ask them which they'd prefer. They'll have a vested interesting in making *their* decision work.

181

Checklist for success

- ☐ Listen more than you talk.

- ☐ Listen reflectively—you'll be amazed at how much you'll learn and how much people will admire you for it!

- ☐ Make sure your body language sends the signals you intend.

- ☐ Emphasise the relationship; if you are both clear that you want a continued good relationship, then you will work harder towards that end.

- ☐ Keep things in perspective by keeping a long-term view in mind.

- ☐ Treat others with respect if you want them to treat you with respect.

- ☐ If you think your ideas, plans or needs are in conflict with someone else's, find out what they want. Then work out how you can both be satisfied.

- ☐ See a difference of opinion as an invitation to learn something new.

- ☐ Make sure you understand the other person's point of view before discussing possible solutions.

- ☐ Look for the common ground and search for solutions that will satisfy you both.

- ☐ If you're stuck, redefine the problem or point of disagreement.

- ☐ If your approach isn't working, try something else.

- ☐ Think 'agreeing', not 'winning'.

- ☐ Don't masquerade your opinions as facts.

- ☐ Create a menu of options to increase your chances of reaching agreement.

Do you recall the **85:15 rule** discussed in Chapter 6? This shows us that 85% of the time, poor performance is outside the employee's control. Often what looks like a performance problem is not really one at all. Less than 15% of cases of poor performance result from employees having a pressing personal or motivational problem that is sapping their ability or willingness to do their job well.

If someone's performance is below par, the first step is always to work through the Five Building Blocks to peak performance and productivity (see Chapter 6):

1. *What to*

2. *Want to*

3. *How to*

4. *Chance to*

5. *Led to*

Box 9.2 Possible causes of poor performance

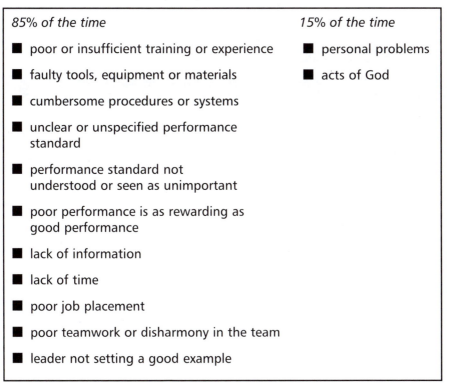

85% of the time	15% of the time
■ poor or insufficient training or experience	■ personal problems
■ faulty tools, equipment or materials	■ acts of God
■ cumbersome procedures or systems	
■ unclear or unspecified performance standard	
■ performance standard not understood or seen as unimportant	
■ poor performance is as rewarding as good performance	
■ lack of information	
■ lack of time	
■ poor job placement	
■ poor teamwork or disharmony in the team	
■ leader not setting a good example	

The **flow chart** shown in Figure 9.2 will guide you in this. If someone needs more training or help with their approach to their job, coaching may be in order (see Chapter 5). If you need to take stronger measures, work through the six steps to perfecting performance discussed below. As a final resort, bring in the 'big guns' and work through an official warning and employment termination procedure, also discussed below.

Six steps to lifting performance

At the end of the day, the choice between improved work performance and continued unsatisfactory work performance (and, ultimately, loss of employment) is the employee's. You can influence that choice by holding a constructive discussion or series of discussions that you have thought through beforehand, following the six steps shown in Figure 9.3.

Step 1: Determine the performance gap
Sweeping statements like: *'Clean up your act'*, *'You're not trying hard enough'* or *'You've got a bad attitude'* won't help anyone improve.

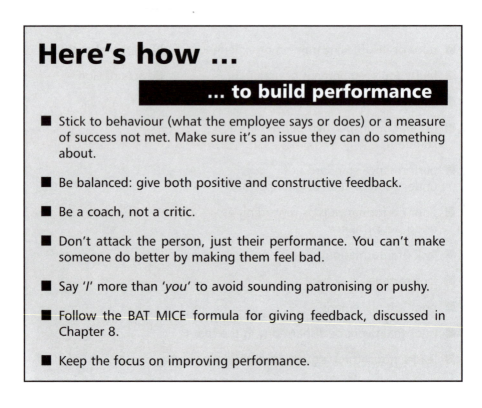

Here's how ...

... to build performance

■ Stick to behaviour (what the employee says or does) or a measure of success not met. Make sure it's an issue they can do something about.

■ Be balanced: give both positive and constructive feedback.

■ Be a coach, not a critic.

■ Don't attack the person, just their performance. You can't make someone do better by making them feel bad.

■ Say '*I*' more than '*you*' to avoid sounding patronising or pushy.

■ Follow the BAT MICE formula for giving feedback, discussed in Chapter 8.

■ Keep the focus on improving performance.

Figure 9.2 Analysing poor performance

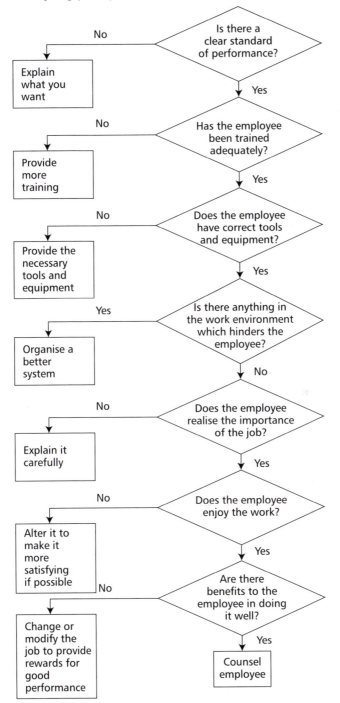

Before saying anything, think: what is the performance shortfall, or **performance gap**? State it specifically; you should be able to quantify it (i.e. put a number to it) or, if it's behavioural, express it using neutral, objective words. To do this, you need a clear **measure of success** (see Chapters 3 and 6) to compare the current with the desired performance.

Box 9.3 Examples of performance gaps

Behavioural	Targets not met
■ Keeping customers waiting more than five minutes without acknowledging them.	■ Arriving 10–15 minutes late two to three times a week for the past six weeks.
■ Speaking abruptly and curtly to customers or colleagues, especially during busy times.	■ Producing the last three reports two days late.
■ Going for a smoke instead of helping team mates complete their work.	■ Not meeting the 95% accuracy target on documents; producing an average of 80% accuracy for the past two weeks.
■ Having to be reminded two or three times a day to complete routine work.	■ Not answering the telephone within four rings and not identifying the department or saying your name.

Step 2: Give good information

Your first few words and the way you describe the performance gap are critical: they will either put the employee off-side and lead to a meeting filled with resistance, denial, accusations, blame and ill will, or to a meeting filled with a willingness to examine and resolve the problem.

Open the discussion with a frame

As discussed above, a framing statement helps you think about what you want to say and flag it to the other person.

Explain the performance gap

Your next task is to provide information about two things: the performance gap and why it is important. Use an 'I' statement (see above) or the *Describe–Explain–Describe* approach:

Two examples
1) Marjorie was concerned with Caroline's continued lateness in submitting a fortnightly standard report. She had spoken to her about it twice in the last six weeks and Caroline indicated she would make an effort to meet the deadline in future. Caroline's other work was accurate and completed on time.

Marjorie opened the discussion with a frame: *'Caroline, I'd like to discuss the fortnightly report. As you know, its accuracy, like that of all your other work, is fine. I'd like to discuss any problems you might be having about its timing. Do you have some time now?'*

2) Scott had disrupted Mario's staff meeting by fooling around, cracking jokes and making comments not related to the items under discussion. Mario was annoyed because he felt this stopped everyone from taking the meeting seriously and it meant he couldn't get through all the items on the agenda.

Here is the frame he used: *'Scott, I'd like to discuss this morning's staff meeting.'*

By framing the discussions this way, Marjorie and Mario made it clear exactly what they wanted to talk about without blaming or accusing Caroline or Scott or damaging their self-confidence. This opened the way for them to work together to sort the problems out.

Describe the behaviour or action.

Explain the effect it has (on service provision, output, yourself, co-workers, customers, efficiency, etc.).

Describe the change you would like to see, and the time frame.

Two examples
1) After her framing statement, Marjorie went on to say: *'Caroline, I need this report on my desk every second Thursday by midday. When it's late, it holds up my analysis for the region and delays my report to the marketing manager. We need to find out what's delaying this report and do something about it.'*

2) Mario said: *'You cracked several jokes and made a number of comments that weren't related to the discussion. This annoyed me because I couldn't get through everything on the agenda. In future, I'd like all comments directed at the item under discussion and jokes saved until afterwards. How about it?'*

> Marjorie moved into problem solving while Mario, who was dealing with a more straightforward performance problem, could simply state what he expected from Scott.

Be precise. If you provide fuzzy information, your message probably won't get across and may be misinterpreted. If someone's attitude is a problem, describe what they're doing and how it affects their performance. Be ready to give specific examples so the person will fully understand what you are saying.

Step 3: Gather good information
Sometimes that's the end of the matter. For example, Scott said: '*Sorry Mario, I wasn't thinking. It won't happen again*'.

If the problem isn't quite so clearcut, hear what the employee has to say. Listen carefully and show that you are listening by making eye

Here's how ...

... to keep discussions on track

■ Present constructive information.

■ If the employee denies there is a performance problem (and you're really sure there is), keep repeating your main point (the performance gap and that it must be rectified).

■ If the employee tries to change the subject, repeat your main point.

■ If the employee uses one excuse after another to justify the performance gap (and you're sure it's an excuse not an explanation) keep asking: '*What can we do to (get the performance we need)?*'

■ Don't be drawn into accusations of favouritism or nit picking. Keep to the point at hand. (Ask yourself whether the employee could be right.)

■ Try stating the problem as a goal.

Here's how ...

... to be a coach, not a critic

- Focus on the future, not the past.

- Ask, don't tell or demand.

- Discuss performance, not the person.

- Be specific not general.

- Find solutions not fault.

- Be positive not negative.

- Focus on remedies, not problems.

- Encourage, don't pressure.

- Say what you *do* want (not what you *don't* want).

- Explain the 'whys and wherefores'.

- Share information rather than accuse or tell.

- Build the employee's self-confidence and self-esteem.

- Offer improvement suggestions.

- Don't lay blame. See what can be learned.

- Find something to compliment.

- Set high performance standards—expect the best.

contact, nodding your head and leaning slightly forward. Repeat what you have understood. Try to put yourself in the employee's shoes and see things from their point of view. You don't need to agree, just to see it their way for a moment. This helps you decide how to proceed and helps the employee because they've had a chance to explain things from their perspective.

Don't interrupt or point out that they are wrong. Keep calm and hear the employee out.

Step 4: Problem solve
When the employee has had their say and accepts that there is a performance gap, use the Five Building Blocks discussed in Chapter 6 to analyse what's preventing the employee from reaching their targets. As much as you can, allow them to come up with solutions and suggest ways you could help them reach their performance goals. Keep focused on a solution.

Step 5: Agree actions
Once you have identified the cause of the performance problem, decide how to deal with it. What will the employee do? What will you do? How will you monitor performance to make sure your strategy is working? Agree specific performance criteria and a review schedule. End on a positive note.

Step 6: Monitor performance and discuss
You should both track whether the employee's performance is improving. If it is, say something to encourage them to keep up the good work. If it isn't, sit down and discuss the problem again.

Don't always expect an overnight improvement, especially if the performance gap is a large one. Rome wasn't built in a day. Don't wait for perfect performance before saying anything. Acknowledge 'small steps' because a series of small improvements grows into great performance if the Five Building Blocks are in place. If people turn around their performance and no one acknowledges it, they'll think it doesn't matter after all and it's likely to slip away again.

What about terminations?
You will occasionally need to terminate someone's employment because of continued unsatisfactory performance. While this is

Figure 9.3 The six step path to perfecting performance

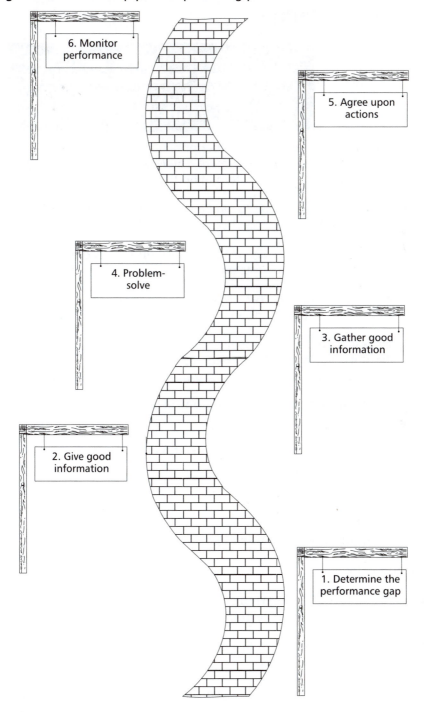

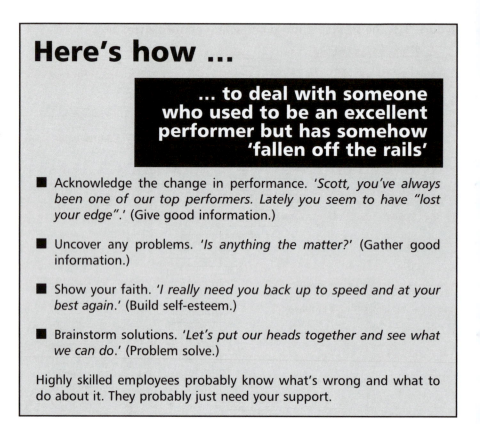

Here's how ...

... to deal with someone who used to be an excellent performer but has somehow 'fallen off the rails'

■ Acknowledge the change in performance. *'Scott, you've always been one of our top performers. Lately you seem to have "lost your edge".'* (Give good information.)

■ Uncover any problems. *'Is anything the matter?'* (Gather good information.)

■ Show your faith. *'I really need you back up to speed and at your best again.'* (Build self-esteem.)

■ Brainstorm solutions. *'Let's put our heads together and see what we can do.'* (Problem solve.)

Highly skilled employees probably know what's wrong and what to do about it. They probably just need your support.

unpleasant, the morale and the output of your department make it necessary.

Most organisations go through a three-stage termination process:

1. Verbal warning

2. First written warning

3. Second (final) written warning

The aim is to:

■ give employees full warning that they are in danger of losing their job if they don't meet certain expectations;

■ allow them a chance to discuss matters and explain things from their point of view; and

■ allow sufficient time for the poor performance to turn around.

If your organisation has a human resources department, involve them from the beginning and follow their guidance.

Only address problems that occur on the job. For example:

- Attendance record
- Safety record
- Behaviour towards co-workers
- Behaviour towards customers
- Job effectiveness, efficiency and output

Never attempt to terminate for the following reasons:

- Temporary absence due to illness or injury

- Union membership or participation in union activities outside working hours or during working hours with employer consent

- Non-membership of a union

- Acting or having acted or seeking to act as an employee representative

- Filing a complaint or participating in proceedings against an employer involving an alleged violation of laws or regulations

- Discriminatory reasons (race, colour, sex, sexual preference, age, physical or mental disability, marital status, family responsibilities, pregnancy, religion, political opinion, national extraction or social origin)

- Absence from work during maternity or other parental leave

- Refusal to negotiate an Australian Workplace Agreement or refusal to make, sign, vary the terms of, or extend one

- Constructive dismissal or forced resignation (where an employee is forced to resign, e.g. by making conditions intolerable or difficult for them)

When you meet with the employee, follow the six steps to perfecting performance shown in Figure 9.3. At each meeting, make sure the employee understands the serious nature of the discussion and that they are in danger of losing their job if their performance doesn't turn

193

around. This is not by way of threat, but of making their options completely clear so there are no misunderstandings.

Apply the *Change–Time–Consequences* formula: if not *this change* by *this time*, this is the *consequence*. The employee must fully understand that if they don't take *this action* or achieve *this standard* by *this date*, they will lose their job. Gather good information (Step 3) by giving them an opportunity to ask questions and explain any difficulties they are facing in reaching their measures of success. You must hear their point of view.

Document each of these three stages, including the verbal warning. Write down the facts regarding the performance shortfall and a summary of each discussion, informal ones too. This provides an authentic record of what has taken place.

Keep a copy for your own files and give a copy to human resources. Give the employee a copy of the written warnings and a chance to respond to them. Write these on company letterhead, and include a date and the information shown in Box 9.4.

If you need to terminate someone's employment, think about what went wrong. Was it a poor job placement? Perhaps the employee never felt part of the work group. Perhaps their job expectations weren't met or they weren't trained properly. Perhaps the quality of your supervision was below par and you need to examine your leadership style. See what you can learn so you can avoid repeating the mistake.

DEALING WITH PERSONAL PROBLEMS

Most supervisors at some stage in their career are faced with an employee who has a personal problem. If their work performance suffers as a result, discuss their performance with them to see how to correct it. If the employee's work performance is unaffected, you could still act as a 'sounding board' to help the employee talk through their personal problems and identify possible options or courses of action.

Be wary of giving advice or in any way telling the employee what to do. Avoid empty reassurances ('Every cloud has a silver lining' or 'Don't worry—she'll be right') because they have a hollow ring to someone who is upset or worried about something. Box 9.5 has some other counselling 'don'ts'.

Box 9.4 Termination checklist

Performance gap?	Describe the performance gap in a factual, measurable, specific way. Keep it free of assumptions, hearsay and your own value judgements.
When?	Times, dates, shifts.
How long?	How long has the problem existed? State this clearly and specifically. State dates of previous performance counselling discussions and what was agreed.
Where?	Clearly and accurately describe locations, if relevant.
Who? To whom?	Names of any others involved.
Substantiated?	What material, sources, witnesses, facts, records, etc. do you have to demonstrate the performance gap?
Work related?	Make sure it is work related and does not include aspects that are not work related.
The Five Building Blocks?	Are each of the Five Building Blocks in place?
Change needed?	What change in behaviour or performance is required?
By when?	How long will the employee be given to meet performance expectations?

Let the employee talk about their problem. Ask questions to help them explore it and identify and assess alternatives for dealing with it. This can help them clarify their thinking, release some tension by 'getting it off their chest', and develop an action plan. If the problem is beyond you (e.g. drug, gambling or alcohol addiction or family violence) direct them to a professional counsellor. Many organisations keep lists and have established links with counselling organisations.

Checklist for success

☐ Don't assume it's the employee's fault if performance is below expectations. Work through the Five Building Blocks to look for the reasons behind performance gaps and identify your best course of action.

☐ Don't delay: address performance shortfalls quickly. Be specific in your details to avoid confusion.

☐ Stick to the facts and don't get personal. Don't expect to change someone's personality. Address only behaviours you can pinpoint and describe with neutral words.

☐ Be constructive and helpful. Make it clear that your primary concern is satisfactory work performance. If people think you're 'out to get them' or 'picking on them', they won't be able to improve their performance.

☐ Use the magic phrase: *'I'll know you're doing a good job when ...'*

☐ Be consistent in your warnings and follow through on them. Don't make idle threats.

☐ Take a 'we' approach and make sure employees accept their responsibility to improve their performance.

☐ Keep it private.

☐ Document all performance counselling discussions (even before you bring in the 'big gun': *Change–Time–Consequences*).

☐ Don't undermine a person's confidence.

☐ Discuss the performance, not the person.

PLANNING AND CONDUCTING PERFORMANCE APPRAISALS

While many performance appraisals don't need to address poor performance and most aren't bristling with conflict, most supervisors consider them 'tough'. How do you tell someone who thinks they're 'tops' that their work is 'average'? How do you tell someone who has been in the job for years that their sullen, uncooperative attitude is getting on your nerves? How do you tell an inexperienced employee

Box 9.5 Counselling don'ts

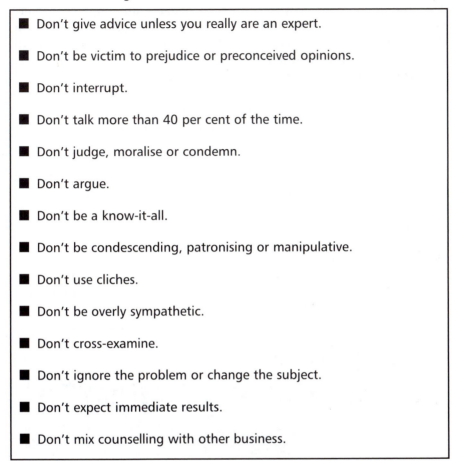

- Don't give advice unless you really are an expert.

- Don't be victim to prejudice or preconceived opinions.

- Don't interrupt.

- Don't talk more than 40 per cent of the time.

- Don't judge, moralise or condemn.

- Don't argue.

- Don't be a know-it-all.

- Don't be condescending, patronising or manipulative.

- Don't use cliches.

- Don't be overly sympathetic.

- Don't cross-examine.

- Don't ignore the problem or change the subject.

- Don't expect immediate results.

- Don't mix counselling with other business.

that there's still plenty of room for improvement, without discouraging them? And what happens if you rate someone's performance as 'excellent' but there's no budget for a salary increase—won't that sap motivation?

Think of annual or bi-annual **performance appraisals** as a regular 'house cleaning': an opportunity to sit down with team members, discuss past performance and plan for the future, and discuss their career aspirations and training needs. Without the discipline a set appraisal provides, it's all too easy to let these important discussions lapse. Of course, they can also be embarrassing to both parties and discouraging to employees if you don't plan and conduct them well.

Looking backwards, looking forwards

The appraisal gives you a chance to discuss an employee's work performance over the preceding period. Make the most of the opportunity to formally compliment areas of excellent performance, acknowledge areas of satisfactory performance and address any areas of poor performance to agree an improvement plan.

Appraisals also provide an opportunity to plan for the future, agreeing measures of success, planning training and development, and discussing possible career moves.

Ideally, appraisals should be two-way. Employees should have the opportunity to offer feedback about their job, further training they may need, additional support that would make their jobs easier or increase quality and so on.

Do your homework

There is no substitute for adequate preparation. Gather as many facts as you can about the employee's performance during the period under

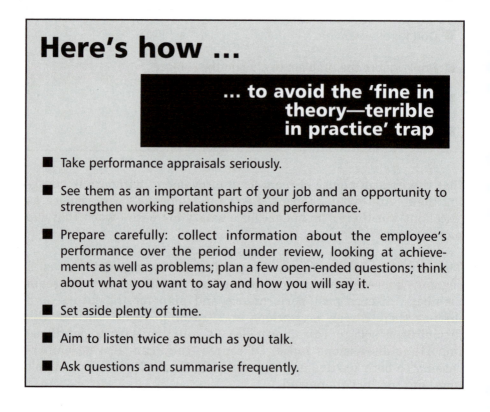

Here's how ...

... to avoid the 'fine in theory—terrible in practice' trap

- Take performance appraisals seriously.

- See them as an important part of your job and an opportunity to strengthen working relationships and performance.

- Prepare carefully: collect information about the employee's performance over the period under review, looking at achievements as well as problems; plan a few open-ended questions; think about what you want to say and how you will say it.

- Set aside plenty of time.

- Aim to listen twice as much as you talk.

- Ask questions and summarise frequently.

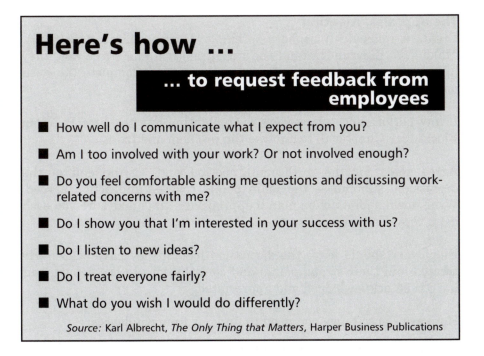

Here's how ...

... to request feedback from employees

- How well do I communicate what I expect from you?

- Am I too involved with your work? Or not involved enough?

- Do you feel comfortable asking me questions and discussing work-related concerns with me?

- Do I show you that I'm interested in your success with us?

- Do I listen to new ideas?

- Do I treat everyone fairly?

- What do you wish I would do differently?

Source: Karl Albrecht, *The Only Thing that Matters*, Harper Business Publications

review, using personnel files, record cards, a summary of on- and off-the-job training, the job description, the agreed **key result areas** and **measures of success** from the last appraisal period and evidence of the extent to which the employee has met them. Think about what the employee does well and what they could do to improve. Think about how to word your feedback so that it is constructive and builds motivation and self-esteem.

Think about where to hold the meeting. Is your office suitable? Perhaps a more neutral place such as a conference room would be less threatening. Arrange to prevent interruptions: ask the switchboard to hold any calls, put your telephone on divert or voicemail, turn your mobile phone off. Allow 45 minutes to an hour for the meeting.

Most organisations use specially designed forms to gather and store the desired information and guide discussions. Give employees a copy and ask them to look through it and think about their comments. Ask them to consider the period under review: What were their successes? Did they have any problems? What might have caused or led to them? What parts of the job do they enjoy most and least? How do they plan to improve their performance and customer service? What help from you or others do they need to do this? What training do they need?

The appraisal meeting

Create a relaxed atmosphere so employees feel able to talk freely. Make sure they understand the rating method and agree how they have performed against performance standards. Complete the form jointly as the discussion progresses.

If any performance areas were disappointing, use the Five Building Blocks (see Chapter 6) to analyse the problem and fix it.

Agree goals for the forthcoming period and, at the end of the discussion, summarise the main points covered and action agreed. Write down a joint action plan if appropriate, and make sure you each get a copy. End on a positive note.

Employees should leave the discussion feeling they have been fairly treated and their strong points and contributions to the department have been acknowledged and appreciated.

Here are some things you need to find out from employees:

■ Attitudes and feelings about their job

■ Ambitions/aspirations

■ Successes

■ Expectations of job, work, rewards, etc.

■ Views on any job changes

■ Self-assessment of performance

■ Main problems faced

■ How you can be of more help as a supervisor

Here are some things employees will want to know from you:

■ Clarification of their job, measures of success, responsibilities

■ Departmental objectives and how they contribute

■ Objectives, standards, targets for the next review period

■ Recognition of good work

■ Constructive help with any problem areas

Ideally, here are some things you should agree together:

- Measures of success for the next review period

- Action plan for future development

- Any training needs

- How you will help, what support you will provide

- An overall assessment of performance

Beware: people tend to hear negative information the loudest, even when most of your comments are positive. If you need to offer a constructive comment, move straight into what you want. Use phrases like *'From now on ...'*, *'In future'* or *'How can we improve this?'*. This is a way of saying: *'Let's not dwell on the past; it's done. Let's get it right from now on'*. It is also a way to make performance improvement more likely.

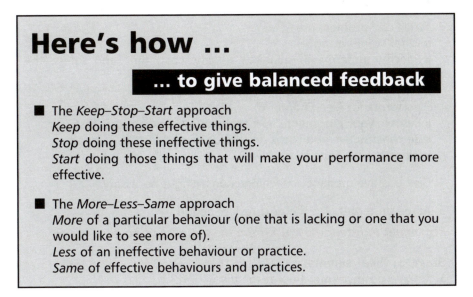

Here's how ...

... to give balanced feedback

- The *Keep–Stop–Start* approach
  Keep doing these effective things.
  Stop doing these ineffective things.
  Start doing those things that will make your performance more effective.

- The *More–Less–Same* approach
  More of a particular behaviour (one that is lacking or one that you would like to see more of).
  Less of an ineffective behaviour or practice.
  Same of effective behaviours and practices.

Follow up

Don't leave it there. Note dates for follow-up reminders to make sure you keep any promises you have made. Keep the channels of communication open so performance appraisals aren't the only 'real' chat you have with employees during the course of six or 12 months.

Box 9.6 The performance appraisal interview

Stage 1: Create the climate
1. Put at ease:
   - Relaxed;
   - Talking freely.

2. Review the purpose of the interview—a discussion about the employee's performance and contributions, and plans for the future.

3. Outline how the interview will proceed.

Stage 2: The main part of the appraisal
1. Review job performance against targets.
   - What should have happened?
   - What actually happened?

2. Give credit and praise where due.
   - Reinforce what went well.

3. Tackle any problem areas.
   - What went wrong?
   - Specify, in terms of quantity, quality, cost, time and safety, the targets that were not met.
   - Why did it go wrong? Review the Five Building Blocks to peak performance (see Chapter 6).
   - Reserve your judgment. Seek the employee's diagnosis first.
   - Be constructive and focus on the future and lessons learned.
   - What can be done to improve?

4. Give positive guidance/coaching/counselling if necessary.

5. Agree on targets for the next review period.

Remember to listen—how is it from the appraisee's point of view?

Stage 3: Final summary
1. Make a positive round-up of the discussion:
   - Confirm the main points covered and the action agreed.
   - Review priorities.
   - Write down agreed joint action plan.

2. Appraisees should leave feeling confident that you have appreciated their strong points and contributions to the department.

3. Use genuine praise and constructive feedback—avoid clichés, 'noises' and paternalism.

Checklist for success

☐ If an employee has a personal problem, take off your 'expert hat' and become a listener. Gently ask questions to help explore the situation.

☐ Avoid saying *'You did a great job, but ...'* People know when they hear 'but' that bad news is about to follow. Instead, say 'and'. *'You did a great job, and one thing you could do to improve it is ...'*

☐ Keep negative aspects of a person's performance in perspective.

☐ Don't forget the 'praise' in ap*praise*.

☐ It's more important to develop strengths than work on areas of weakness.

☐ Be positive, constructive and future focused during appraisal and counselling meetings.

☐ Do what you can to make appraisal and counselling meetings as relaxed as possible.

CHAPTER TEN

ACHIEVE GOALS IN MEETINGS
Leading and attending meetings

Meetings strengthen your position as the group's leader. They strengthen the group too. Sometimes the only time employees exist as a 'group' and not a collection of individuals is when they meet together. Meetings can create commitment and help people understand their joint aims and how their own roles fit in and contribute.

Meetings can help the group revise, update and add to what it knows and does, developing a pool of shared knowledge. They're also a great way to keep people informed, harvest their ideas, and discuss problems and plan ways to resolve them.

But if you run meetings poorly or call them unnecessarily, they will waste time, slow down decisions and damage morale.

SHOULD YOU HOLD A MEETING?
Before calling a meeting make sure that some other method of communication such as the telephone, a series of short face-to-face discussions, *ad hoc* informal chats, a memo or an e-mail wouldn't achieve your purpose equally well.

PLAN YOUR MEETING CAREFULLY
Multiply how long your meetings last by the average pay per hour of those attending and you'll see how expensive they are. This alone makes them worth planning carefully.

What do you want your meeting to achieve?
What results do you want from the meeting? Once you know this you can select the correct type, structure (following a formal, rigid agenda or a simple list of discussion/decision points) and style of meeting

Here's how ...

... to decide whether to hold a meeting

Hold a meeting if:

- There is no better or less expensive way to achieve your objectives.

- The information you want to present is better coming from you in person.

- You need to gain your group's commitment and understanding.

- You need your group's involvement or input in solving a problem, reaching a decision and so on.

- You want to generate discussion or ideas.

Skip the meeting if:

- There is nothing specific to discuss.

- You don't need others' input.

- Involving others would only complicate matters.

- It's just a substitute for real work or a stalling device.

- It's only to rubber-stamp a decision or make you feel like a leader.

(formal/informal), develop a suitable **agenda**, invite the right people and lead it appropriately.

What type of meeting should it be?

There are many types of meetings, each suited to a different purpose. Hold an *information-giving meeting* when you need to provide information that is complex or controversial, has major implications for meeting participants, is best heard from you in person, has symbolic value in being presented personally, would benefit from discussion or information exchange or needs clarification or comments to help people make sense of it.

Team briefings cascade the same information through an organisation and keep everyone up to date on matters of importance. You are

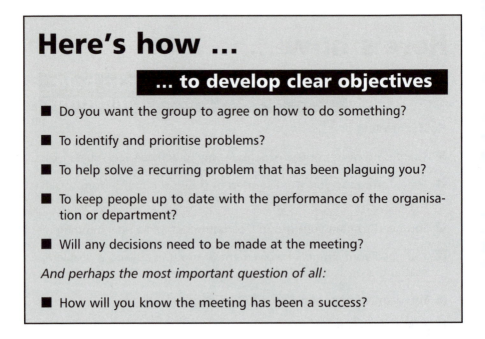

Here's how ...

... to develop clear objectives

■ Do you want the group to agree on how to do something?

■ To identify and prioritise problems?

■ To help solve a recurring problem that has been plaguing you?

■ To keep people up to date with the performance of the organisation or department?

■ Will any decisions need to be made at the meeting?

And perhaps the most important question of all:

■ How will you know the meeting has been a success?

briefed by your own manager and brief your team in turn, using headings such as: *Progress* (how we've performed against key measures of success), *People* (new appointments, visitors), *Policy* (any changes to policy or procedures) and *Points for Action* (what's coming up, what we'll do in response to other points).

Since several brains working together are often better than one, use *ideas-gathering* and *information-exchange meetings* when you need a lot of ideas or want to develop new concepts or ways of doing things, and when you want people to contribute and combine their knowledge, experience and ideas, and work creatively together. Use **brainstorming** techniques to get people thinking and explore, refine and develop ideas. Ask questions such as 'What are our options?' and 'How could we...?'

If the whole group is affected by a problem or will be implementing a solution, call a *problem-solving and decision-making meeting* so they can help explore it, develop and evaluate possible solutions and select the best one. Problem-solving meetings typically go through three phases:

1. Exploring the problem by defining and then analysing it and setting objectives for its resolution.

2. Searching for solutions.

3. Evaluating alternatives and selecting the most suitable one(s).

This process may take place over a series of meetings if the problem is complex and is often followed by a planning meeting.

Planning meetings begin with a desired outcome or goal to be accomplished and end with a clear action plan to achieve it. Guide the group to set priorities, decide who will do what, when and how, and establish follow-up procedures.

Quality, value-adding or customer service meetings combine ideas-gathering, problem-solving and decision making and planning meetings to identify ways to improve productivity and customer service. They aim to identify problems, make improvements to work systems and provide better service to internal and external customers.

Use *introducing change meetings* to explain change, help your team to understand the reasons for it and gain their support. Since change is disturbing to most people, explain it fully and clearly and allow time for questions, discussion and dissent. If there is a great deal of dissent, it is tempting (but a mistake) to close the meeting with a *'Well, that's the way it is!'*. It is unrealistic to expect quick and easy acceptance of large-scale change, so be ready, willing and able to discuss the issues involved and allow people time to air and adjust their thoughts and opinions. (See also Chapter 16.)

Plan your agenda carefully

Are meetings indispensable when you don't want to achieve anything, as US economist John Kenneth Galbraith once said? A good agenda can help make sure your meetings *do* achieve something.

Unless you are calling a meeting to achieve only one purpose, you will need an **agenda**. This shows the running order for a meeting, listing what you want to cover and why, and the time you have allocated to each topic. It can be as simple as a list of topics and expected outcomes for yourself and the group to refer to (see Figure 10.1).

Agendas like this help focus a meeting and provide a sense of direction. They indicate what you want the meeting to achieve and highlight what is, and is not, relevant to discuss. Specify start and finish times. Emphasise the outcome you intend by beginning

Figure 10.1 A sample action agenda

> ### The 'A' Team Action Meeting
> Wed. 13 June 2002, 9.30 sharp
> Conference Room B
>
> | TIME | TOPIC | ACTION |
> |------|-------|--------|
> | 9.30 | Welcome | |
> | 9.33 | Discuss last month's results | |
> | 9.43 | Agree on our key goals for next month | |
> | 9.53 | Agree upon venue for Kelly's farewell | |
> | 10.03 | Close of meeting | |

each agenda item with a verb: discuss, plan, decide, generate ideas, etc. Circulate the agenda and supply any relevant background information before the meeting—but keep it brief!

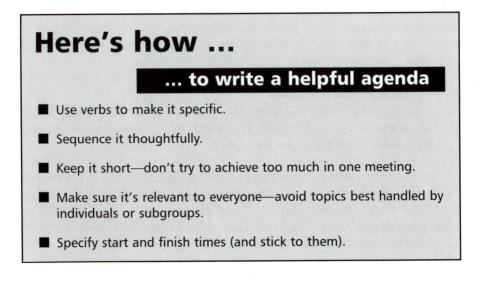

Here's how ...

... to write a helpful agenda

- Use verbs to make it specific.

- Sequence it thoughtfully.

- Keep it short—don't try to achieve too much in one meeting.

- Make sure it's relevant to everyone—avoid topics best handled by individuals or subgroups.

- Specify start and finish times (and stick to them).

The way you order agenda items is important too. Try to sequence them logically, so that they build on each other. Here are some other ideas:

■ Sequence items from the easiest to the most difficult or controversial, or the most to the least urgent.

■ Put items that will require a lot of mental work first (people tend to be more lively and creative during the early part of a meeting).

■ Schedule items of great interest to everyone for the lull in the meeting that seems to come 15–20 minutes after its start.

■ Put the most important item second on the agenda to allow people to warm up.

■ Put routine matters and *For Your Information* items towards the end.

Be aware of the choice and make it consciously. Try to end a meeting with an item that will give people a sense of unity and/or with an item that will achieve something positive.

Here's how ...

... to plan a meeting

Ask yourself these five questions:

1. What do I want the meeting to accomplish?

2. How can we best accomplish it? Is a meeting the best way or is there a better way?

3. Who should attend?

4. When is the best time to hold the meeting?

5. Where is the best place to hold it?

Who should you invite?

If the meeting is purely an information-giving meeting or a team briefing, numbers really don't matter that much; you just need to organise a venue to accommodate people comfortably.

However, keep your numbers down if you want people to contribute. Four to seven participants are ideal, 10 is a tolerable number and 12 is usually considered the outside limit. More than this can make the meeting difficult to control and inhibit effective discussion. If your group consists of more than 12 people, you could hold more than one meeting, or you could invite representatives from different areas to keep the numbers down.

Sometimes you will invite everyone in your work group; sometimes, only some of them will need to attend. You might also invite specialists from other departments, suppliers or customers, if they could contribute to your meeting.

Use the *two-thirds rule* to decide who to invite: each participant should be directly involved in, affected by or able to contribute to two out of every three agenda items. If people do not have the opportunity or the reason to contribute, their attention will quickly fade.

When and where to hold your meeting?
A general rule to follow is to hold the meeting during working hours at a time convenient for everyone.

Gear your start-time to the desired length of the meeting and ensure a minimum of interruptions. People might be fresher in the mornings. They might be less 'talkative' towards the end of the day or just before lunch.

Checklist for success

☐ Don't hold meetings so often that people get bored with them; hold them often enough that they feel part of the group, know what's going on in their department and the organisation generally and have a voice.

☐ Make sure the meeting is necessary and you know what you want it to achieve.

☐ Develop a clear, results-oriented agenda and stick to it.

☐ Don't try to cover too much—keep the number of items within reasonable limits.

☐ Avoid topics best handled by individuals or subgroups.

Where will you hold the meeting? A neutral conference room? A formal meeting in your office? An informal meeting around a lunch table? The appropriate setting depends on your purpose and the venue you select will be important in determining the general atmosphere of the meeting. (If you decide to use a conference or meeting room, don't forget to book it.)

Discussions are smoother when people can see each other easily, which makes circular, square and rectangular seating arrangements popular. Do you want to focus attention on yourself? Try a semicircle. Do you want to give information and minimise discussion? Try a theatre-style seating arrangement. Do you want a short, sharp meeting? Don't sit at all—gather everyone together and remain standing. For a short, informal team-briefing meeting, people might be just as content perched on furniture around your office or in the kitchen or main work area of your department.

How long should the meeting last?
To avoid people becoming restless try to keep meetings to 30 to 45 minutes. If a meeting must go on longer schedule a short break so that people can refresh themselves.

Notifying participants
How much notice should you give people of a meeting? It all depends on the purpose of the meeting and how much preparation they will need to do. For group meetings, three days is usually sufficient warning.

If participants need to prepare for the meeting, or to set a more serious or formal tone for the meeting, distribute the agenda along with any other background information people will need beforehand.

For informal meetings you can post the agenda in the meeting room (e.g. as an overhead or on a whiteboard). Make sure everyone can see it so they know where the meeting is heading.

Do your homework
Think about whether you want your meeting to be formal or informal in tone. Consider the general approach you will take, your opening remarks and how you will introduce each topic on the agenda. Gather any materials (visual aids, handouts, etc.) that you will need.

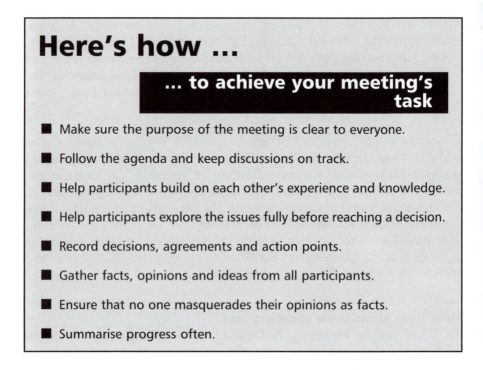

Here's how ...

... to achieve your meeting's task

■ Make sure the purpose of the meeting is clear to everyone.

■ Follow the agenda and keep discussions on track.

■ Help participants build on each other's experience and knowledge.

■ Help participants explore the issues fully before reaching a decision.

■ Record decisions, agreements and action points.

■ Gather facts, opinions and ideas from all participants.

■ Ensure that no one masquerades their opinions as facts.

■ Summarise progress often.

Will you need to sound people out in order to anticipate issues, concerns and disagreements that may arise? Try to anticipate questions and various points of view so you won't be taken by surprise.

LEADING MARVELLOUS MEETINGS

Well-run meetings build the team, create commitment and understanding and get people working together. To accomplish this you need to be clear about two things: *what* you want to achieve and *how* to achieve it.

Task and process issues

As we saw in Chapter 8, the purpose of a meeting, its **task**, is what you are trying to achieve. This might be to solve a problem, reach a decision or inform people about a new procedure. To succeed at the task we need people. The way people communicate and work together to achieve the task is called the group **process**. (See Figure 10.2.)

When people work well together it usually doesn't happen by itself. The way you lead your meetings sets the tone. It shows other members of the meeting what behaviours are valued and appreciated.

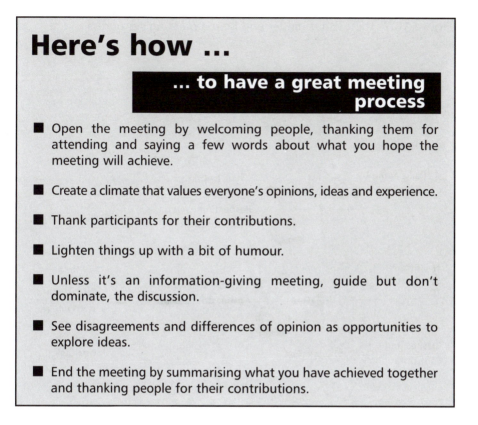

Here's how ...

... to have a great meeting process

■ Open the meeting by welcoming people, thanking them for attending and saying a few words about what you hope the meeting will achieve.

■ Create a climate that values everyone's opinions, ideas and experience.

■ Thank participants for their contributions.

■ Lighten things up with a bit of humour.

■ Unless it's an information-giving meeting, guide but don't dominate, the discussion.

■ See disagreements and differences of opinion as opportunities to explore ideas.

■ End the meeting by summarising what you have achieved together and thanking people for their contributions.

Opening the meeting

Try not to make a grand entrance by sweeping into the room after everyone has assembled. Instead, establish a relaxed and friendly atmosphere that promotes discussion and cooperation by being there first to greet people as they arrive.

Starting a meeting late punishes those who were on time and encourages them to turn up late for your next meeting. Start on time, even if some of the participants haven't arrived. This conveys a clear message and people will soon learn to arrive on time.

Begin by welcoming everyone and thanking them for being there. Then draw people's attention to the agenda. This signals its importance and gives people a chance to orient themselves to it. It also creates a shared understanding of the purpose of the meeting and reinforces what topics are and are not open for discussion. You may also want to check whether there are any items anyone would like to add to the agenda.

Figure 10.2 Things that hinder and help a meeting's progress

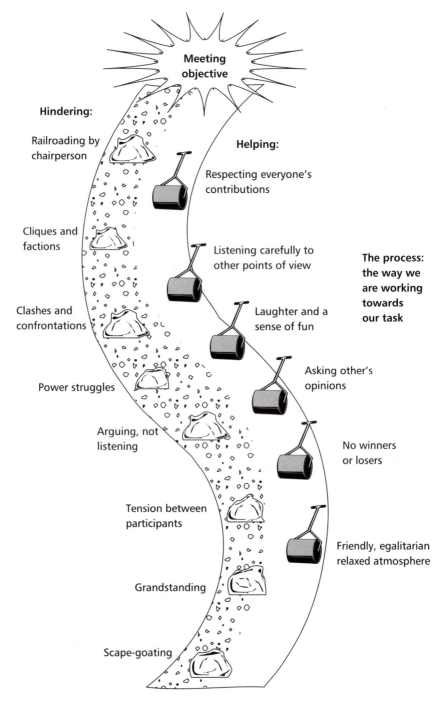

Leading discussions

People on a power trip lead lousy meetings! This is not a time to hog the discussion or the limelight. Unless it is a straightforward information-giving meeting, establish an atmosphere where people feel free to discuss, question and work together. Guide a focused discussion that does not ramble, digress from the topic, repeat ground already covered or contain irrelevancies.

Keep you own ideas until last. Encourage everyone to contribute, the quiet ones as well as the more talkative ones. Give each person their say so that all sides have equal 'air time' and all issues and points of view are explored. Listen carefully so you can keep discussions on track.

Most of us have short attention spans—less than 10 minutes, in fact. Frequent summaries help people focus their thoughts and keep a meeting rolling. If you are listening carefully, you will hear the main points and be able to summarise them, enabling the group to move on. If you can see people are losing focus, suggest a five-minute break and let people get up and move around.

When agreement or **consensus** is reached, summarise and move on. Don't end a discussion before all the points have been covered or before agreement is reached. Suspend a discussion if it is clear that:

■ you need more facts or information before you can make further progress;

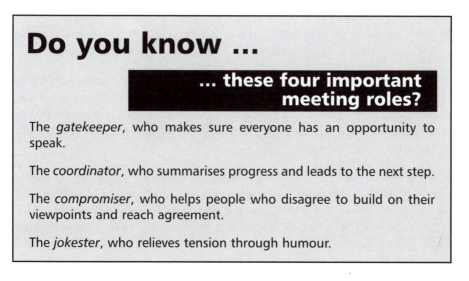

Do you know ...

... these four important meeting roles?

The *gatekeeper*, who makes sure everyone has an opportunity to speak.

The *coordinator*, who summarises progress and leads to the next step.

The *compromiser*, who helps people who disagree to build on their viewpoints and reach agreement.

The *jokester*, who relieves tension through humour.

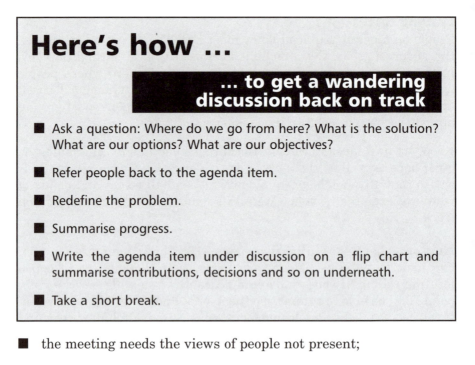

Here's how ...

... to get a wandering discussion back on track

■ Ask a question: Where do we go from here? What is the solution? What are our options? What are our objectives?

■ Refer people back to the agenda item.

■ Redefine the problem.

■ Summarise progress.

■ Write the agenda item under discussion on a flip chart and summarise contributions, decisions and so on underneath.

■ Take a short break.

■ the meeting needs the views of people not present;

■ members need more time to think or discuss something with colleagues not present;

■ events are changing rapidly and are likely to alter the basis of discussion quite soon;

■ there is not enough time to discuss the issues fully; or

■ two or three members can settle the topic being discussed outside the meeting without taking up the time of everyone present.

It's important that agenda items aren't discussed and then left 'up in the air'. Reach a conclusion, even if it's only to decide to suspend the discussion until the next meeting. *Warning*: Don't assume silence means agreement. Check it out. If necessary go around and ask people in turn for their thoughts.

Keep notes on action items and consider whether you wish to follow them up before the next meeting to ensure that action is proceeding as agreed. If there are a lot of action items, make sure everyone gets a list of who is to do what by when. If a working party or subcommittee is to act on an issue, nominate someone to convene the group and report on its behalf by a certain date.

Here's how ...

... to encourage participation

■ Ask each person for their thoughts, one at a time.

■ If the topic is non-confrontational and doing so won't set up a win–lose climate, ask for a show of hands. Otherwise use the nominal group technique.

■ Use the **nominal group technique** to make sure everyone has an equal voice in a decision. If the number of options is small, each person assigns a number to each option to indicate their preferred choice (e.g. 3 for third choice, 2 for second choice, 1 for first choice). If you have a large number of options use the *half plus one* rule: rank half plus one of the options; for example, if you have 22 choices, rank 12 of them by giving each person 12 points to distribute among the options. This clearly shows the wishes of the group without creating 'winners' and 'losers'. (See also Chapter 14.)

■ Ask an open-ended question.

■ Ask quiet members by name: *'Pat, we haven't heard from you on this—what are you thinking?'*

Closing the meeting

End the meeting on time, clarifying what will happen next and who is responsible for any items needing action. Check that all decisions and action items have been recorded and confirm you will distribute them to participants.

Check whether there is anything else anyone would like to bring up before moving on to schedule the next meeting and, if appropriate, fixing a date, time and place. End the meeting on a positive note, with a sense of accomplishment.

After the meeting

Unless it has been an official meeting or it is part of your organisation's meeting etiquette, you probably don't need to write up a set of formal **minutes**. You should, however, make a few notes covering the main points discussed, what was decided and any actions to be taken for each agenda item. You might also want to post your notes or circulate them to your group.

If you have a lot of group meetings set up a lever arch or electronic file for the minutes and other papers.

Here's how ...

... to lead a formal meeting

- Begin by introducing yourself if necessary, thanking participants for attending and reviewing the agenda.

- If participants are not familiar with the venue, for example if it is off-site or if external participants or guests are present, review emergency procedures: what the alarm sounds like, safe exit pathways, where to assemble and so on. Indicate where the toilets and other facilities are.

- Follow the agenda in sequence: read apologies, approve minutes of the previous meeting and so on.

- Manage time carefully.

- Liaise with the minute taker, providing appropriate direction prior, during and after the meeting.

- Take a few notes to keep focused on the discussion, help you summarise key points and check the minutes when they're drawn up.

Handling problems and difficult participants

Do you need to prevent difficult participants from wasting everyone's time, dragging your meeting off course and irritating and lowering the energy and enthusiasm of the rest of the participants? Here are some ideas to help these people make a more positive contribution.

Interrupters
- Quietly ask them to wait and give them an opportunity to speak when the other person finishes.

Talkers
- Break in and thank them for their contribution,

summarise it and ask the rest of the participants what they think.

■ Try seating them to your extreme left or right; this makes it easier to avoid seeing their attempts to get the floor.

■ If they do get the floor, let them have a reasonable amount of time, then interrupt by saying, '*You've got some good points there. Now let's hear what others think*'.

Digressers

■ Gently draw their attention to the agenda and move on.

■ Try to tie their comments in to the item under discussion.

■ Ask how their comments pertain to the item under discussion. '*This is an interesting observation. How does it fit into our problem?*' This helps return to the topic under discussion.

■ Gradually tie in their remote comments with the problem at hand.

■ Summarise what has been said so far to reorient members and focus their attention on the main discussion.

■ Point out that '*This discussion is interesting, but I suggest we postpone it until next month's meeting when we will discuss that topic*'.

■ If none of this works you might have to rule the discussion out of order and move on with the agenda.

Big mates

■ Gently interrupt them and ask if they would like to share their comments with the rest of the meeting.

■ Try pausing until they have finished and say that you want to keep everyone 'together'.

■ Say that you only want to have one person speaking at a time.

■ Say to the talkers, '*If you have something to say, please speak up so that everyone can have the benefit of your comments*'.

Non-contributors ■ Consider whether they really need to attend or whether they could send a nominee.

■ Try speaking to them privately to find out what the problem is.

Shy people
■ Call on them by name and ask their opinion if you think they have something to contribute to the topic at hand.
■ Thank them when they do contribute.

Critics
■ Ask them what they see as the positives.
■ Make their role the official 'devil's advocate'.
■ Ask them how their objection could be overcome.
■ Rephrase or restate their negative comment so it sounds more acceptable to the group **norms** you are trying to build.
■ Ask them what they do like about a suggestion, or to explain how they think it could be improved.
■ Treat their caustic comments and criticisms as though they were normal and routine.
■ Rephrase and restate the criticisms so that they appear to be conforming with the group and ask for a response from other members: *'Terry feels that this approach wouldn't be the best use of our time. What do the rest of you think?'*
■ Consider not having the critics at your next meeting, but bear in mind that with a bit of 'retraining' they may have a useful role as devil's advocate.

Show-offs
■ Quickly and briefly summarise each of their contributions and thank them whenever they do make a good point—often all they want is acknowledgement for their cleverness.

Unprepared people
■ Remind them to prepare before the meeting and let them know you don't intend to make a habit of doing their remembering for them.

Broken records
■ Gently remind them that you have already noted their views.

For chronic problem participants, speak to them privately before your next meeting. Explain the behaviours you expect in a meeting and ask for their cooperation.

Checklist for success

☐ Start and finish on time.

☐ Keep meetings short enough to hold everyone's attention.

☐ Invite the right people.

☐ Hear everyone's point of view. Don't let anyone dominate or use the meeting as a 'soapbox'.

☐ Don't waste time on irrelevant side issues, hobbyhorses, going over old ground and so on.

☐ Don't lose or ignore good ideas. Note down important ideas, decisions and actions to be taken and follow through on them.

☐ Deal with one issue at a time.

☐ Make sure people hear each other out without interrupting.

☐ Make sure no one feels pressured to compromise their feelings and opinions.

☐ Don't compromise or dictate—go for **consensus**.

☐ Focus on facts and on understanding and exploring points of disagreement.

☐ Focus on the future, not on the past (e.g. not on why something went wrong but on what to do about it now and how to prevent it happening again).

☐ In addition to achieving a task, use meetings to build a sense of belonging, shared responsibility, shared goals and team spirit.

☐ Allow group members to explore all sides of the issues fully. To prevent confusion, clarify and summarise regularly.

☐ Ask people to discuss what they know, not what they don't know. Don't ask for input on matters the group knows nothing about, has no expertise in or has no solid data or information about. People might be willing to share their opinions but you may then find yourself having to ignore those opinions.

☐ When you need to reach a decision, avoid accepting 'the lowest common denominator', the 'easy way out' or rushing into a poor or rash decision.

☐ Keep your own ideas until last, since your team may not want to disagree with you openly or challenge your opinions.

☐ When a decision is reached, be clear about what it is and how it will be implemented.

PARTICIPATING IN MEETINGS

Meetings ... are rather like cocktail parties.
You don't want to go but you're cross not to be asked.

Jilly Cooper, author

If you're participating in a meeting you also have some work to do. It's no secret that how you participate in meetings is an important factor in how you are perceived in the organisation and hence in your career success.

Don't just take up space, participate. Follow what's going on. Don't fidget, gaze out of the window, roll your eyes, constantly check your watch, tap your feet or drum with your pen. This can break people's flow of thought and talk and make you very unpopular.

Stick to the point and keep your contributions relevant to the subject under discussion. Make your comments clear and loud enough to be heard. Omit personal stories unless they make a point, and skip 'inside jokes'. When speaking, address the entire meeting (or the chair in a more formal meeting). Don't play 'devil's advocate' for the sake of it.

Don't dump data. Have supporting evidence by all means but don't bore people with it. Make your point succinctly; if people have questions pull out some of your detailed information.

If you're asked to contribute and you don't have something to say, don't say it. '*I can't add anything to what's been said*', or '*I don't know anything about that and I don't want to confuse the issue*' are perfectly acceptable.

Develop your listening skills. Encourage good ideas suggested by others. Follow through on any promises you make or actions you agree

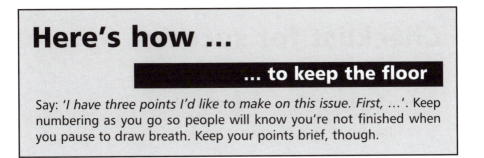

Here's how ...

... to keep the floor

Say: *'I have three points I'd like to make on this issue. First, ...'*. Keep numbering as you go so people will know you're not finished when you pause to draw breath. Keep your points brief, though.

to take. Don't accept tasks that do not properly belong to you or your work group.

VIRTUAL MEETINGS

Does your organisation partner with others around the globe? Is it part of an international consortium? Perhaps you're even part of or leading an international project team.

As the world shrinks we find ourselves working with people not in the next office or next city, but a continent away. Meeting face to face becomes time consuming and expensive and the mechanics of keeping in touch can create problems. Technology allows us to meet virtually

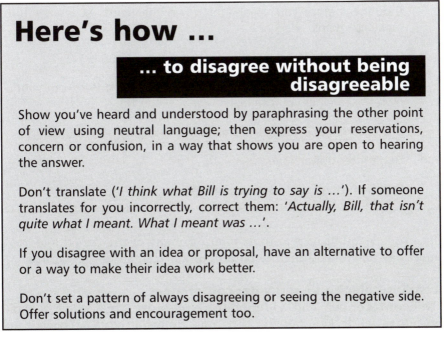

Here's how ...

... to disagree without being disagreeable

Show you've heard and understood by paraphrasing the other point of view using neutral language; then express your reservations, concern or confusion, in a way that shows you are open to hearing the answer.

Don't translate (*'I think what Bill is trying to say is ...'*). If someone translates for you incorrectly, correct them: *'Actually, Bill, that isn't quite what I meant. What I meant was ...'*.

If you disagree with an idea or proposal, have an alternative to offer or a way to make their idea work better.

Don't set a pattern of always disagreeing or seeing the negative side. Offer solutions and encouragement too.

Checklist for success

☐ Arrive on time and fully prepared.

☐ Turn off your mobile phone, beeper or pager.

☐ Stay focused on the discussion at hand.

☐ Keep your body language positive and supportive.

☐ Don't hold side conversations.

☐ Don't take up more than your fair share of speaking time.

☐ Leave your special interests, hidden agendas, problems and distractions outside the meeting room.

☐ Speak up when you have something to contribute; hold your tongue when you don't.

☐ Address and make eye contact with everyone, not just one other meeting member or the meeting leader.

☐ Project a positive professional impression by collecting your thoughts before you speak—jot down the points you want to make if it helps.

☐ Return promptly from breaks.

☐ Listen carefully to people whose points of view differ from your own to see what you can learn.

☐ Use differences of opinion as a chance to explore alternatives.

☐ Don't interrupt anyone.

☐ Follow through on tasks assigned to you.

face to face, often in real-time, offering many of the benefits of 'real' meetings and smoothing the path of productivity and collaboration.

Leading telephone and videoconferences

Teleconferences and **videoconferences** are great ways to hold meetings while keeping the time and financial costs of travel and accommodation down. In addition to following the guidelines above, here are some other tips.

Before you begin, clarify people's roles. Who will operate the camera if it's a videoconference? Who will telephone the others in case the connection breaks? Who will introduce the others and keep discussions on track?

Send out the agenda and any background information about a week in advance. For videoconferences, include large name cards in the meeting documents if participants don't know each other. Stress the importance of preparation; to keep the meeting flowing participants will need to be ready to ask and answer questions.

Begin as usual by outlining why the meeting is being held, how long it will last and exactly what needs to be accomplished during the meeting. Unless you're sure all participants know each other, go around and introduce them or ask them to introduce themselves, and provide a bit of background information so everyone knows how the other members can potentially contribute. Review the procedure for gaining the floor to ask a question or make a comment.

E-meetings
Multimedia conferences, also known as *data conferencing* or *e-meetings,* use collaborative computing to allow several users to meet over great distances.

An early form of e-meetings is the *bulletin board*, where a series of e-mails is presented like a conversation. You can read through what others have said and add to it. If you're designing a new procedure, you can put the background information, people's comments and successive versions on the board. They don't work in real-time, which can be an advantage if you're working with people in different time zones.

Net meetings are in real-time. You can converse with people in three ways: typed text (called 'chat'), spoken voice or a video link. You can put photos (or live video pictures) of each member on each person's screen as they log on. Or you can post photos and click on one to begin a quick chat, or drag them together for an informal meeting.

Virtual meetings let you simultaneously exchange, view, work on and collaboratively edit or update whiteboards and other software such as a document or spreadsheet, a presentation or CAD (computer-aided design) drawings.

If you join or form a team using e-meetings, make sure the procedures and etiquette for contacting each other and responding to each other are clear to everyone. Spend a bit of time getting to know each other as people so that trust can develop; without this your e-team can't be effective.

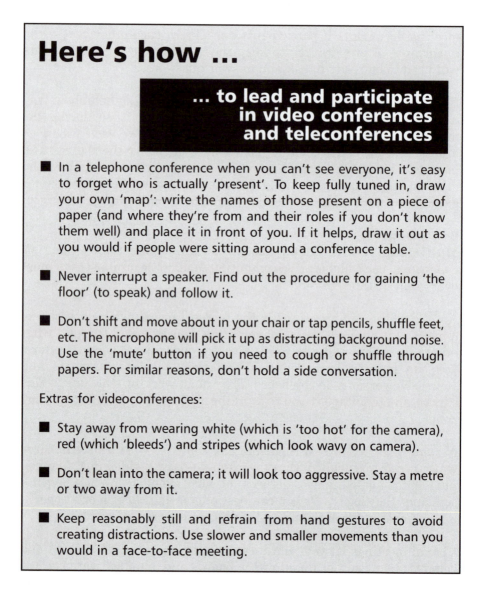

Here's how ...

... to lead and participate in video conferences and teleconferences

■ In a telephone conference when you can't see everyone, it's easy to forget who is actually 'present'. To keep fully tuned in, draw your own 'map': write the names of those present on a piece of paper (and where they're from and their roles if you don't know them well) and place it in front of you. If it helps, draw it out as you would if people were sitting around a conference table.

■ Never interrupt a speaker. Find out the procedure for gaining 'the floor' (to speak) and follow it.

■ Don't shift and move about in your chair or tap pencils, shuffle feet, etc. The microphone will pick it up as distracting background noise. Use the 'mute' button if you need to cough or shuffle through papers. For similar reasons, don't hold a side conversation.

Extras for videoconferences:

■ Stay away from wearing white (which is 'too hot' for the camera), red (which 'bleeds') and stripes (which look wavy on camera).

■ Don't lean into the camera; it will look too aggressive. Stay a metre or two away from it.

■ Keep reasonably still and refrain from hand gestures to avoid creating distractions. Use slower and smaller movements than you would in a face-to-face meeting.

Career tip

Get comfortable with virtual meetings.

CHAPTER ELEVEN

ASSIGN WORK AND DELEGATE TO INDIVIDUALS AND TEAMS
Spreading the workload

uccessful supervision has been defined as the talent for assisting others to accomplish goals. Allocating and delegating the right duty to the right person is part of this, and a skill you can use every day.

TWO KEY PRINCIPLES
If you follow these two important principles you won't go far astray:

1. Explain the big picture.

2. Make sure doing the task is in some way rewarding for the employee.

Explain the big picture
Whenever you assign a task, explain why it is important. Place it in the context of the wider work and objectives of the department and organisation. Tasks in isolation destroy motivation and can easily overwhelm people and seem meaningless.

How will what you're asking someone to do add to profitability, productivity, quality, customer service, cost reduction or market leadership, image or presence? In short: *How will it make a difference?* While the difference may be direct or indirect, we all need to feel that our contributions support something worthwhile.

Horses for courses
Select the right task for the right person:

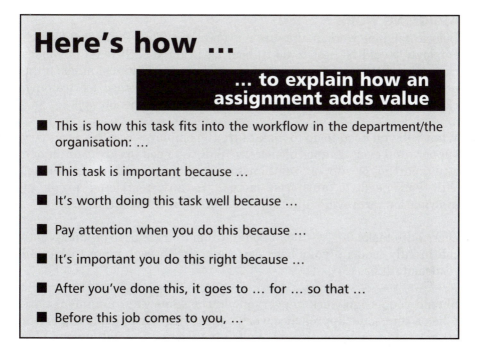

Here's how ...

... to explain how an assignment adds value

- This is how this task fits into the workflow in the department/the organisation: ...

- This task is important because ...

- It's worth doing this task well because ...

- Pay attention when you do this because ...

- It's important you do this right because ...

- After you've done this, it goes to ... for ... so that ...

- Before this job comes to you, ...

- Who in your work team enjoys repetitive work and who craves variety?

- Who has a good eye for detail and who is better at seeing 'the big picture'?

- Who is good at working cooperatively with others and who works best on their own?

- Who handles the unexpected well and who prefers a predictable, stable routine?

As we saw in Chapters 2 and 4, it's important to achieve a good match between what people enjoy doing and what they do well, and the tasks we assign them.

Career tip

Always explain why a task needs to be done, where it fits in, and how it contributes to the team, the department or the organisation.

ASSIGNING WORK

Before assigning work, make sure it is necessary. Then think about which employee would be best to do it, bearing in mind each team member's current workloads, skills, knowledge, attributes and interest areas. If the person doesn't already know how to do the job, arrange for training. Ensure they will have the resources they need to do the job well.

What will you need to do to make sure the employee has the necessary support and every chance of success? Will you need to clarify or amend any reporting or support relationships and communication channels? Will you need to authorise access to any restricted areas or information or provide additional resources or information?

Distribute tasks fairly—it can be tempting (but counter-productive) to continually load up your best performers with ever more tasks and responsibilities.

Should you assign work to everyone in the same way? Common sense tells us that some approaches work better with some people than with others. Giving a dogmatic and explicit instruction to a willing and able employee is likely to result in animosity. An uncooperative employee might ignore an implied request.

Using the descriptions in the box on the next page, decide how to assign the work. This also applies to 'reminders' to complete a task or tidy up a work area, and other instructions. Base your choice on the urgency and importance of the task and the skills and motivation level of the individual receiving the assignment. If you choose correctly, your assignments will be understood, accepted and carried out properly.

Give full and clear information so the employee knows exactly what you want and doesn't have to second-guess. Explain why the task is important and how it fits into the work of the department or how it will contribute to the organisation.

People often like to know why they have been selected to do something. Take this opportunity to provide some positive feedback.

Specify the overall objective and measures of success. Clarify the resources available and any constraints or restrictions. Agree measures of success and monitoring and reporting procedures. Then find out if the employee has any questions or concerns.

Here's how ...

... to allocate work in five different ways

Explicit assignments	These leave no room for discussion, choice or initiative. They specify who is to do something, what is to be done, when it is to be done and how it is to be done. Use them when it is important the employee follows a particular procedure or safety instruction and in emergency situations. Use them with inexperienced employees, careless employees, employees who continually fail to follow standard procedures or safety rules, chronic objectors and people who refuse to do what you ask with no good reason.
Outcome assignments	These allow latitude and flexibility in how the task is done. Assigning only the end result allows people to think for themselves. They are good with employees whose skills and motivation are reasonably high.
Requests	These begin with something like *'Would you...'* or *'How about ...'*. They encourage cooperation and don't upset relationships. Use them with employees who are motivated and skilled and with older and sensitive employees.
Implied requests	Use indirect requests such as *'We need to ...'* when you are looking for an end result but are willing to leave it up to the employee to decide when and how to achieve it. They draw on people's ideas and invite cooperation. Use them with experienced employees who have an understanding of the situation and who assume responsibility easily.
Open requests	These don't specify who is to do something but, rather, call for volunteers. State what is required and why, especially for tasks 'beyond the call of duty'.

Here's how ...

... to avoid the most common mistakes when delegating and assigning work

- *Rushing.* Take the time to explain the assignment fully.

- *Mixed messages.* Show that you are confident in the employee's ability.

- *Arrogant or overly authoritative attitude.* Treat the employee respectfully and build confidence.

- *Voice tone.* Don't 'bark out an order'.

- *Insufficient detail.* Fill in all the blanks: measures of success, timelines, etc.

- *Vague and unclear.* Take the time to check that the employee understands the assignment.

What if someone refuses an assignment?

To avoid 'losing your cool' and getting into an argument, count to 10 and give yourself time to consider whether the assignment was a reasonable one. Are they clear about what you are asking? Do they have the skill, ability and time to carry it out in the required fashion?

If you cannot understand why an employee won't do what you request, ask what the trouble is: maybe they have a good reason; maybe they misunderstood; maybe something you said or the way they interpreted it annoyed them. Ask questions to get to the heart of the matter.

Softly does it

Consider your options before deciding what to do. Bear in mind that your job is to get work accomplished, and to do this well you need to work with, not against, your team. Trying to enforce your authority or using bribes to gain compliance aren't likely to be very effective in getting the job done or ensuring future support and they could make a hero of the erring person in the eyes of workmates.

Start with a 'whisper' and slowly escalate as necessary, aiming for cooperation, not mere compliance. Asking questions so you can see things from the employee's point of view and spending more time explaining what you're asking, the importance of the task and why your directions need to be carried out, are 'whispers'.

If this doesn't work escalate to other options such as modifying your request to get the job done in the short term. This might get the employee back to work, and you can talk privately and constructively later.

You may need to bring out the 'loud hailer' and hold a performance counselling interview and begin termination proceedings (see Chapter 9). Do this only when everything else has failed.

After dealing with the immediate situation, think through what happened and learn from it so you won't have to face a similar situation in the future.

The northbound bus approach
If an order or instruction is reasonable, particularly when a change in policy or procedure is concerned, try 'the northbound bus' approach. When we get on a bus going north, we will go north too. If we don't want to go north we should get off that bus and try another one.

Organisations often alter course to head in a new direction: they might establish a new customer service philosophy or new procedures and work methods based on a new technology, or reorganise and change established reporting structures. Symbolically, they are now heading 'north'. Some employees may have trouble accepting this new direction. If an employee refuses to 'head north' with everyone else, the northbound bus approach may be a last resort. Clearly, this is a 'loud hailer' tactic to be adopted only when other approaches have failed.

What if the job is done poorly?
Don't confuse 'poorly' with 'differently'. People often change a bit here, adjust something there, modify things in some way. This isn't sabotage, stupidity, resistance or rebellion—it's a natural part of life. People need to be creatively involved in their work. Think about this the next time someone modifies one of your instructions!

However, if someone hasn't completed an assignment to the expected standard, use Figure 11.1 to select the best course of action. Each square suggests a possible cause and a possible approach.

233

Figure 11.1 Poor job performance?

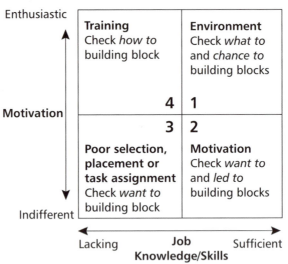

In the first square, the employee is motivated and has sufficient knowledge or skills, so look to the environment or the *chance to* building block for a clue: perhaps the employee has inadequate resources (tools, equipment, time or information) or is working with cumbersome systems. Also, make sure the employee was clear about what you expected—the *what to* building block (see Chapter 6).

In the second square, the employee has sufficient job knowledge but lacks willingness, so the problem is either a motivational or a leadership one. Work through the *want to* and *led to* building blocks.

In the third square, the employee lacks not only skills and knowledge but also willingness. This suggests that you have assigned the task to the wrong person. If the individual does many tasks poorly, examine your selection procedures or job placement (to stop this happening in the future) and consider transferring the employee to other, more suitable work. As a last resort you may have to consider termination of employment.

In the fourth square, the employee is willing but lacks job knowledge or skill, so training is probably the answer; work through the *how to* building block to peak performance and productivity. Provide constructive feedback by clarifying the preferred way of doing something, showing what to do next time to improve and offering hints, advice, assistance or further training. Focus on the future and on making sure performance improves.

Here's how ...

... to give constructive feedback

Use these phrases:

- From now on ...

- Next time ...

- In future ...

- Let me show you how to do this faster/more simply/more easily.

- That's fine, and here's how to make it even better ...

Follow the BAT MICE feedback formula discussed in Chapter 8 to give helpful and useful feedback. Keep it:

Balanced. Offer praise as well as improvement suggestions.

Actionable. Focused on something within the person's control.

Timely. Don't wait too long!

Meaningful. Focused on behaviour or success measures not achieved.

'I' language. So you don't sound pushy or patronising.

Constructive. Be a coach, not a critic.

Empathic. Put yourself in the other person's shoes. Praise in public, criticise in private.

Who should assign work to your employees?

In 1916 Henri Fayol published his 14 principles of management, most of which are still applied today. One of the most important was **unity of command**. This stated that employees should receive assignments from only one person. This was to avoid conflict and confusion over what to do and whose instructions should have priority.

This is a good general principle: try to ensure that you are the only person who gives orders to your employees. If others often pass instructions to people reporting to you, ask them, or your employees, to keep you informed so you can keep tabs on your employee's workloads and commitments. If they burn out, not only they but the team and the task will suffer.

With some of the newer organisation structures, a chain of command cannot always be applied. For example, does your organisation operate on a team basis? Or perhaps you work in a matrix organisation where people report to two or more bosses, each for a different project or activity. In organisations like these employees must learn to cope with the ambiguity, conflicting priorities and stimulation of having two or more supervisors. If this is the case where you work, each supervisor should manage only clearly defined, and different, aspects of a person's job, with no overlap. If this is not the case, confusion and conflicts can arise.

Passing on directives

When you are asked to relay instructions and information from your manager to your work team, don't refer to a third person: *'He told me ...'* or *'They want ...'*. This makes you seem to be dodging responsibility and will lower your prestige in the eyes of your staff.

Accept responsibility for the directive and for seeing it is carried out. Try to make them come from you by saying *'We'* or *'I'*. This shows you have confidence in the request.

If you need more background information to pass on an instruction accurately, ask for it. If you have concerns about it or can see a better way of achieving the intended results, explain your concerns or ideas. If in the end the directive stands, accept it graciously and do your best to implement it.

What if you disagree with an instruction?

An easy response would be to accuse management of being 'out of touch' and to pass on the information or instructions, adding something like: *'I know it's crazy and won't work but that's the way they want it done'*. Rather than creating harmony within the work group, this will only make it harder to enlist your team's cooperation.

Look for 'the big picture' and try to understand the overall reasons behind an instruction or a change in policy or procedure. Realise that sometimes a 'tough' decision must be made, despite the fact that it is likely to be unpopular.

Talk through any concerns with your manager. State your opinions calmly, slowly and clearly. Cite any relevant examples, facts or figures to illustrate your points. Avoid being purely negative—try instead to be constructive in your remarks. In other words, don't just say *'It will never work'*. Explain why you think this and offer some alternative approaches.

If, at the end of the discussion, your manager still requires that you relay the instructions, it is your job to do so, provided that no organisational policies or legal issues (e.g. discrimination or environmental regulations) are contravened. If you truly believe that rules are being breached, raise the matter again with your manager or, if necessary, with your manager's manager. If there is no breach of the law or company policy, carry out the assignment or pass it on to your team, explaining the reasons behind it as fully as possible. Remember that you are part of the management team and are expected to be a supportive member of that team.

Checklist for success

☐ Match the person to the task.

☐ Explain the task, objective and measure of success; think about quality, quantity, time and safety.

☐ Explain why you have selected this person and why the task is important.

☐ When you want an employee to do something, think: What's in it for them? What can I supply in return for good performance? Cooperation is a two-way street.

☐ Use the Five Building Blocks to peak performance and productivity to make sure the person will be able to do the job assigned. Use them to analyse unexpected below-standard performance, too.

☐ Monitor the workload of employees to make sure it's within acceptable bounds.

☐ Support your manager when you need to pass on an instruction.

DELEGATING

Delegation refers to assigning one of your own tasks or duties to an employee. This is a great way to reduce your workload, but don't overload your employees in the process! Here are the four steps to delegating effectively.

Step 1: What to delegate?

Recurring, routine and occasional duties are ideal to delegate provided they are not confidential, needed in a hurry or of critical importance. Here are eight types of tasks that are suitable for delegation:

1. Tasks that will train and extend a team member's skills and experience.

2. Tasks that would increase the delegate's job interest.

3. Tasks that need a special skill that you don't have but an employee does or could develop easily.

4. Tasks that need to be done but you can't squeeze in, such as a small project and portions of larger projects (data collection, research, etc.).

5. Things that don't require your personal input, provided they are not boring, 'go-for' tasks.

6. One-off tasks.

7. Tasks where you're not adding any value by doing them personally.

8. Non-critical, non-urgent tasks.

When new work comes in, ask yourself whether you could delegate it.

Step 2: Who to?

Delegate a task to:

 someone who is already able and willing to do it;

 someone who wants to learn it;

 someone you want to prepare for promotion or to be your successor;

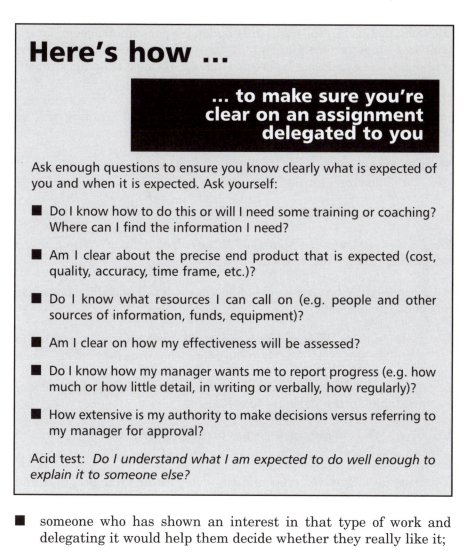

Here's how ...

... to make sure you're clear on an assignment delegated to you

Ask enough questions to ensure you know clearly what is expected of you and when it is expected. Ask yourself:

- Do I know how to do this or will I need some training or coaching? Where can I find the information I need?

- Am I clear about the precise end product that is expected (cost, quality, accuracy, time frame, etc.)?

- Do I know what resources I can call on (e.g. people and other sources of information, funds, equipment)?

- Am I clear on how my effectiveness will be assessed?

- Do I know how my manager wants me to report progress (e.g. how much or how little detail, in writing or verbally, how regularly)?

- How extensive is my authority to make decisions versus referring to my manager for approval?

Acid test: *Do I understand what I am expected to do well enough to explain it to someone else?*

- someone who has shown an interest in that type of work and delegating it would help them decide whether they really like it;

- someone whose job skills you want to increase, for example to multiskill or cross-skill employees;

- increase someone's motivation by giving them an interesting and challenging assignment; or

- someone who could add it to their other duties without becoming overwhelmed with work.

Don't delegate a task that is well beyond someone's training or experience. If you need to train the delegate before they can take on the work, do this carefully, patiently and in portions small enough for the trainee to master (see Chapter 5). Give them enough time to build confidence and experience before moving onto the next training segment.

It may take some time to explain or train someone to do a recurring task. However, the time you spend explaining and training will be repaid many times over in the future.

Step 3: Delegate
Give the following information:

1. *Goal.* What end result do you expect?

2. *Reason.* Why is it important? Where does it fit in? Why are you asking *this* person to do it?

3. *Standard.* What measures of success will tell you the person has done the job well?

4. *Time frame.* When do you expect the delegate to start and to complete the task? Are there any time constraints?

5. *Resources.* What resources (e.g. people, funds, equipment) are available for the delegate to call on?

6. *Help.* Who should the delegate turn to for help or advice if you're not available?

7. *Progress.* How will you and the delegate monitor progress and effectiveness?

Work through the Five Building Blocks to peak performance and productivity (see Chapter 6) to make sure you've covered everything.

Did you know ...

US President John F. Kennedy told NASA to *'get a man to the moon by the end of the decade and bring him back safely to earth'.* There were two parts to this: *what* he wanted done and the *results* he expected.

Now *that's* how to delegate!

Train and coach the employee as necessary and inform anyone the delegate will be liaising with as they carry out the delegated duty.

Keep a delegation log. Note down every assignment you delegate. Create a special file in your electronic task manager or put it on a special section of your *To Do* list.

Step 4: Monitor results

You may have delegated the task, but you can't delegate your responsibility for ensuring it is done correctly, safely and on time. Monitoring stops you losing control. Keep track of whatever is important, for example time frames, that procedures are being followed correctly, the end result or stages being completed correctly and on time.

Try to let delegates monitor themselves and meet with them from time to time for a progress report. Maintain open lines of communication so that any problems can be discussed. Treat any mistakes and problems as learning opportunities. Help people solve problems they run into but don't solve them for them. Turn their questions around and help them think through possible solutions.

If people run into difficulties in the process of completing their assigned work, sit down with them and work through the Five Building Blocks to find out why.

PLANNING WORK FOR THE TEAM

Sometimes it isn't enough to agree individual contributor's **job purposes**, **key result areas** and **measures of success** with them. You might also need to plan out the work of your work group or a special-purpose team such as a project team or a cross-functional team. You may be redesigning the workflow through your department due to a resignation, restructuring or re-engineering project or introducing a new process or key team responsibility. Whatever your reasons for planning your team's work, follow the three steps below.

Know your goals

Establish measures of success. What must the team and its members achieve, together and individually? The measures you select might be financial, quality, quantity, safety, accuracy, service or time related. They might be derived from enterprise standards, benchmarks or comparison with other teams or projects, or they might be standards

Figure 11.2 Five degrees of monitoring

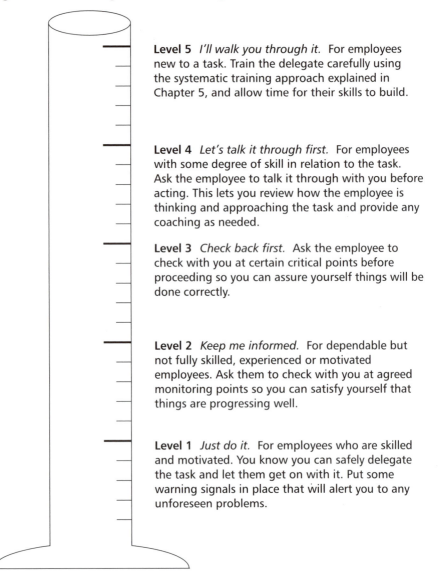

Level 5 *I'll walk you through it.* For employees new to a task. Train the delegate carefully using the systematic training approach explained in Chapter 5, and allow time for their skills to build.

Level 4 *Let's talk it through first.* For employees with some degree of skill in relation to the task. Ask the employee to talk it through with you before acting. This lets you review how the employee is thinking and approaching the task and provide any coaching as needed.

Level 3 *Check back first.* Ask the employee to check with you at certain critical points before proceeding so you can assure yourself things will be done correctly.

Level 2 *Keep me informed.* For dependable but not fully skilled, experienced or motivated employees. Ask them to check with you at agreed monitoring points so you can satisfy yourself that things are progressing well.

Level 1 *Just do it.* For employees who are skilled and motivated. You know you can safely delegate the task and let them get on with it. Put some warning signals in place that will alert you to any unforeseen problems.

you agree with your manager, work group or project group. (See also Chapter 12.)

Once you know your objectives, the next question is: What is the best way to achieve these goals within the timelines?

Checklist for success

☐ Don't use the lame excuse *'It's quicker to do it myself'* for not delegating.

☐ Select the right person for the job.

☐ Use delegation to motivate, develop and extend employees' skills and heighten job interest.

☐ Don't delegate all the best jobs to a select few employees. Distribute tasks and assignments evenly among employees.

☐ Explain the complete picture, including the importance of the task, why you chose that person, any constraints, the standards and time frame.

☐ Provide the necessary resources (including time).

☐ Delegate in plenty of time so you can explain and train properly.

☐ Let delegates know they can come to you if they get stuck.

☐ If the task is long or complex, or if the delegate has a tendency to procrastinate, focus on starting the job, not on finishing it. For example, instead of saying *'And I'd like to have that report in a month'*, say *'When do you think you can start writing a rough outline to show me?'*.

☐ Except for people you are training, stress results, not details. In other words, delegate the thinking as well as the doing.

☐ Don't hover. Let the employee get on with the task. If you think the delegate will need a lot of help, plan plenty of monitoring and coaching sessions, or give the task to someone better equipped to do it.

☐ Don't 'hit and run'. Periodically monitor the progress of assigned and delegated tasks.

☐ Remember that when you delegate, you delegate the right to make a mistake. Use any mistakes as learning opportunities.

☐ Thank delegates when they've completed a task successfully.

☐ Don't pile so much of your work onto your staff that they can't get their own work done.

Sequence the activities

Establish a logical sequence of activities to be carried out and set time frames for starting and completing them. You might find that individual and group tasks depend upon each other and that it makes sense to sequence them using a **Gantt** or **PERT chart** (see Chapter 14) or a **flow chart**.

You can do this on your own, although involving your manager, your work group or the individuals who will be carrying out the plan usually yields better ideas and greater commitment.

Flow charts

If the job is complex, you may want to write it in flow-chart form. Most offices have software programs that do this. As Figure 11.3 shows, flow charts display the sequence of steps visually, inside boxes (for activities), diamonds (if a decision is needed) or circles (for the first and last steps). Arrows connect the boxes, showing the sequence of activities. Each activity has one arrow leading into it and one arrow coming from it, leading to the next activity or step. Decision diamonds have two arrows, one leading to a 'yes' action and the other to a 'no' action.

Flow charts are valuable tools for designing procedures and training people to use them. Because they are pictorial representations they often make problems such as omissions, doubling up of efforts and so on obvious. This helps identify problems and streamline procedures. Use flow charts rather than checklists or standard operating procedures if a system requires several decisions. (See also Chapter 15.)

Figure 11.3 Flow chart

Fine tune

Monitor your plans and adjust and readjust them as necessary, in order to take changing circumstances and events into account.

PART THREE

MANAGING OPERATIONS

Just when things seem to be settling down and working well, something shatters the peace. If it isn't a people issue, it's bound to be an operational one— delivering better quality at lower cost, introducing and managing change, solving the myriad of problems that seem to plague every first-line manager, finding ways to do more with less. The more gracefully you can 'roll with the punches', the more effective, and appreciated, you'll be.

CHAPTER TWELVE

DELIVER QUALITY—EVERY TIME
Identifying your customers and meeting their needs

Without customers we wouldn't have jobs. That's been said many times in many ways and yet many of us seem to have forgotten this basic principle. Knowing your customers, finding out what they want and providing it in ever-better ways, will keep you, and your staff, in jobs.

If you think this applies only to supervisors and departments that deal directly with external customers, read on … It applies to you, too!

EVERYONE IS A CUSTOMER!
Retailers and hoteliers have customers. Who else has customers? Does a mail clerk have customers? How about an orderly in a hospital? A garbage collector? A factory worker? A volunteer for the Salvation Army? Does a human resources or an information technology department have customers? How about a finance department or a purchasing department?

Everyone has customers. Whatever sector we work in, whether we work directly with customers or behind the scenes, every employee has customers and every department has customers.

Think of all the people and groups who are affected in some way, directly or distantly, by your department's work. They are your customers. They fall into two groups: **external customers**, the people who buy or use your products or services; and **internal customers**, your colleagues who work with you as employees or contractors. They are part of your organisation's **customer–supplier chain** that makes and supplies its goods and services.

Be aware of other important **stakeholders** too: your suppliers, your closer community and the wider society. How well your department performs also affects them.

External customers

Clearly, the *ultimate consumers* or *end-users* of your goods or services, whether as purchasers or through some other relationship, are customers. They may be individual customers, such as the shopper who purchases a box of cornflakes. They may be the organisations we supply, for example the supermarket chain that purchases the cornflakes in bulk or in pallets of prepackaged boxes.

You may deal directly with them or through a chain of other employees. However far removed they are, the quality of your

Figure 12.1 They're all customers!

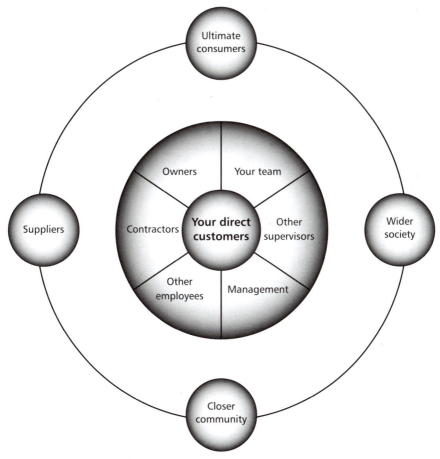

department's work still affects them and therefore your organisation's success.

From a broader perspective, the *wider society* and *closer community* need to be satisfied too. We have a responsibility to obey the laws of the land, to care for the environment and to support our organisation in being a responsible community member. The more highly regarded an organisation is as a good 'corporate citizen', the more secure its future.

Does it seem odd to think of *suppliers* as customers? They are part of your customer–supplier chain too. The better you can get to know each other's needs and expectations, the more effectively you will be able to work together. This will make both you and your suppliers stronger and your joint futures will be more secure.

How effectively and cooperatively does your department work with its external suppliers? The clear trend is to form strong bonds with our suppliers. This approach is often referred to as a **trading partnership**: suppliers and customers working cooperatively to strengthen their businesses.

What good does it do an organisation, for example, to beat down a supplier's price so much that it goes out of business? That only creates the problem of finding a new supplier who can meet your needs, and the trials and tribulations that 'getting it right' with the new supplier entails.

Internal customers

External customers 'pay the rent' but without the internal customer–supplier chain, we couldn't meet their needs.

Concepts such as *servant leadership* and *upside-down organisation charts* reinforce the idea that an organisation's leaders symbolically support the rest of the workforce to help them do their jobs to the best of their ability. Have you ever thought of the people in your work group as your customers?

How about the other supervisors, managers, employees and contractors you come into contact with in the course of your duties? They're your customers too. The better you do your job, the better they can do theirs.

Who owns your enterprise? If you work for a large corporation in the private sector, the owners may be shareholders; if you work for a private company or professional firm, the owner may be one or more individual owners or partners. If you work for the government or a local council, the taxpayers or ratepayers would be your 'owners'. If you work for a non-profit organisation, you could consider the main funding bodies to be your 'owners'. How does your department meet their expectations and goals?

Who benefits most directly from the work of your group? This is your department's primary or principal customer. Unless your department is front line, working directly with your organisation's external customers, your most direct customers are probably people in another department. The more effectively you supply them, the better they will serve their customers in turn and the more your organisation will prosper.

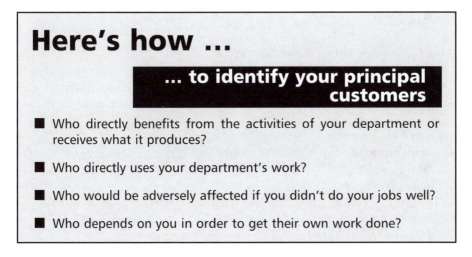

Here's how ...

... to identify your principal customers

■ Who directly benefits from the activities of your department or receives what it produces?

■ Who directly uses your department's work?

■ Who would be adversely affected if you didn't do your jobs well?

■ Who depends on you in order to get their own work done?

The weak link

In some organisations, departments seem to operate in a vacuum. The left hand doesn't know what the right hand is doing.

■ 'What! You needed this urgently? No one told me!'

■ 'The salespeople keep sending in orders requiring uneconomic production runs. We just save them up until there's enough to make a run worthwhile.'

■ 'How can I meet my deadlines if people don't give me the right information?!'

What's it like in your organisation? Instead of seeing each other as parts of an interdependent chain, do departments operate in isolation and protect their 'turf'? Does marketing fight with production, production blame purchasing and supply for its problems and sales battle with distribution? When departments act like this, it disrupts work, diverts energy and efforts away from the real problems and does nothing to satisfy customers.

What if departments didn't battle with each other but saw themselves as suppliers and customers of each other? What if production were a customer of purchasing, administration were a supplier to marketing and so on? The entire organisation would become a strong customer–supplier chain. All departments, and everyone working in them, would work to satisfy their customers. Is that what it's like in your organisation? As everyone knows: a chain is only as strong as its weakest link. The standard to which you each perform will strengthen, or weaken, each of you.

The customer service riddle: What ...
... is intangible and ephemeral?
We can't 'touch' it as we can other products, and it has no shelf life. It is only as good as what is being delivered *right now*.

... can't be undone?
If something goes wrong, we can only try and make up for it.

... is subjective?
It is only as good as an individual customer perceives it to be.

... defines the whole but is delivered by one?
Although it is part of an organisation's or department's identity and image, it is not given by organisations and departments, but by individuals.

... is a moving target?
Whether your primary customers are internal or external, quality customer service is no longer an add-on. It's expected. Once it was a 'nice thing to do'; now it's an essential thing to do. And what was once seen as 'good' service is now perceived by many as the 'bare minimum'.

Our definition of 'good service' is constantly changing and for the most part the bar is continually being raised. Organisations and depart-

Here's how ...

... to find out how customer focused you and your staff are

Ask:

- Does our behaviour, our equipment and our workplace inspire confidence in us personally and in our department as a whole?

- Do our customers believe we can meet their needs properly?

- Are we willing to help customers courteously and promptly? Do our customers see us as courteous and prompt?

- Are we known for delivering what we promise?

- Do we give our customers the attention they deserve?

- Do we talk to our customers about what we do in 'plain English'?

- Do we listen to and act on what our customers tell us?

ments that don't provide continually higher levels of customer service will wither. We will look at how to keep getting better in Chapter 13.

Customer service maths

Is getting all the elements of this riddle right worth the effort? According to research conducted by the Harvard Business School, the International Customer Service Association in Chicago, Illinios, and PIMS (Profit Impact of Marketing Strategy), the answer is a resounding 'Yes'. Here's what their research shows:

- A 5% increase in customer retention equals between 25% and 80% increase in profits.

- Increasing your customer retention rate by 2% has the same effect on profits as cutting costs by 10%.

- Organisations that emphasise customer service see 12 times the return on sales as those that put a lower priority on service.

- Companies with a reputation for great service are able to charge

THE SUPERVISOR'S SURVIVAL GUIDE

up to 9% more for the goods and services they offer and, on average, grow twice as fast.

Your department may or may not deal directly with external customers. If you're not, you're probably serving someone who is.

Here's how ...

... to avoid patchy customer service

You and your team should ask each other these questions, and give the same answers:

- ■ Why does our department exist?

- ■ What do we do? Why?

- ■ Who are our customers?

- ■ Who else benefits from our efforts? Who else uses the services or products we provide?

- ■ Who are our most important customers? Why? How do we know this?

- ■ What do they want from us? How do we know?

- ■ What do our customers care about most? How do we know?

- ■ How well are we satisfying them now in what they care about? How do we know?

- ■ How does the way we operate make it easy or difficult to work with us?

- ■ Are we doing anything for our customers they'd rather we didn't or that they find irrelevant or unnecessary?

- ■ Are we making their life easier?

- ■ Are we making it harder in any way?

- ■ What opportunities do we have to delight our customers?

How well is your department helping them succeed with your organisation's external customers?

Customer service might be full of paradoxes but it can make or break your organisation and your department. It is one of the most direct tools we have for building loyalty, attracting repeat business, generating word-of-mouth (free) business and boosting profits.

Did you know ...

Do you think quality is a fad? It isn't. Here's how so-called 'fads' work:

A few organisations begin to use a technique to improve their business and their position in the marketplace. They gain a competitive advantage. So the rest use it too. The playing field is level again, and the bar is raised. We need something else to gain further competitive advantage. A new technique is 'discovered'. Failing to use it will be a disadvantage; using it will level the playing field.

Is quality a competitive advantage? It was once but no more. It's mandatory. Offering quality won't ensure success but if you don't offer it you're sure to fail.

The penalties for not keeping up with the new ways of creating and sustaining competitive advantage can be severe.

Quality customer service doesn't happen by itself. It is the result of a carefully thought-out and well-managed process. If it is to be more than mere pleasantries and smiles and really contribute to your organisation's mission and success, do these three things:

1. Find out what your customers really need and want.

2. Set yourself up to deliver it.

3. Measure the level of service each of your customers actually receives and work to continually improve it.

Checklist for success

☐ Focus on treating your most profitable external customers so well they wouldn't dream of going elsewhere.

☐ If your customers are internal, make sure your department proves itself so valuable to them every day that you'll have a job for life because they wouldn't even consider outsourcing your services.

☐ Don't assume you know what your customers want without asking them.

FIND OUT WHAT YOUR CUSTOMERS WANT

Here's how Joseph Juran, one of the founders of the Total Quality movement, defined quality:

Quality is whatever the customer says it is.

That pretty much sums it up. We might think we're providing fantastic service, but if our customers don't agree, we aren't.

A quality service is one that reliably meets or exceeds its customers' expectations. Reliable means dependable and consistent; getting it right once in a while isn't enough.

Do you know who your customers are, what they want and how to supply it? Do you really? When was the last time you asked them what they want from you and whether they're happy with what you're providing? When was the last time you asked if they'd like anything different from you, or for you to provide it differently?

Ask the customer

Your customers can be the first to alert you to problems, potential problems or changing needs if you are willing to listen and if you keep the lines of communication open.

SET YOURSELF UP TO DELIVER *STAR* QUALITY

This involves three things:

1. Establishing STAR measures of success.

2. Getting your internal processes right.

Here's how ...

... to delight your customers

■ Do what you say you'll do, when you say you'll do it.

■ Do a little bit more than they ask for.

■ Use checklists and a *To Do* list to make sure you remember to do everything you say you will.

■ Act on their feedback.

■ Get the details right.

■ Work to their preferred communication style: in writing, verbally, by e-mail.

■ Work to their preferred working style: for example, don't pester them with details they don't want to know about. Give them plenty of details if that's what they want.

■ Keep them informed.

■ Use your own initiative to do things that will help them do their jobs well.

■ Make it a pleasure to work with you.

3. Aligning them and your department's culture so they support the behaviours and service levels you know your customers want.

Establish STAR measures of success

Once you clearly know your customers' expectations, you can decide **measures of success** for timelines or speed of delivery, cost, quality,

Career tip

Become known as a 'can do' person and a 'can do' department. Anticipate, respond to and surpass your customers' expectations.

Here's how ...

... to find out what your customers think of your service

Ask a few of your key customers to tell you what they think you do best and what you need to improve on. Listen carefully and look for any patterns.

Make sure your measures of success reflect what your customers say is most important to them.

Ask your customers how easy it is for them to request your help and how satisfied they are with the promptness, quality and pleasantness of your response.

Ask questions like these:

■ What do we do well?

■ What could we do better?

■ What suggestions would you make for the future?

■ What could we do that we don't do?

■ What do we do that we don't need to?

■ What could we do more? Less?

volume, accuracy and quantity. Use the STAR standard (see Chapters 3 and 6):

S *Specific*—measurable or quantifiable in some other way.

T *Timelines* are specified.

A You can *assemble* performance information quickly and easily.

R *Realistic*, or achievable.

Here's how ...

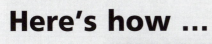

... to prevent problems before they occur

Whenever possible, monitor **lead indicators**, not **lag indicators**. (See also Chapter 14.)

Lead indicators tell you how things *are* going. Lag indicators tell you how they *went*.

Lead indicators are more valuable because they help you identify problems quickly and fix them before they spoil your service. If you only use lag indicators, it will often be too late to prevent problems.

Agree upon your measures of success with your customers and ensure your work group understands them and can easily monitor them themselves.

Streamline your processes

Are your systems customer friendly or customer hostile? If they are designed to benefit you they're probably customer hostile. If they benefit your customers they're probably customer friendly.

Focus them on providing your customers with what they want in a way they want it, not on your department's ease and convenience. Customer-friendly systems and policies build strong relationships with your customers.

To succeed, they also need to be sensible and streamlined. Cumbersome systems make people feel like they're banging their heads against a brick wall; they will soon give up trying.

Moments of truth

In his book, *Moments of Truth* (Harper & Row, Sydney 1987), Jan Carlzon explains how he took Scandinavian Airline Systems from a loss of nearly $20 million to a profit of $54 million in 12 months. The cornerstone of this recovery was making the most of 50 000 **moments of truth** every day. These are any contact a customer has with an organisation. Moments of truth for your department are any contact any of your customers have with your department. They often involve you or one of your group members: a moment of truth has occurred each time you or someone in your work group speaks or has contact with a customer on the telephone, via e-mail or in person.

Moments of truth are not always 'up close and personal', though. They also occur when a customer opens a parcel of documents you send—how well presented and easy to navigate are they? Is there a clear covering note? Moments of truth also occur when a customer reaches the voicemail of someone in your department: is there a clear and friendly outgoing message and are incoming messages returned promptly? Or is the voicemail left on constantly? Slow responses to e-mails or requests for information are negative moments of truth while prompt responses are positive moments of truth.

Observing the many small moments of truth with your customers is another way to assess the effectiveness and quality of the customer service you and your group provide. Do the moments of truth your department provides delight customers?

Get your ducks in a row
Make sure your department's culture, tools and equipment, and the other Building Blocks we looked at in Chapter 6, not just *allow* but actually *encourage* people to provide quality customer service.

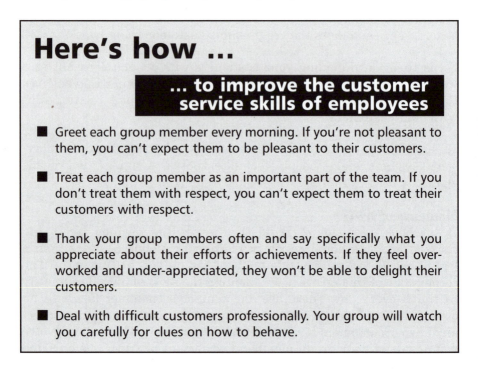

Here's how ...

... to improve the customer service skills of employees

- Greet each group member every morning. If you're not pleasant to them, you can't expect them to be pleasant to their customers.

- Treat each group member as an important part of the team. If you don't treat them with respect, you can't expect them to treat their customers with respect.

- Thank your group members often and say specifically what you appreciate about their efforts or achievements. If they feel over-worked and under-appreciated, they won't be able to delight their customers.

- Deal with difficult customers professionally. Your group will watch you carefully for clues on how to behave.

Are you and is everyone in your department focused on your customers and providing what they want? Are the people on your team professional? Are they thoughtful? Do they go the extra distance? Do they look after their customers in ways the customers appreciate? Do they take pride in their work? Do the stated objectives and end results of the work people do keep the focus on customers?

How do you 'take care of your customers' before you provide the product or service? While you are providing it? After you have provided it? You may set the standards but it is up to each individual employee, every day, to meet them.

How aware are your staff of the effect their behaviour has on your business and the image of your department? Could they clearly state what level of customer service they are expected to provide and how important it is to provide it?

Oops!
We need to identify and address problems quickly and carefully, preferably before our customers are forced to draw them to our attention.

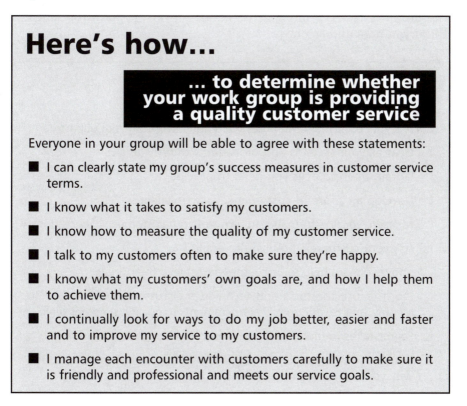

Here's how...

... to determine whether your work group is providing a quality customer service

Everyone in your group will be able to agree with these statements:

- I can clearly state my group's success measures in customer service terms.

- I know what it takes to satisfy my customers.

- I know how to measure the quality of my customer service.

- I talk to my customers often to make sure they're happy.

- I know what my customers' own goals are, and how I help them to achieve them.

- I continually look for ways to do my job better, easier and faster and to improve my service to my customers.

- I manage each encounter with customers carefully to make sure it is friendly and professional and meets our service goals.

If a problem occurs find out whether customer expectations have changed in any way. If they have, adjust your measures of success and see whether you need to alter the sequence of operations, modify your procedures, acquire more resources or train anyone.

If expectations have not changed, gather your team together and use the Five Building Blocks explained in Chapter 6 and the tools and techniques discussed in Chapter 15 to find the source of the problem, analyse it and fix it.

Celebrate achievement
Recognise improvement and celebrate achievements. If you don't people are likely to think it doesn't really matter after all and curb their efforts as a result.

Develop an informal recognition program for both individual contributors and the group. Stress whichever will best build the culture you want: reward the whole group if you want to emphasise teamwork, and individuals if you want to highlight individual responsibility and action. Every once in a while celebrate the fact that the group is reliably meeting its service levels: a pizza for lunch, a thankyou note and so on.

Checklist for success

☐ Ask your customers what they want and need from your department.

☐ Gear all your systems and procedures to providing it.

☐ Obtain the resources you need to provide it.

☐ Develop a culture of customer service excellence.

☐ Measure your performance in terms of your customers' expectations.

☐ Ask your customers how you're doing.

☐ Show you can help your customers achieve their goals.

☐ Learn to use the tools and techniques discussed in Chapter 15 to identify, analyse and remove impediments to quality customer service.

☐ Fix mistakes immediately above and beyond what is required.

☐ Set a positive example for your staff to follow and treat them the way you expect them to treat their customers.

CHAPTER THIRTEEN

DO MORE WITH LESS
Making continuous improvements

Whatever industry or sector we work in, if we're not getting better, we're getting worse. Without perpetual progress, our competitors will eventually overtake us, no matter how good we are right now.

In Chapter 1 we talked about being mindful, not mindless, as a way to boost personal productivity. It also boosts departmental and organisational productivity.

The inflexible, mechanical thinking of mindlessness blinds us to opportunities as well as to solutions to recurring problems and hassles. Mindfulness, on the other hand, allows us to take a flexible and creative approach that helps us find solutions. It encourages us to examine constantly what we're doing to find ways to do it better, differently, more efficiently, more easily, more quickly, at less cost. How can I streamline this? How can I add more value? Mindfulness helps us make continual improvements and work out how to do more with less.

ENHANCEMENTS ARE ESSENTIAL

There are three ways to improve an organisation. First, we can make a *capital investment*; we can purchase new computers and software or buy the latest production machinery or technology. This is expensive and because it's expensive, it's one-off: we can't afford to do it too often.

The second is *cost reduction*. This can work initially, but then what?

The third way to improve an organisation is to *improve our systems*. There are two ways to do this: the **kaizen** way and the

re-engineering way. The first leads to lots of incremental 'small-step' improvements and the second to one major 'big-step' improvement.

Little-step improvements: perfect your systems and procedures

Kaizen is a Japanese word meaning *continuous incremental improvements*, or making small improvements, all the time. Lots of small improvements soon add up and make a big difference.

Of all the approaches to improving organisations, *kaizen* is the cheapest and most reliable. It gets everyone involved—employees, suppliers and customers.

Kaizen is no longer an option but a necessary part of everyone's job. If we don't practise *kaizen*, we will probably find our service and products slipping backwards relative to our competition's. Constant improvement safeguards our future and the future of our organisation.

Have you heard the saying 'If it ain't broke, don't fix it'? Rather than 'leave well enough alone', the *kaizen* goal is continuous improvement. How can we make things a little bit better? How can we 'tweak' them, refine them and polish them, even when they're already working well? *Kaizen* aims to do 100 things 1% better rather than one thing 100% better. To this end, we keep examining everything we do and see how we can improve on it.

Did you know ...

A rule of thumb says:

A problem that costs $1 to fix in advance

will cost $20 to fix during a process

and $50 to fix afterwards.

Conclusion: *kaizen* saves money.

The big payoff comes from improving systems and procedures so they will meet customer requirements more reliably and efficiently. The way to do this is to use the tools and techniques described in Chapter 15 to simplify and streamline systems and procedures, remove unnecessary activities and duplication of effort and make it possible for people to 'get it right first time'. The *kaizen* approach is to do this continuously.

If something does go wrong, look to the system to see why it happened. Use the tools and techniques described in Chapter 15 to fix the system, not lay blame.

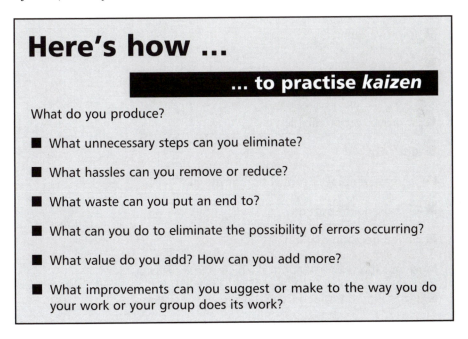

Here's how ...

... to practise *kaizen*

What do you produce?

- What unnecessary steps can you eliminate?

- What hassles can you remove or reduce?

- What waste can you put an end to?

- What can you do to eliminate the possibility of errors occurring?

- What value do you add? How can you add more?

- What improvements can you suggest or make to the way you do your work or your group does its work?

Kaizen helps us determine the best ways of doing things. It helps us strengthen our systems so they produce at the required quality levels more dependably. It helps us design procedures that reduce the chance of error and increase consistency. It helps us spot and reduce or eliminate activities that don't 'add value' but are needlessly taking up time, effort and 'space'. It shows us where there is duplication and unnecessary work and helps us eliminate it. It helps develop and establish standards against which to monitor performance.

Big-step improvements: redesign your systems from scratch

In some organisations re-engineering, or **core process redesign**, is synonymous with mindless retrenchments, mistrust and lowered morale among employees at all levels. If managed properly, however,

Here's how ...

... to improve systems

Ask these questions of each step in a process.

Does it:

- Add value to the product or the customer?

- Improve quality?

- Improve service?

- Improve productivity?

- Improve communication?

- Cut costs?

- Increase employee motivation or morale?

- Encourage innovation?

- Speed decision making?

More questions to ask about each step in a process.

- What would happen (*really*) if it didn't get done?

- Who does it? (Look for duplication of effort.)

- When did we start doing it? Why? (It may have made sense once but ...)

- Could someone else (inside or outside the company) do it better? More easily? Faster? More economically?

it can offer a way to make major improvements in the way we produce and offer our products and services.

It is more than the 'little-step' *kaizen* approach of improving a process or system by streamlining it to do things more quickly or more efficiently. It involves radically rethinking your processes, systems and procedures from top to bottom. It aims at great leaps forward in all measures of operating efficiency.

First, we identify our customers and what they want. Then we work backwards, using technology and systematic analytic methods to radically redesign processes and operating procedures to achieve dramatic improvements in productivity and serve the customers more efficiently.

We end up seeing departments not as independent fiefdoms but as part of a web of work relationships and information systems throughout the organisation.

The end result of process re-engineering is usually:

■ Less specialisation

■ Less 'isolationism' of departments

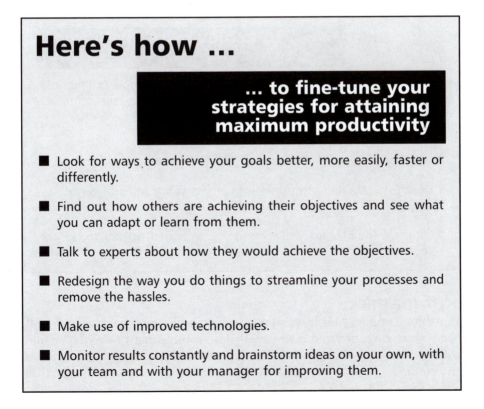

Here's how ...

... to fine-tune your strategies for attaining maximum productivity

■ Look for ways to achieve your goals better, more easily, faster or differently.

■ Find out how others are achieving their objectives and see what you can adapt or learn from them.

■ Talk to experts about how they would achieve the objectives.

■ Redesign the way you do things to streamline your processes and remove the hassles.

■ Make use of improved technologies.

■ Monitor results constantly and brainstorm ideas on your own, with your team and with your manager for improving them.

- Fewer non-value-adding activities

- Lowered overhead costs

- Increased responsiveness to customer needs

- Increased productivity

Aim high with Six Sigma

Six Sigma efforts added an estimated US$600 million to GE's bottom line in 1998. Sigma is a statistical measure of variation used to measure defects per million. The greater the sigma number, the fewer the defects. Most major companies have a defect rate of around four sigma, or more than 6000 defects per million. Organisations at the Six Sigma level have just 3.4 defects per million. This is a huge leap forward in productivity, profits and customer satisfaction.

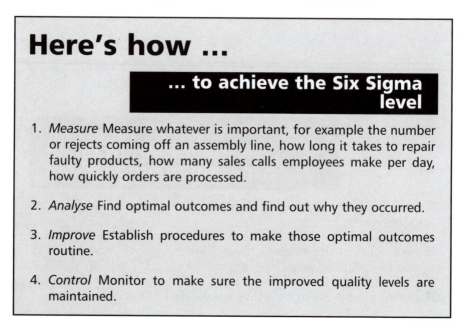

Here's how ...

... to achieve the Six Sigma level

1. *Measure* Measure whatever is important, for example the number or rejects coming off an assembly line, how long it takes to repair faulty products, how many sales calls employees make per day, how quickly orders are processed.

2. *Analyse* Find optimal outcomes and find out why they occurred.

3. *Improve* Establish procedures to make those optimal outcomes routine.

4. *Control* Monitor to make sure the improved quality levels are maintained.

DO IT TOGETHER

To achieve ongoing improvements, enlist the help of your team. You'll need shared values and a shared vision, commitment to goals, people willing to learn, change and develop and able to operate in a team environment, and a supportive open supervision style to make this work. (See Chapter 8.)

As well as benefiting from several brains, approaches and a storehouse of experiences and ideas, this will develop a departmental culture that places quality, teamwork and continuous improvement at its centre.

Career tip
Keep looking for ways to do things better, more easily, faster, cheaper ...

People don't change their attitudes and become quality-conscious continuous improvers overnight. They need training in the skills of team working and participating in meetings, and in the systematic, analytical techniques to identify and solve problems discussed in Chapter 15.

... you must realise that you will stay ahead competitively only if you acknowledge that no advantage and no success is ever permanent. The winners are those who keep moving.

John Browne, CEO of BP
quoted in *Harvard Business Review*, Sept.–Oct. 1997

ANTICIPATE PROBLEMS AND TRENDS
You've probably heard the saying 'A stitch in time saves nine'. It's a good idea to put on your 'doom and gloom' spectacles once in a while to look for things that could go wrong. *'What if ...'* and *'How can I best safeguard this or avoid that?'* are your basic questions.

Foresee developments
If you want to be ready for anything, keep your eyes open. Stay in touch with your customers and colleagues, their jobs and how they are doing them and expect to be doing them in the future. What changes do they expect to introduce? What are their chief concerns? Their greatest satisfactions? Staying in tune with issues like this will highlight any changes and trends that might affect what customers expect from you and your department.

What is happening in the marketplace? What changes are your counterparts in other organisations or your competitors introducing?

Are they planning to introduce any new technology or methods? An awareness of things like this will highlight changing needs.

Link with your industry organisation and keep up to date in your profession so you stay in touch with trends you'll need to know about and perhaps incorporate into the way you and your department work.

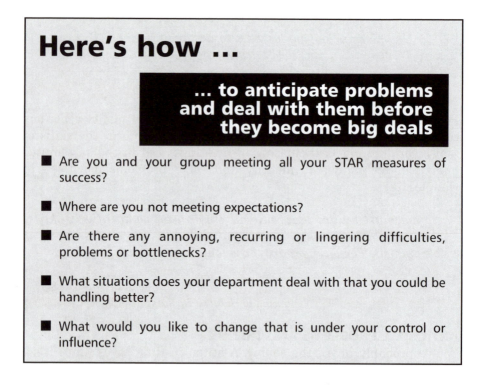

Here's how ...

... to anticipate problems and deal with them before they become big deals

- Are you and your group meeting all your STAR measures of success?

- Where are you not meeting expectations?

- Are there any annoying, recurring or lingering difficulties, problems or bottlenecks?

- What situations does your department deal with that you could be handling better?

- What would you like to change that is under your control or influence?

THE PDCA CYCLE

Have you ever thought that you'd improved how something was done and the new methods worked for a while but then mysteriously evaporated? The **PDCA cycle**, or Plan–Do–Check–Act, is a great way to prevent this from happening. Also called the Deming Wheel, the sequence was actually developed by Walter Shewhart, a contemporary of Edwards Deming and a fellow Total Quality proponent. Its purpose is to ensure that we make improvements in a consistent way and that, once made, we retain them.

Step 1—Plan   Planning is the first step in the cycle. Identify a problem or concern, collect factual information about it and set a target to improve it.

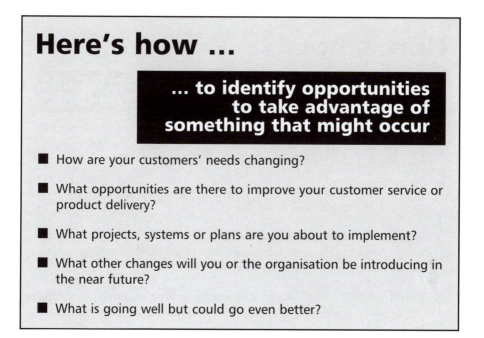

Here's how ...

... to identify opportunities to take advantage of something that might occur

- How are your customers' needs changing?

- What opportunities are there to improve your customer service or product delivery?

- What projects, systems or plans are you about to implement?

- What other changes will you or the organisation be introducing in the near future?

- What is going well but could go even better?

Step 2—Do   Analyse your information, form tentative conclusions, decide how to achieve your improvement target and test your ideas in a trial run.

Step 3—Check   Check your results. Did it work? Does it need to be refined?

Step 4—Act   Take action to incorporate the change(s) into the standard operating procedure. This might involve training, altering the design of a machine, moving the location of equipment or changing supplier specifications. Standardise the changes, build them into the process, communicate them and document them. This way, they won't mysteriously evaporate.

PRACTISING *KAIZEN* ON YOURSELF

If you really want to increase your ability to add value and your earning potential, get in the habit of practising *kaizen* on yourself, not just with your procedures. If you do this daily your performance will blossom and your results will burgeon.

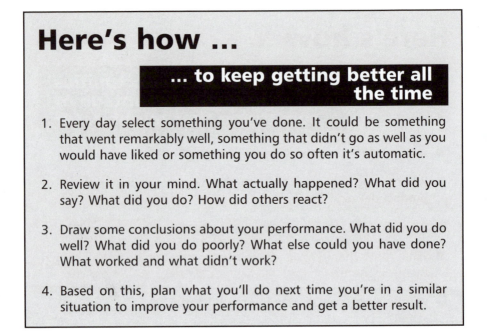

Here's how ...

... to keep getting better all the time

1. Every day select something you've done. It could be something that went remarkably well, something that didn't go as well as you would have liked or something you do so often it's automatic.

2. Review it in your mind. What actually happened? What did you say? What did you do? How did others react?

3. Draw some conclusions about your performance. What did you do well? What did you do poorly? What else could you have done? What worked and what didn't work?

4. Based on this, plan what you'll do next time you're in a similar situation to improve your performance and get a better result.

OOPS! WHAT SHOULD YOU DO WHEN YOU MAKE A MISTAKE?

Many people dream of success. To me, success can only be achieved through repeated failure and introspection. In fact, success represents one per cent of your work, which results from the 99 per cent that is called failure.

Soichiro Honda (1906–91)
Japanese industrialist

The only way never to make a mistake is to do nothing. We'd be like a ship in harbour and, as William Shedd observed, '*A ship in harbour is safe but that's not what ships are built for*'. If we never try anything out we would probably avoid making mistakes but we wouldn't make anything better or learn anything either!

'*There are no mistakes, only feedback*' is a useful maxim.

It frees us to try out new ways of doing things, create ideas and test them out and approach problems from different angles. The more we try out new things, the more mistakes we're bound to make. And the more successes we're bound to have too.

Figure 13.1 The PDCA cycle

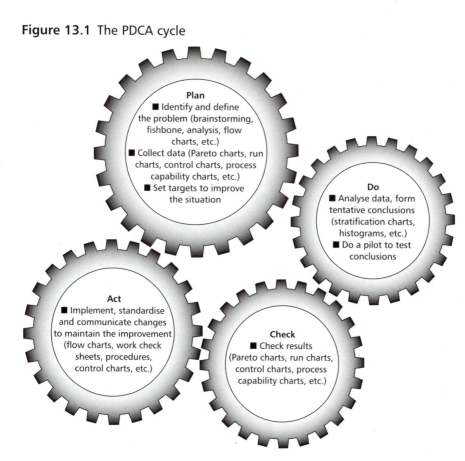

When you make a mistake, and you will, don't ignore it, cover it up, make excuses or find someone else to blame. Do two things. First, concentrate on ways to fix it. Analyse what went wrong and decide what corrective action to take; then take it. Second, learn from your mistake. Find out where you went wrong. What could you have considered that you didn't, what should you have done or said that you didn't, how else might you have approached it? This isn't so you can beat yourself up but so you'll know what went wrong. Then you can make sure you don't make the same mistake again.

Checklist for success

☐ Keep getting better if you want to 'stay in the race'.

☐ Review your systems to identify hazards, hassles, wasted effort or materials and unnecessary or cumbersome steps and remove them.

☐ Find ways to do things better or differently to achieve the same ends more efficiently, effectively and economically.

☐ Explore options for upgrading resources and services using improved technology, methods or systems.

☐ Continually upskill and cross-skill yourself and group members so everyone can do their jobs better and better.

☐ Keep up to date with current trends and new, improved ways of doing things (e.g. by reading professional journals, joining a professional association and attending seminars).

☐ Share what you've learned with others so they can improve too.

☐ Talk to people and listen to their ideas on what's wrong and how to improve things.

☐ When you make a mistake, acknowledge it, correct it, learn from it and carry on.

CHAPTER FOURTEEN

DEAL WITH THE HEADACHES THAT SURROUND EVERY SUPERVISOR
Planning, solving problems and making decisions

 o you ever find there isn't enough time to solve all the problems facing you? Do you find problems come back again and again, and sometimes flow on to other departments?

Without a methodical and logical process for dealing with the day-to-day and out of the ordinary problems that crop up, you will end up applying 'quick fixes' that never really work, 'solving' the same problems over and over again and often creating new ones in the process. Once you're on the 'fix it quick' treadmill, you'll find it hard to get off. Genuine problems and timely plans will take a back seat while you put out fires. Problems will spiral into crises. Ultimately, your performance and that of your department will disintegrate.

How can you make sure you don't end up running around like the proverbial headless chook? By thinking things through. Combining the systematic procedures for planning, solving problems and making decisions outlined in this chapter with sound time management (see Chapter 3) will ensure you avoid crisis management and fire fighting.

PLANNING AHEAD
Plans channel us towards our objectives. Just having a plan, of course, doesn't guarantee success. However, without planning the probability that you will achieve your goals other than by accident is remote.

Setting goals and establishing plans

What do you want to achieve? Make your goal a general statement describing your broad purpose or intent, expressed in positive language—what you *do* want, not what you *don't* want.

Then establish measures of success to tell you whether or to what extent your plans are succeeding in achieving your goals. Follow the STAR formula: make them *specific*, with *timelines,* easily and inexpensively *assembled* and *realistic*, or achievable (see Chapter 3). This concentrates your thinking towards a desired outcome, shows you where you're heading and tells you whether you've arrived.

As shown in Figure 14.1, the third step is to decide what tasks or action steps need to be carried out to achieve your plan. Try **brainstorming** or use the five Ws and one H 'triggers' (What? Who? Where? When? Why? How?) to determine what needs to be done, who will do it and all the other details.

Sequence the activities in the order in which they should occur using the planning tools discussed below. Assign target dates and, if appropriate, individual responsibilities to each activity.

Figure 14.1 Making a plan

Figure 14.2 Gantt chart for painting a house

Activity	Time				
	Monday	Tuesday	Wednesday	Thursday	Friday
Scrape and sand bad spots	------------------------------	---------			
Prime bare spots		----------------------			
Paint house			----------------------------------		
Trim house					------------------

------- Planned   .... Actual

The more complex the plan is the more you will benefit from bringing several minds to bear on it. If your work group will be affected by the plan or implementing it, they will probably be more cooperative if you involve them early on.

Finally, check your progress against the plan and measures of success to make sure your original targets and time frames are being achieved. This is your insurance. Aim to find out in plenty of time if things are going off the rails so you can take effective corrective action.

Communicate your plans
To increase your chances of success make sure everyone who will be involved in or affected by your plan is aware of it. Explain clearly what you intend to achieve, how they can help, the standards and timelines you are aiming for and so on. Do you need to inform anyone as a courtesy (for instance your manager or other supervisors)?

Planning and monitoring tools
Planning aids can be as simple as a diary, *To Do* list, checklist or schedule, or they can be as detailed as a **flow chart** (see Chapter 11), **Gantt chart, PERT diagram** (discussed below) or some of the techniques described in Chapter 15. Don't rely on your memory—use a mixture of tools to keep things running smoothly.

Gantt charts
Gantt charts, developed by Henry L. Gantt in the early 1900s, were first widely used by supervisors during World War I to aid in planning and controlling operations in war materials plants.

You can easily construct a Gantt chart like the one in Figure 14.2, which shows a plan for painting a house. List each activity at the left side of the chart (vertically). Show time horizontally (in hours, days, etc.). Note that the plan calls for the scraping and sanding to be completed by midday on Tuesday. As work starts and progresses, fill in the *actual* line below the *planned* activity. The actual time required to scrape and sand was all day on Monday and Tuesday.

PERT diagrams

PERT stands for Program Evaluation and Review Technique. Like Gantt charts and flow charts, PERT diagrams also show a plan as a 'picture' so that everyone can see all the activities and how they relate to each other at a glance. And like Gantt charts, PERT diagrams help monitor your plans. They also show which activities depend on the completion of other activities before they can begin. You can draw a simple PERT diagram yourself, like the one in Figure 14.3 (showing the activities required to relocate a small office); however, special software is available for plotting complex plans.

PERT diagrams are particularly useful when time is tight because they show the *critical path* of a plan. This is the longest path (in time) through the diagram. Monitor activities along this path carefully in

Figure 14.3 PERT diagram for relocating an office

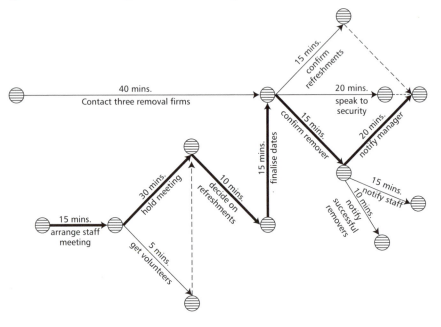

order to complete your plan on time. Activities not on the critical path have some leeway in their timing.

Monitoring your plans

The unexpected always seems to happen. Fortunately, if you've made a plan showing what should have been done, who should have done it, how it should have been done and when and where it should have been done, it's easy to take prompt remedial action and avert a major catastrophe.

In addition to the above tools, **bar charts**, **run charts**, **process capability charts** and **control charts** can also help to monitor your plans. As we see in Chapter 15, they chart your progress over time for comparison with the results you expected or planned.

Four steps to monitoring

Step 1: Establish areas where monitoring is needed
Monitor what is most important: output, cutting costs, improving quality, increasing sales, delivering on time, improving customer satisfaction, lowering employee turnover, reducing stock levels. Monitor the danger points. Monitor what would cause the most damage if it went wrong.

Step 2: Establish specific measures to monitor
Select measures that give you a lot of information easily and quickly. Wherever possible, make these **lead indicators**, not **lag indicators**. Lag indicators measure is the results *after* the process is completed, when it's too late to correct any problems. They are the scorecards that sales results, market share reports, profit results, cost of production reports, mystery shopper surveys, financial reports and many human resources monitoring systems measure.

> *We don't win matches*
> *by keeping our eye on the scoreboard.*

If all we monitor is the scoreboard we are faced with taking retrospective corrective action, which is always more difficult than taking timely countermeasures.

> *We win by keeping our eye on the ball.*

Lead indicators are the 'ball' we should keep our eye on. They provide an early warning when things are not going as expected. They measure what *is* happening as our plan progresses. While lag indicators tell us only whether we *have achieved* our targets, lead indicators show us whether we *are achieving* them. If results are unsatisfactory, we can take corrective action quickly, before more serious problems arise. Lead indicators are the ones to measure and monitor if you can.

To decide which lead indicators to measure, identify the critical tasks needed to complete your plan satisfactorily. Then design measures to track their progress.

Step 3: Compare what is *happening with what* should be *happening*
Some amount of variation will always occur. Decide which variations warrant moving onto Step 4, taking action.

Step 4: Take action as necessary
If your results are disappointing, you will need to do something:

1. *Interim action* buys you time to find the cause of the substandard performance and correct it. However, like the Dutch boy with his finger in the dyke, it is merely a stopgap action.

2. *Adaptive action* allows you to live with the inevitable when, for any number of valid reasons, you cannot live up to your original performance targets.

3. *Corrective action* eliminates the cause of the substandard performance and gets your plan back on the rails.

4. *Preventive action* removes the cause of a potential performance shortfall.

5. *Contingency actions* are stand-by arrangements that you can put into place to remedy a difficulty that may (or may not) occur. If monitoring shows a negative trend or hints that performance might be dropping below expectations, you would put your contingency plans to work.

Protecting your plans

You've no doubt heard Murphy's law: 'Anything that can go wrong will go wrong.' Perhaps you've also heard O'Toole's corollary: 'Murphy was an optimist'.

Here's how ...

... to ensure that your monitoring system is effective

- Bear in mind the overall goals and targets of your department and organisation when deciding what to monitor.

- If you can, involve the people whose performance will be measured in establishing monitoring systems and procedures.

- Whenever possible, incorporate employees' own desire to do a good job into your monitoring systems.

- Try to incorporate management by exception, where you will be advised as soon as a critical activity deviates from the plan.

- Make sure your monitoring information can be collected or produced and used relatively quickly and easily. It must be worth the time and effort to collect and document it, and worth the time and effort to analyse and make use of it.

- Ensure that monitoring feedback will alert you quickly of any deviations from the plan. It need only be accurate enough to provide sufficient information to enable you to identify and act on problems.

- Make it clear who is responsible for taking any corrective or other action that may be required.

- Coordinate what is being monitored to avoid duplication.

- When your monitoring system shows that things are going according to plan, don't forget to thank the people who have helped.

Plans are seldom perfect. The more important it is that your plan goes well, the more important it is for you to put on your doom and gloom spectacles and look for things that could go wrong. Then you can develop a preventive plan to stop it from occurring, a contingency plan so you will know what to do if it does go wrong, or an adaptive plan to live with it if you must.

Here are four questions to ask yourself once you have formulated your plan:

1. What could go wrong? Which are the most likely? Which would be disastrous? (These are the ones to work on.)

2. How will I know if it is about to happen?

3. What can I do now to prevent it from happening?

4. What can I do if it does happen?

Career tip

Don't leave anything to chance and don't jump to conclusions! Think things through, gather the information you'll need and plan carefully.

Force field analysis

A force field analysis can protect your plan by highlighting *resisting forces* (that might jeopardise it) and *driving forces* (that will help it succeed). You can then eliminate or minimise the resisting forces and capitalise on the driving forces. A **force field analysis** can also help identify the implications of your plans and see how they could affect people, systems and procedures and so on. Conduct them on your own or with a group.

Figure 14.4 Force field analysis

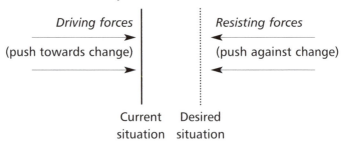

Here are some areas to consider when identifying driving and resisting forces:

- Internal forces:
  - the task
  - the team
  - individual employees
  - policies
  - procedures
  - organisation culture
  - influential parties (e.g. management or unions)
  - administrative practices
  - financial and other resources
  - leadership styles
  - tools and equipment
  - time and information

- External forces:
  - customers
  - technology
  - competition
  - changing government regulations
  - the economic environment
  - changing marketplace conditions
  - community pressures

Here's how ...

... to conduct a force field analysis

1. *Define both the current and the desired situation clearly.* For example, for the current situation you might describe the problem and its symptoms, and for the desired situation you might describe what you want to be happening instead.

2. *Draw and label a vertical line to represent the current situation and a dotted line to represent the desired situation.*

3. In any situation there will be driving or favourable forces pushing us in the direction we want to go, and resisting forces working against us, holding us back from reaching our goals. To the right and left of the lines, *brainstorm the driving forces* that are 'pushing' you *towards* your desired situation and the *resisting forces* that are 'pushing' you *away from* your desired situation.

4. *Circle the most important resisting and driving forces.*

5. *Decide how you can minimise or remove those resisting forces and make the most of those driving forces.*

Checklist for success

☐ Think it through and plan it out. Before doing anything of importance, know why you're doing it, how you'll do it and what you'll need to do it well.

☐ Keep a watchful eye on progress.

☐ Measure what counts most: establish what is really important and monitor that.

☐ Don't over-monitor. Track only those things with the greatest bearing on results.

☐ Stay alert for trouble that might be brewing and do something about it long before it becomes a crisis.

SOLVING PROBLEMS

Planning prevents problems but sadly, not all of them. As Scottish poet Robert Burns (1759–96) said in his poem *To a Mouse*:

The best-laid plans o' mice an' men
Gang aft a-gley,
An' lea'e us nought but grief an' pain
For promised joy.

In short, no matter how careful we are, our plans often go pear shaped, leaving us with disappointment and misery instead of the security and happiness we planned. When your plans 'gang a-gley' here are seven steps that will prevent 'grief an' pain'.

Step 1: What is the problem?

Don't waste your time solving problems that don't exist or 'curing' symptoms. Before doing anything sit down and think. Ask around. Look at the problem from as many angles as you can. This ensures you aren't 'blinkered' in your approach and prevents you from jumping to the 'obvious' conclusions and solutions. Ask yourself these questions:

Who or what is the problem?   *When does it occur?*

Where does it occur?   *When did it first appear?*

How serious is the problem?

Is it getting worse?

What are the technical aspects of the problem?

What are the staff and customer aspects?

How is the work or task affected?

What is related to the problem but is not a problem itself?

What are people's opinions and feelings about the problem?

Box 14.1 shows how these questions can be applied. Based on the understanding you gain from these questions, develop a clear, one-sentence description of the problem.

Box 14.1 Questions to specify and clarify the problem

General problem	Questions to ask
'Too many equipment breakdowns'	How many breakdowns?
	Which equipment?
	What is the nature of the breakdowns?
	When do they occur?
	What is happening when they occur?
	Who is involved?
	How regularly has the equipment been serviced?
	Has anything changed?
'Too many accidents'	What is the specific nature of the accidents?
	Where are they located?
	When do they occur?

Step 2: What caused the problem?

Once you have explored the problem thoroughly and have a good understanding of it, establish how it came to exist. What *caused* it? Don't proceed until you have answered this question.

Beware of symptoms

Have you ever 'solved' a problem only for it to pop back up again in another, or even the same, form? Thinking back, you'll probably find that what you 'solved' was a symptom of the problem and not the problem itself. When we're in a hurry or not thinking clearly it's easy to confuse a symptom with a real problem.

A symptom alerts us that a problem exists. It results from a problem but it doesn't cause it. Fixing symptoms and not the real problem is like closing the barn door after the horse has bolted. It leaves the real problem unsolved, to recur again and again, and often creates new problems. This is probably the most common cause of problem-solving failures.

To fix a problem, remove its cause. Don't jump to conclusions. Study the problem, separate it from its symptoms and gather facts, ideas and opinions that may help in your analysis. You probably won't be able to get all the facts, but use those you have plus those you can obtain without too much trouble or expense.

Figure 14.5 Problem solved

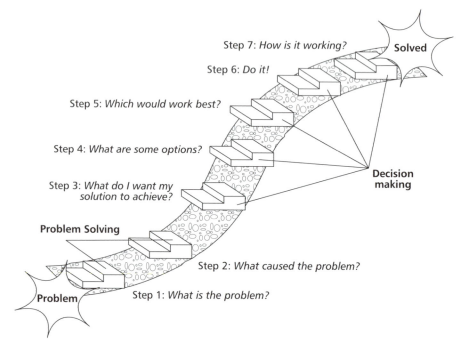

Step 7: *How is it working?* — **Solved**

Step 6: *Do it!*

Step 5: *Which would work best?*

Step 4: *What are some options?*

Decision making

Step 3: *What do I want my solution to achieve?*

Problem Solving

Step 2: *What caused the problem?*

Problem

Step 1: *What is the problem?*

You may need to use some of the tools and techniques discussed in Chapter 15 to gather information about the problem and find out exactly what you are dealing with:

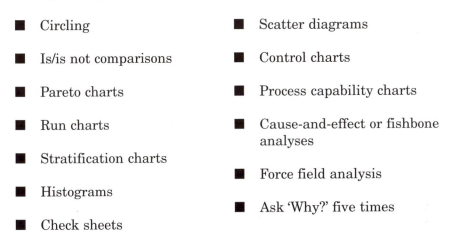

- Circling
- Is/is not comparisons
- Pareto charts
- Run charts
- Stratification charts
- Histograms
- Check sheets

- Scatter diagrams
- Control charts
- Process capability charts
- Cause-and-effect or fishbone analyses
- Force field analysis
- Ask 'Why?' five times

If the problem is complex, break it down into its component parts and solve each aspect of it separately.

Knowing the cause of a problem can save a lot of time and trouble. In fact, it will often point directly to a problem's solution. If you can't solve the problem by removing its cause your next best option is to decide how best to minimise it and live with it.

Step 3: What do you want your solution to achieve?
Here's where the decision-making process begins. Just as you do when developing a plan, establish your goals and measures of success upfront. Stating the problem as a *How to* will help you frame clear objectives and keep you on track. It also puts the problem in its wider context and provides a sound basis for selecting the most suitable solution (Step 5) and evaluating results (Step 7).

What must this decision do or the solution to the problem achieve? What position do you want to be in after you have taken action? How will you know if your action is working? Incorporate any constraints you must work with, such as time or financial restrictions, into your objectives.

For complex or very important problems, divide your criteria into *musts* and *wants*: what must your decision do for you and, ideally, what would you like it to do? This puts you in a good position to select the best alternative and determine how well it is working.

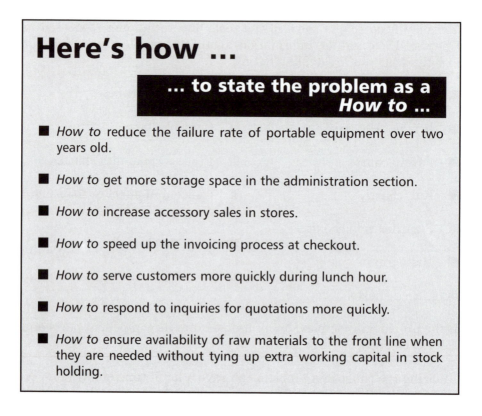

Here's how ...

... to state the problem as a *How to ...*

■ *How to* reduce the failure rate of portable equipment over two years old.

■ *How to* get more storage space in the administration section.

■ *How to* increase accessory sales in stores.

■ *How to* speed up the invoicing process at checkout.

■ *How to* serve customers more quickly during lunch hour.

■ *How to* respond to inquiries for quotations more quickly.

■ *How to* ensure availability of raw materials to the front line when they are needed without tying up extra working capital in stock holding.

Step 4: What are some options?

Solutions are subtle and elusive. They don't announce themselves with trumpets and drums and they are generally hard to find. We usually need to develop several possible solutions and keep an open mind to all of them, even though setting aside our fixed ideas about what might have caused a problem or how it should be solved can be difficult.

Sometimes the best solutions come not from logical thinking but from creative thinking. Seemingly 'wild' or 'crazy' solutions can lead to some great ideas. This is why it's essential to keep Step 4, generating solutions, completely separate from Step 5, evaluating them.

Don't settle for the first action that occurs to you and don't stop thinking when you've thought up one or two ideas—keep going. Generate several solutions. Your chances of success increase when you have a number of alternatives to choose from. If you are having trouble developing options, keep asking *'How can we best ...* (achieve the objectives we established in Step 3)?'.

Did you know ...

Some of us are 'satisficers' and some of us are 'optimisers'. 'Satisficers' stop at the first answer; they stop searching the haystack when they find the first needle. 'Optimisers' keep searching until they find all the needles. Which are you?

Look beyond the obvious. Question everything, especially your own assumptions. There is usually more than one 'right' answer.

Step 5: Which would work best?

Use the criteria you established in Step 3 to decide which alternative will best achieve your objectives. How practical is each? How likely is each to work? What are their costs (not just in terms of money but all your resources, including people)? Do the benefits outweigh the costs? Which solution would fit best with your organisation's accepted procedures and overall goals? Would it cause any waves? How would your customers react? Visualise each in action; does it 'look' good? Does it seem feasible?

Finally, if it's an important decision a quick force field analysis will help identify which factors will promote the success of your decision and which will work against it, and highlight any implications of your favoured option.

Step 6: Do it!

Implement your decision or solution. If it's complicated, apply the third step of the planning process, (see Figure 14.1). If you have been working on your own, brief anyone who will be affected or involved.

Step 7: How is it working?

Follow-up is critical. Is the solution or decision working? If it is, what can you do to keep it working? For example, you might want to include it in a standard procedure or make it part of a regular training or induction course. Perhaps there are some refinements you can add that will make it work even better.

If things are not working as well as expected, find out why and decide what to do. Go back to Step 1 and reassess the problem.

Helping others solve problems

Have you ever thought that, because you're the supervisor, it's your job to solve people's problems for them? Wrong. We learned in Chapter 5 that accepting other people's 'monkeys' is not the way to go. Help people benefit from your experience by showing them how to solve their own problems; otherwise you'll wind up being a full-time problem solver and doing everyone's job except your own.

Show people how to apply these seven steps. Ask questions to help them think their problem through. Help them focus on what they want to happen (not on what they don't want to happen), on solutions and on finding a way forward. Support them, but don't do it for them.

The 'yes, but ...' trap

Have you ever offered anyone advice only to hear something like 'Yes, that's a good idea, but ...'. It's as if they don't really want to solve their problem—just moan about it.

If your help is being butted away with 'Yes, buts', stop offering advice. Switch to asking questions, listening and summarising. Use the STAR formula (see Chapter 3) to help the person establish a goal or objective for solving their problem. If they don't really want to solve the problem it will soon become clear.

MAKING DECISIONS

When you need to decide something important follow Steps 3 to 7 of the problem-solving model explained above and summarised in Figure 14.5. Begin at Step 3 by stating your decision as a *How to ...* and then establishing *must* and *want* criteria.

Avoiding your brain's traps

When we deal with complexity our brains go through mental routines called **heuristics** that can sabotage our decisions. The Here's how box on page 290 lists six common heuristics and explains how to avoid them.

What about 'tough' decisions?

It has often been said that supervision is not a popularity contest. This is most apparent when we must make decisions that we know will not be popular with all or some of our staff. Think through the implications, particularly the possible effects on others, so you can use tact when communicating your decision. Try to see the situation from others' points of view and understand their feelings so you will be able to explain difficult decisions in the most effective way.

Checklist for success

☐ Know precisely what your plan, solution or decision should achieve.

☐ Try to get underlying assumptions out into the open.

☐ Don't attempt to fix a problem until you know what caused it.

☐ Shun 'quick fixes' and easy solutions.

☐ Break big problems down and solve them one portion at a time.

☐ Gut-feel diagnosis is fine, as long as you supplement it with systematic planning and problem-solving tools and techniques (see Chapter 15).

☐ If your first attempt doesn't fix the problem, remove it and try something else.

☐ Don't patch up a problem. If you can't fix it properly, leave it until you can. Give it a high priority if it's important.

☐ Keep an open mind when you're looking for solutions and options.

☐ Seek information from several sources.

☐ Don't overestimate or underestimate the value of other people's opinions. Ignoring advice can be just as bad as accepting it without question.

☐ Don't overvalue or undervalue your own opinions or instincts, either.

☐ Be on the lookout for potential problems. Plan to prevent them or know what to do if they come to pass.

☐ Examine problems from all angles and review 'the big picture'. Learn to cope with 'soft' and limited information.

☐ Focus on solutions, not problems. If all you can see is the problem, you'll never find a way around it. Pause, decide on your objectives and work out ways to achieve them.

Here's how ...

... to avoid our treacherous mental programs

Anchoring. To avoid giving too much weight to what we see or hear first, beware of your first impressions and information. View problems from different perspectives and don't automatically stick with whatever occurs to you first. Stay open-minded and seek a variety of information and opinions. Be careful of anchoring your team members with your own opinions.

Sticking with the *status quo*. Don't continue with things as they are just because it seems simple, safe and comfortable. Keep your objectives clearly in mind; ask yourself: *'Would I select the current situation if it were just another alternative?'*.

Not cutting your losses. Have you ever made a mistake and rather than cut your losses, stuck with it? Set aside your previous choice if it isn't working. Don't base future actions on a misguided attempt to recover your investment in time or money or turn a poor decision into a good one; prolonging a mistake only compounds its error. As well-known investor Warren Buffet says: *'When you find yourself in a hole, stop digging'*.

Selective vision. To avoid seeing what you want to see, be aware of your expectations and biases and don't accept confirming evidence without question. Find someone to play devil's advocate and argue against your preferred decision. When asking others' opinions don't ask leading questions.

Framing. The way we state a problem or decision is important. It can guide us down one path or another. Don't automatically accept the way a problem is presented to you: look for distortions caused by frames. State problems in neutral ways that reflect different reference points. Try wording your problem or decision differently to see if your thinking would change.

Estimating and forecasting. It's difficult to estimate uncertain, unusual or unfamiliar events accurately. To overcome this consider the extremes. Examine all your assumptions, try not to be guided by impressions and use accurate facts and figures when you can. Avoid becoming over-confident or over-cautious, or relying too much on past events or dramatic events which have left a strong impression.

If you're really concerned over the possible effects of a decision, ask yourself: *'What is the worst that could happen as a result of this decision?'*. Sometimes you will find the effects are not as dire as you imagined. At least you will know what to expect and can make some preventive, contingency, interim or adaptive plans.

The next time you have to make an unpopular or unpleasant decision, think about the best supervisor you know. How would that person go about reaching the decision? How would they communicate it? How would they deal with any negative consequences? Use this supervisor as a role model to help you decide how to proceed.

INVOLVING YOUR GROUP

Do you think it's quicker and easier to make a decision yourself? Or that you *should* make the decision yourself since you are accountable for the results?

Checklist for success

- ☐ Decide whether the decision is a big or a small one. If you have a big decision to make or a big problem to solve, follow the procedure outlined in this chapter. If the decision or problem is small, don't spend hours agonising over it at the expense of more important matters.

- ☐ Don't be too impatient. 'Decide in haste, repent at leisure' is good to remember when making important decisions. On the other hand, don't wait until you can make a perfect decision, either.

- ☐ Get on with it! Don't put off making a decision or solving a problem until it becomes a crisis.

- ☐ If you do have a crisis, remember that you are the leader and employees are looking to you for clear thinking and calm direction. Stand back and consider the situation. Ask yourself when the decision has to be made. Then use the time available to make the best decision.

- ☐ Actively look for the weak points in your chosen decision or course of action.

- ☐ Know the warning signals that might indicate your decision is failing, and keep alert for them so that you can alter course if necessary.

There are three important benefits to involving people. It can enhance the outcome: more brains, more ideas. Because they have taken part, understood the constraints and seen what was considered, peoples' understanding of the course of action and their commitment to making it work increase. People working together can also provide enthusiasm.

When to involve the team

Does this mean that your work group should participate in every decision? Two types of decisions in particular are not suited to a group solution: those where the answer is obvious and those that have no real effect on the group. If either is the case, make the decision yourself and announce or explain it.

However, if any of the following four factors are present, involve your group if you can:

1. *The need for acceptance.* The more you need your team to accept your decision or plan, the more you should involve them.

2. *Its effect on the group.* The more the problem, decision or plan affects the group, the more you should involve them.

3. *Their involvement in implementing it.* If your team will be implementing or carrying out the decision or plan, involve them.

4. *The ability and desire of the group to become involved.* If your team wants to become involved, try to involve them, particularly if they have knowledge or expertise in the relevant issues. Even if they do not, their participation could be useful training and development for them.

Another rule of thumb is that if you suspect the answer will not be straightforward, involve others. Complex problems and decisions usually benefit from the application of several people considering them from their different viewpoints and experiences.

How to involve the team

You can involve others to varying degrees, as shown in Figure 14.6.

There are two factors to consider when you use this model to decide how much to involve your work group:

Figure 14.6 Degrees of team involvement

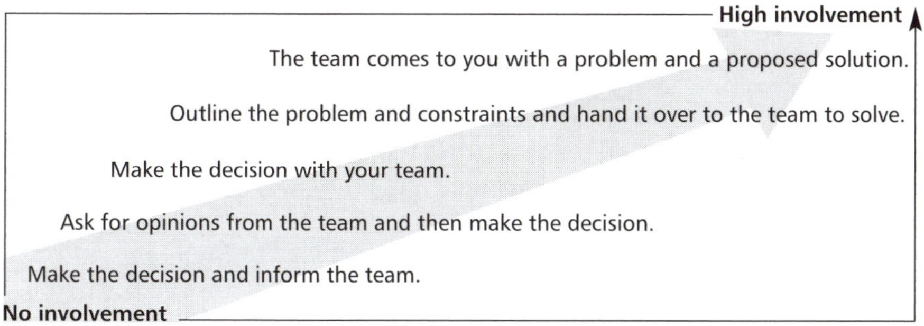

1. The more complex the problem or decision is, the bigger its implications for your customers or the company, or the tighter time is, the more involvement you should have, so move slightly to the left in the model.

2. The greater your group's knowledge, skills and commitment, the less involvement you need, so you can move slightly to the right in the model.

Call a meeting or series of meetings (see Chapter 10) and use the techniques shown in Chapter 15 to gather information, analyse it and reach your decision. You will find **brainstorming** and the **nominal group technique** useful.

Brainstorming
Brainstorming is a good way to tap creativity, ferret out aspects of a problem you might otherwise miss and develop lots of options quickly.

Nominal group technique
Have you ever noticed that it is often the person with the loudest voice, the most articulate person or the most senior person who gets their way? Others lose heart and interest because they feel their point of view will never be 'heard'. (See the Here's how box on page 295.)

The **nominal group technique** is a way of making sure this doesn't happen. It gives everyone in the group an equal say in decision making. It also clearly shows the wishes of the group without creating 'winners' and 'losers' the way straight voting does.

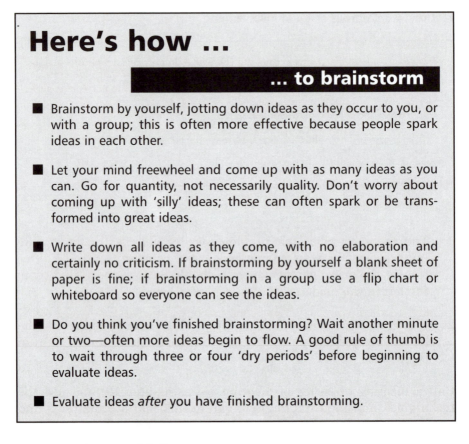

Here's how ...

... to brainstorm

■ Brainstorm by yourself, jotting down ideas as they occur to you, or with a group; this is often more effective because people spark ideas in each other.

■ Let your mind freewheel and come up with as many ideas as you can. Go for quantity, not necessarily quality. Don't worry about coming up with 'silly' ideas; these can often spark or be transformed into great ideas.

■ Write down all ideas as they come, with no elaboration and certainly no criticism. If brainstorming by yourself a blank sheet of paper is fine; if brainstorming in a group use a flip chart or whiteboard so everyone can see the ideas.

■ Do you think you've finished brainstorming? Wait another minute or two—often more ideas begin to flow. A good rule of thumb is to wait through three or four 'dry periods' before beginning to evaluate ideas.

■ Evaluate ideas *after* you have finished brainstorming.

Beware of groupthink

Feeling there is safety in numbers, people in groups can be willing to take greater risks than they would on their own. And sometimes, when groups have worked together for a long time and have good team spirit, people are loathe to disagree with what seems to be the majority view or to act as devil's advocate and argue a different point of view. This is when **groupthink** can occur: coming to an unwise and even dangerous decision because no one is game to stand up and speak out.

To avoid groupthink actively seek alternatives, different opinions and evidence both for and against your conclusions.

If you suspect groupthink might be at play, appoint one or two people to the role of devil's advocate. Bring in some outsiders for their opinions and experience. Consciously look for alternatives, different points of view and downsides to your current plans. Otherwise you might all end up with egg on your faces.

Here's how ...

... to apply the nominal group technique to group problem solving

1. Brainstorm problems that need to be resolved. Specify each one clearly so that everyone has the same understanding of it. Make sure you haven't listed the same problem more than once using different words. (See Box 14.2 on the next page.)

2. Assign a letter to each problem. (See Box 14.3 on the next page.)

3. Each person assigns a number to each problem according to how they weight its importance. For example, if there are five problems each member assigns a 5 to the problem they believe is most important, a 4 to the next most important problem and so one, ending with a 1 next to the least important problem. (See Box 14.4 on the next page.)

   If you are discussing a large number of problems, follow the 'half plus one' rule. Instead of ranking each problem, rank only half plus one of the problems listed. For example, if 22 problems are listed rank 12. Each member would assign a 12 to the problem they believed most important, an 11 to the next most important problem and so on.

4. Tally the ratings. The problem with the highest score is the one the team thinks is the most important problem to work on first. (See Box 14.5 on the next page.)

Another version of the nominal group technique is to brainstorm ideas to a flip chart and when finished, give everyone coloured dots to put beside the ideas they like.

Box 14.2 Stating problems clearly

Examples of problems	*Problems stated clearly*
■ Storage space	■ Lack of storage space
■ Tools	■ People not putting tools away
■ Safety procedures	■ Safety procedures not always followed
■ Housekeeping	■ Poor housekeeping due to lack of time and unclear priorities
■ Customer complaints	■ Increasing customer complaints re late delivery

Box 14.3 Problems labelled

A. Lack of storage space

B. People not putting tools away

C. Safety procedures not always followed

D. Poor housekeeping due to lack of time and unclear priorities

E. Increasing customer complaints re late delivery

Box 14.4 One team member's rating

Which problem is most important?

A. 1

B. 4

C. 5

D. 3

E. 2

Box 14.5 Team rating

Tally the ratings

A. *1 3 2 2 3* = 11

B. *4 5 3 3 2* = 17

C. *5 4 4 4 5* = 22

D. *3 1 1 5 4* = 14

E. *2 2 5 1 1* = 11

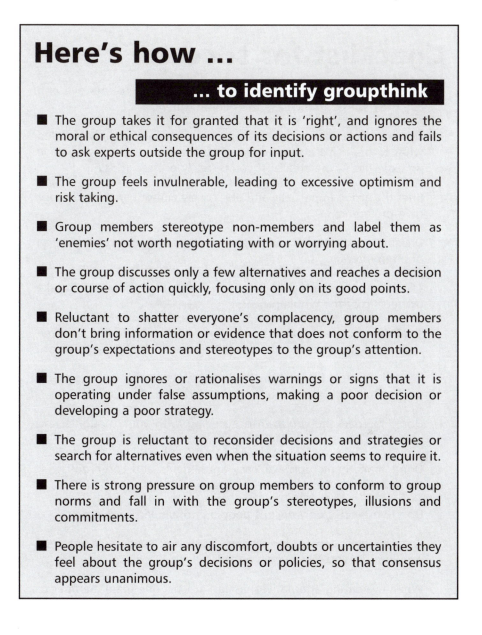

Here's how ...

... to identify groupthink

■ The group takes it for granted that it is 'right', and ignores the moral or ethical consequences of its decisions or actions and fails to ask experts outside the group for input.

■ The group feels invulnerable, leading to excessive optimism and risk taking.

■ Group members stereotype non-members and label them as 'enemies' not worth negotiating with or worrying about.

■ The group discusses only a few alternatives and reaches a decision or course of action quickly, focusing only on its good points.

■ Reluctant to shatter everyone's complacency, group members don't bring information or evidence that does not conform to the group's expectations and stereotypes to the group's attention.

■ The group ignores or rationalises warnings or signs that it is operating under false assumptions, making a poor decision or developing a poor strategy.

■ The group is reluctant to reconsider decisions and strategies or search for alternatives even when the situation seems to require it.

■ There is strong pressure on group members to conform to group norms and fall in with the group's stereotypes, illusions and commitments.

■ People hesitate to air any discomfort, doubts or uncertainties they feel about the group's decisions or policies, so that consensus appears unanimous.

Checklist for success

☐ Involve your group members whenever you can to improve and use their skills and increase their commitment.

☐ Don't involve your group members if you have already decided what to do, if it's a simple, straightforward decision, if they have no expertise in the area or if you're really pressed for time.

☐ Brief the group impartially and objectively without advocating your own preferences.

☐ Develop an atmosphere of open inquiry and careful consideration of alternatives.

☐ Take your time, don't push too hard—encourage the group to take ownership of the whole process.

☐ Treat differences of opinion as a way to gather additional information, clarify issues and force the group to seek better information.

☐ Keep the group focused on the objectives, on the future and on solving the problem or reaching the decision.

☐ Don't railroad the group into agreeing with your thoughts and ideas.

☐ Don't make early, quick or easy agreements and compromises— these are often based on wrong assumptions.

☐ Don't vote—this only divides people into winners and losers.

☐ Keep an eye open for longer-term customer needs and potential problems so you're one step ahead.

☐ When evaluating alternatives, assign at least one team member to play the role of devil's advocate.

CHAPTER FIFTEEN

FIND, ANALYSE AND FIX PROBLEMS
Using systematic, analytical tools and techniques

O pinions and intuition are fine but they need to be supported by solid facts and information. That's the only way we can be confident in our decisions. Collecting and displaying genuine information is neither as time consuming nor as difficult as you might think. In the long run it will actually save time because you will know exactly where you are in what can otherwise look like one big muddle.

The main ways to gather and present information to help find problems, analyse them and monitor results are explained below.

FINDING PROBLEMS
Perhaps you're thinking that you don't need to go looking for problems because they find you easily enough. However, by the time problems find you they have developed in magnitude. Finding them first makes them easier to resolve, keeps you on the continuous improvement track and ensures you add real value to your job.

Make it your business to find problems early on. When you know or suspect you've got a problem and it seems complex, analyse it. If necessary, break it into subproblems that are small enough to solve.

Qualitative methods
If we're listening, people's experience, logic, judgement, intuition and opinions can point us to problems, potential problems and their solutions. In Chapter 12 we looked at how the techniques of *ask the customer* and managing **moments of truth** can alert us to problems. Here are two more ways to spot trouble.

Flow charts

These pictorial representations of a system or process are great for highlighting where value is (or is not) added and potential difficulties. Because they help us 'see' each step and how it relates to other steps, we can spot deviations from the ideal path a process should follow.

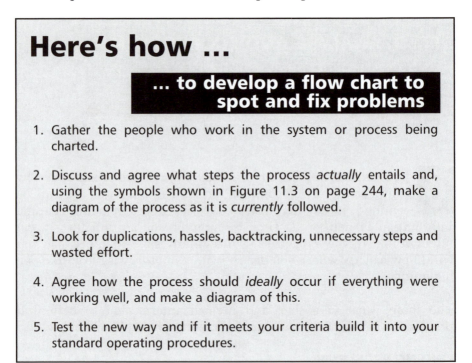

Here's how ...

... to develop a flow chart to spot and fix problems

1. Gather the people who work in the system or process being charted.

2. Discuss and agree what steps the process *actually* entails and, using the symbols shown in Figure 11.3 on page 244, make a diagram of the process as it is *currently* followed.

3. Look for duplications, hassles, backtracking, unnecessary steps and wasted effort.

4. Agree how the process should *ideally* occur if everything were working well, and make a diagram of this.

5. Test the new way and if it meets your criteria build it into your standard operating procedures.

Make sure everyone is clear about the process that is being flow charted, including where it begins and ends. Make sure every feedback loop in the chart has an escape. There is usually only one output arrow out of a process box. If you need more it indicates that a decision diamond might be needed.

Ask the team

Asking questions is a great way to identify problems. Here are some questions that will help you spot problems early on:

■ What difficulties did you run into this week?

■ What took longer than it should have?

■ What took more effort than you expected?

■ What was surprisingly complicated?

■ What did you do this week that seemed just plain silly?

■ What caused complaints or irritation this week?

■ What was misinterpreted?

■ What involved too many people?

■ What cost too much?

■ What was wasted?

■ What involved too many steps or actions?

Remember, you're asking these questions for a reason—to find and fix problems. Keep that in mind so you don't set up a climate of negativity and fault finding.

Quantitative methods

Sometimes we need hard, or quantitative, data. Numbers alone aren't enough though; we need 'good numbers'. To be sure you can rely on the validity of your data, collect enough information, over a long enough period and from enough sources. Always date your information and note down who collected it, over what time period and where the figures came from.

Check sheets

Check sheets show how often something is happening and highlight where things are going wrong. They are a good starting point because they help identify problems and show which occur most often. If your customers are complaining that your section's output is often late or contains flaws, you could use a **check sheet** to find out exactly what is going on.

Figure 15.1 shows that problem A occurred seven times, problem B occurred 13 times and problem C occurred six times. It seems that we should focus our attention on problem B, particularly as the number of times the problem occurred each week is consistent. If one week stood out from the others as having far more or fewer problems occurring, we would want to examine what happened during that week to see what we could learn from it.

Figure 15.1 Check sheet

Problem	Week			Total
	1	2	3	
A	II	III	II	7
B	IIII	JHT	IIII	13
C	II	I	III	6
Total	8	9	9	26

collected by: A. Smith   period: 1–30 November 2002   location: Central administration

Here's how ...

... to make a check sheet

1. Agree on, and define precisely, the events you will monitor so that everyone is looking for the same thing.

2. Decide how long you will collect data; this might be several hours or several weeks. Collect enough data over a long enough period to be as representative as possible, but not so much data that collecting them becomes an end in itself. Make sure your observations and samples are homogeneous—that is, from the same machine, person, etc. If this is not the case, stratify or group the samples first (see stratification charts, below) and sample each one individually.

3. Design a form that is clear and easy to use, labelling each column clearly and making sure there is enough space to record your observations.

4. Collect the data. Ensure that people have time to collect them.

Make sure your form is clear and easy to use, that you clearly label the columns and that you leave enough space to enter the data. Display the information you collect in chart form, for example **bar charts**, **run charts** or **Pareto charts**.

Run charts and bar charts

These are good for charting trends or progress over time and comparing performance with **measures of success**. Seeing how things vary over time (are they getting worse, staying the same or improving?) can help identify and describe a problem or monitor a process.

To make a run chart, show the units of measure vertically and time horizontally. Plot what you are measuring as points on the graph and then connect the points. Plot the measurements in the order you made them, since you are tracking them over time (see Figure 15.2).

Pay attention to any wide variations because they might highlight a problem in a process or procedure. Run charts can also highlight shifts in the average results. For example, when you're monitoring a process an equal number of points should fall above and below the average. When this is not the case, it probably indicates that an unusual 'event' or change has occurred or that the average has changed. If the shift is favourable find out why so you can make whatever has changed a permanent part of the system. If it is unfavourable find out why and eliminate the possibility of it happening again. Also examine any steady increase or decrease in a trend, since this would not be expected to occur randomly and would also indicate an important change that needs to be investigated.

Figure 15.2 Run chart

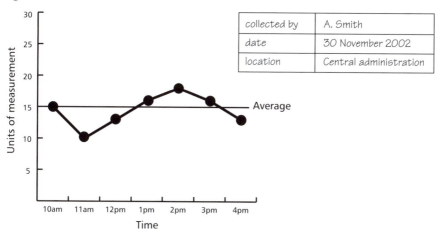

Bar charts are useful for showing differences between categories or types of activities. Show the categories horizontally and the units of measurement vertically. The bar chart in Figure 15.3 shows the number of different types of processed documents; this would then be compared with the expected figures.

Figure 15.3 Bar chart

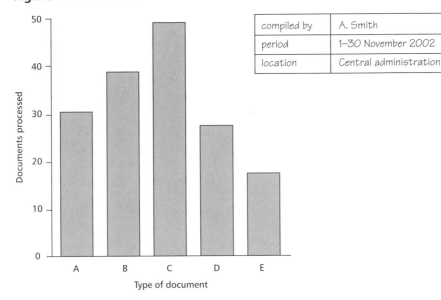

compiled by	A. Smith
period	1–30 November 2002
location	Central administration

Control charts

Control charts are run charts that show upper and lower statistically expected limits (usually calculated by specialists using complex statistical formulae). The upper and lower control limits are drawn on either side of the average (see Figure 15.4).

Don't confuse the upper and lower limits of a **control chart** with specification limits. The former tells you what a process *can do* consistently and the latter reflects your targets, or measures of success. Control limits may be tighter than your targets (are you putting too much effort into this process?) or they may be looser (you'd better fix the process).

When drawing control charts, show categories (quantities or time) horizontally and units of measurement vertically.

All processes and systems have natural variation, but too much variation results in unreliable quality and increased costs. Control charts will show how much variation exists in a process, whether this

Figure 15.4 Control chart

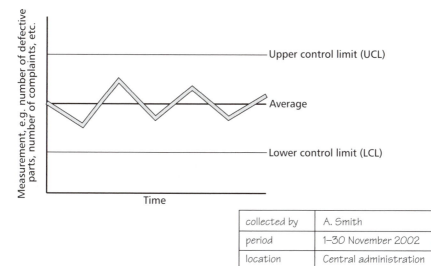

collected by	A. Smith
period	1–30 November 2002
location	Central administration

variation is random or follows a pattern and whether or not the process is in statistical control. In short, they will indicate whether a problem exists and help implement and monitor solutions. For example, control charts can show:

- how machine A's productivity and quality compares with machine B's;

- the running speeds, temperatures, pressures and other factors in a process;

- how long it takes to complete a process (e.g. answering a customer query, resolving a customer complaint, sending out an invoice, making a sale, assembling an car);

- when/how often delays are occurring.

If the averages fall within the control limits your process is in control. If any of the points fall outside the control limits or form unlikely patterns, your process is statistically 'out of control' and you need to fix it. Find out what event or events caused a result to be outside the control limits (remember the 85:15 rule from Chapter 6) and fix it so that it won't happen again.

Figure 15.5 gives several indications of a process that is 'out of control' and suggests questions you could ask.

Figure 15.5 An out-of-control system

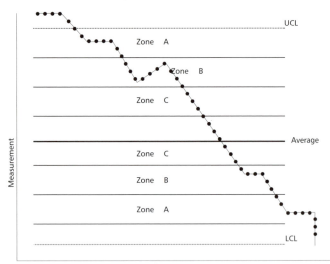

collected by	A. Smith
period	1–30 November 2002
location	Central administration

A process is 'out of control' if:

- one or more points fall outside the control limits;
- two out of three successive points occur on the same side of the centre line in Zone A;
- four out of five successive points occur on the same side of the centre line in or outside Zone B;
- nine successive points occur on one side of the average line;
- there are six consecutive points increasing or decreasing;
- there are 14 points in a row alternating up and down; or
- there are 15 points in a row within Zone C.

Questions to ask with an out-of-control process:

- Are the methods used changing?
- Did the samples come from different methods, machines, shifts or operators?
- What has changed in the process or the environment (e.g. maintenance procedures, training, overtime levels, raw materials)?
- Could the environment be affecting the process (temperature, humidity, etc.)?
- Could the equipment need maintenance?
- Have different measuring instruments been used that may not have the same degree of accuracy?
- Is everyone trained in how to carry out the process?
- Are the raw materials, information or other process inputs different?

You can also use control charts as a monitoring tool by taking samples at regular intervals and plotting them on the control chart. This ensures a process doesn't change in important ways and remains reliable. It will also highlight any non-conformances, or variations outside the control limits, that you should investigate.

306

Pareto charts

Pareto charts are a good way to display the relative importance of the problems or events you are examining. They are vertical bar charts that show problems in descending order. This helps identify problems and clearly shows which ones to start working on first—the biggest ones!

In the example shown in Figure 15.6 we would want to investigate why raw materials run out to try to stop this occurring. Then we would want to find the causes and sources of faulty raw materials and discuss this with our suppliers; we may even consider changing to a more reliable supplier. Next, we would want to investigate the causes of machine breakdowns and see what we could do to stop or reduce them.

Compile Pareto charts from check sheets or other forms of data collection.

Figure 15.6 Pareto chart: defects found at in-process inspection

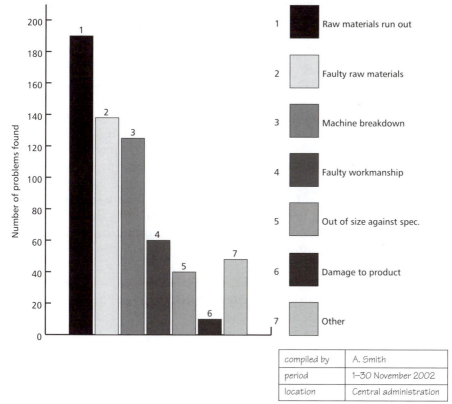

compiled by	A. Smith
period	1–30 November 2002
location	Central administration

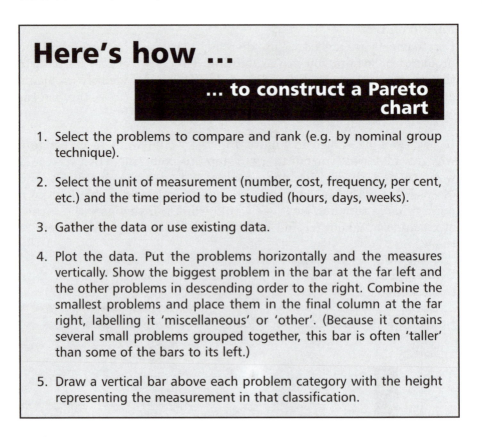

Here's how ...

... to construct a Pareto chart

1. Select the problems to compare and rank (e.g. by nominal group technique).

2. Select the unit of measurement (number, cost, frequency, per cent, etc.) and the time period to be studied (hours, days, weeks).

3. Gather the data or use existing data.

4. Plot the data. Put the problems horizontally and the measures vertically. Show the biggest problem in the bar at the far left and the other problems in descending order to the right. Combine the smallest problems and place them in the final column at the far right, labelling it 'miscellaneous' or 'other'. (Because it contains several small problems grouped together, this bar is often 'taller' than some of the bars to its left.)

5. Draw a vertical bar above each problem category with the height representing the measurement in that classification.

Pareto charts can provide surprising insights. For example, the two charts in Figure 15.7 show the importance of examining a problem from different perspectives: resolving the most frequently occurring problems first might not be the most cost-effective way to proceed.

Figure 15.8 shows that we sometimes need to use our imagination when measuring problems and information. Showing defects by type and by machine doesn't give us very much information, but showing defects by shift really gives us something to investigate.

Figure 15.9 shows how to use Pareto charts to measure the impact of changes, with before and after comparisons. In the example shown the number of complaints dropped markedly after the introduction of a revised process flow.

Pareto charts can also help break down a problem, as Figure 15.10 shows. This can be great when you need to isolate the causes of problems from their symptoms.

Figure 15.7 Using Pareto charts to identify the most important problems from different perspectives

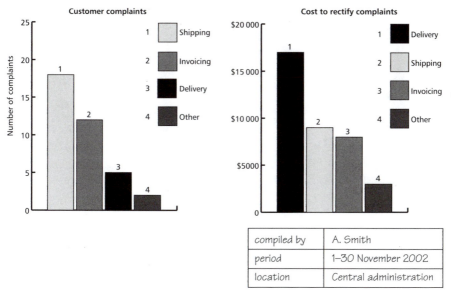

compiled by	A. Smith
period	1–30 November 2002
location	Central administration

Figure 15.8 Using Pareto charts to analyse information in different ways

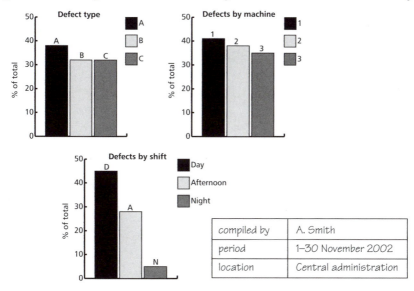

compiled by	A. Smith
period	1–30 November 2002
location	Central administration

Use your common sense when constructing and analysing Pareto charts. For example, it may pay to resolve a recurring complaint from a major customer before resolving numerous other complaints from small customers.

Figure 15.9 Using Pareto charts to measure the impact of change

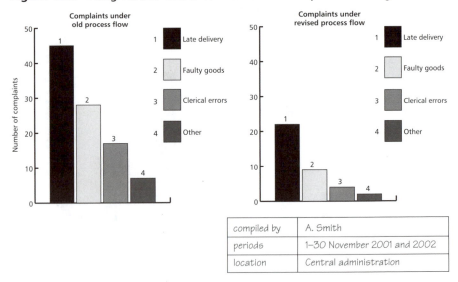

Figure 15.10 Using Pareto charts to break down a problem

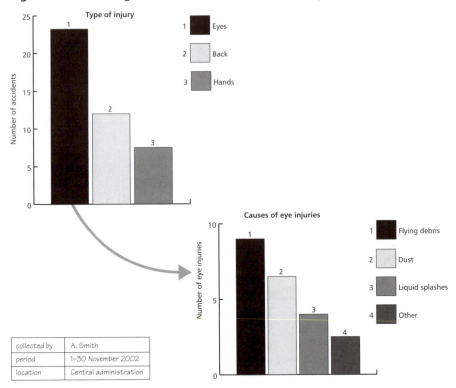

Pie charts

If you are dividing data up where the starting point is 100% use a **pie chart**. This is a circular way of displaying information. The entire circle represents 100%, with 'slices' showing the relative sizes (frequencies, amounts, etc.) of the data you are examining.

Like a Pareto chart, this helps describe a problem and can show where to begin your problem-solving efforts. Be sure to mark the subject matter clearly, showing the percentages within the slices and what each slice represents.

Figure 15.11 Pie chart: time usage of sales representatives

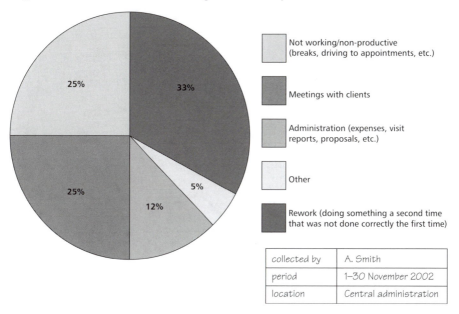

Stratification charts

Stratification is a good way to analyse data to identify problems and find improvement opportunities. It helps sort out confusing numbers that actually mask the facts. This might happen, for example, when the recorded data are *non-homogeneous* (from many sources but treated as one number). Stratification can break these down into categories that are more meaningful, and focus on and monitor corrective action.

The run chart in Figure 15.12 shows, for example, that the number of minor injuries in a factory has been steadily increasing over the last 12 months. However, this is the total of all minor accidents. We don't

Figure 15.12 Stratification chart

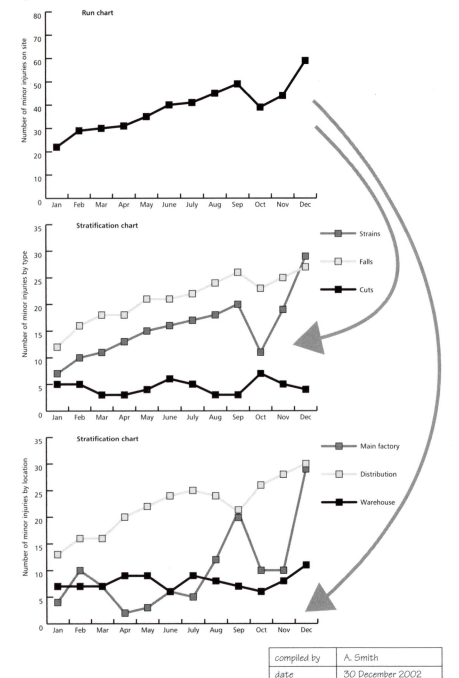

compiled by	A. Smith
date	30 December 2002
location	Central administration

know what type of accidents (scratches, cuts, bumps, burns) they are, where they are occurring (which department, which machines, which processes), when they are occurring (which shift, day of the week) or any other potentially important information.

Stratification charts can show this information, making it easier to isolate the real problem and resolve it. The first stratification chart in the example shows that we should investigate the cause of falls first and try to reduce them, and then move our attention to strains. The second stratification chart shows that Distribution seems to be a particularly bad area for minor injuries and we should focus our attention there, at least initially. It also indicates that the main factory had far higher number than average of minor injuries in September and December, which we should investigate.

Checklist for success

☐ Don't confuse statistics with information. Statistics can provide information, but not all statistics give information.

☐ Look at problems through the eyes of all your customers, competitors, co-workers, management—everyone who has an interest.

☐ Seek the help of others when in doubt. Ask other people what they think, especially informed people whose judgement you trust. If necessary, bring in experts; that's what they're there for.

ANALYSING PROBLEMS

The more complex a problem is, the more carefully we need to examine it to find out what is really happening. This usually means collecting more information or data about the problem or breaking it down into its component elements.

Does this sound like a lot of work? If you don't do it you may find yourself fixing a symptom and leaving the real source of the problem unchanged. What a waste of time and effort!

These are jumping-off points for thinking about and discussing problems you have identified. Try to look at them from every possible angle.

Qualitative methods

Sometimes thinking a problem through, applying your judgement, experience, insight and logic, can tell you a lot. If it's a large, complex or highly troublesome problem you'll probably want to enlist the help of experts, other supervisors and/or your group members.

Fishbone analysis

Some problems are too big to deal with as a whole: we need to break them down into their component parts and deal with them one at a time. A **fishbone analysis** (also called **Ishikawa diagram** after the person who developed the technique and **cause-and-effect diagram**, which describes its purpose) helps accomplish this.

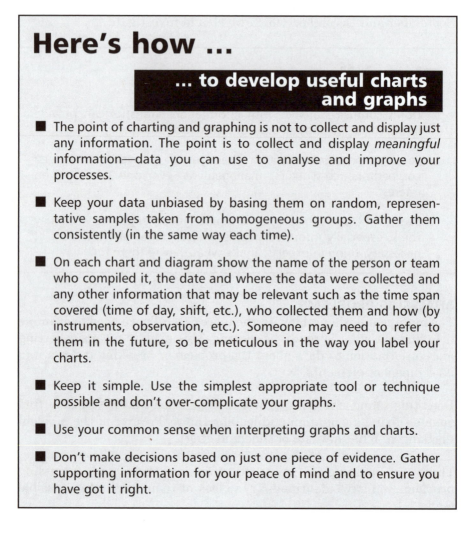

Here's how ...

... to develop useful charts and graphs

■ The point of charting and graphing is not to collect and display just any information. The point is to collect and display *meaningful* information—data you can use to analyse and improve your processes.

■ Keep your data unbiased by basing them on random, representative samples taken from homogeneous groups. Gather them consistently (in the same way each time).

■ On each chart and diagram show the name of the person or team who compiled it, the date and where the data were collected and any other information that may be relevant such as the time span covered (time of day, shift, etc.), who collected them and how (by instruments, observation, etc.). Someone may need to refer to them in the future, so be meticulous in the way you label your charts.

■ Keep it simple. Use the simplest appropriate tool or technique possible and don't over-complicate your graphs.

■ Use your common sense when interpreting graphs and charts.

■ Don't make decisions based on just one piece of evidence. Gather supporting information for your peace of mind and to ensure you have got it right.

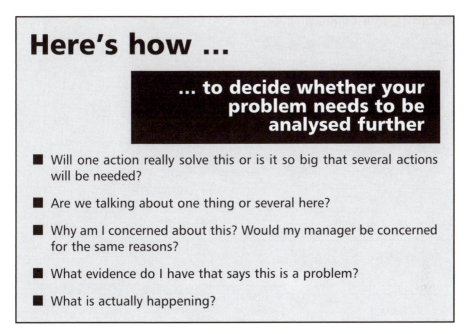

Here's how ...

... to decide whether your problem needs to be analysed further

■ Will one action really solve this or is it so big that several actions will be needed?

■ Are we talking about one thing or several here?

■ Why am I concerned about this? Would my manager be concerned for the same reasons?

■ What evidence do I have that says this is a problem?

■ What is actually happening?

Making a diagram of a problem allows us to 'see' it from all angles, sort out a maze of facts, identify its most important elements and isolate its most likely cause(s). It is relatively quick to do, usually enjoyable and can be done alone or with a small group of people. Either way, you will be relying on the technique of **brainstorming**.

Figure 15.13 shows a cause-and-effect analysis for the problem of high staff turnover. You know it is higher than the other businesses in your area, and higher than other offices in your company across the country. You want to stem the problem because you know turnover is expensive and reduces customer service levels.

You will see that four aspects of the problem, or possible causes, have been considered: employees, work environment, equipment and rewards. These possible causes may not suit every problem, so choose from the diagnostic areas shown in Box 15.1 or create your own. It is usual to break a problem down into four components, but don't let this constrain you—use three or five categories if you prefer. Do whatever suits analysing your specific problem best.

If you think of a possible cause of the problem that could go under more than one category on your diagram, don't worry—put it down somewhere. The main thing is to ensure you are looking at your problem from all angles, which is critical to sound problem analysis.

315

Figure 15.13 Fishbone analysis

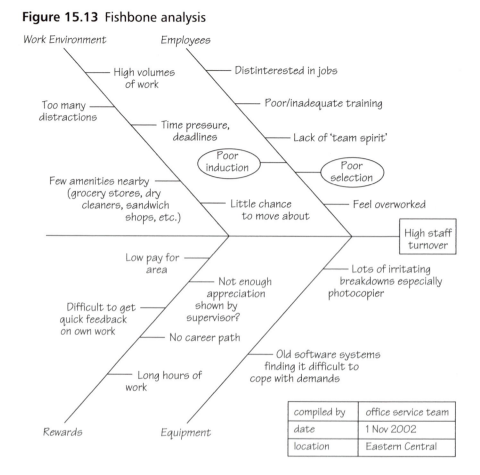

Once your initial analysis is complete, stand back and consider it. Which elements seem most important? Circle them to highlight the ones you intend to begin working on or investigating further.

Ask 'Why' five times

This is a great technique for tunnelling to the cause of a problem. It works like this:

1. State your problem clearly.

2. Brainstorm possible causes.

3. Decide the most likely cause(s).

4. Ask 'Why?' five times for the most likely causes.

Box 15.1 Aspects of problems

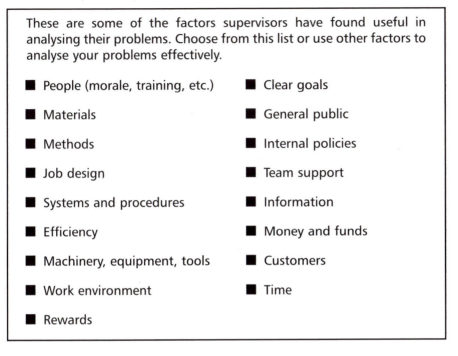

These are some of the factors supervisors have found useful in analysing their problems. Choose from this list or use other factors to analyse your problems effectively.

- People (morale, training, etc.)
- Materials
- Methods
- Job design
- Systems and procedures
- Efficiency
- Machinery, equipment, tools
- Work environment
- Rewards

- Clear goals
- General public
- Internal policies
- Team support
- Information
- Money and funds
- Customers
- Time

Keep asking 'Why?' until you can go no further. 'Why does this happen?' or 'Why is this a problem?' are variations on the 'Why?' question.

Take the high staff turnover problem considered in Figure 15.13. You decided the two most likely possible causes were poor selection and poor induction.

Your 'Why?' chain for poor selection might look like this:

- *Why?* I've hired the wrong people.

- *Why?* I'm not applying recruitment and selection techniques.

- *Why?* I'm not confident in them.

- *Why?* I need more training.

This is the logical end to this 'Why?' chain. Four 'Whys?' were enough to arrive at a possible solution.

317

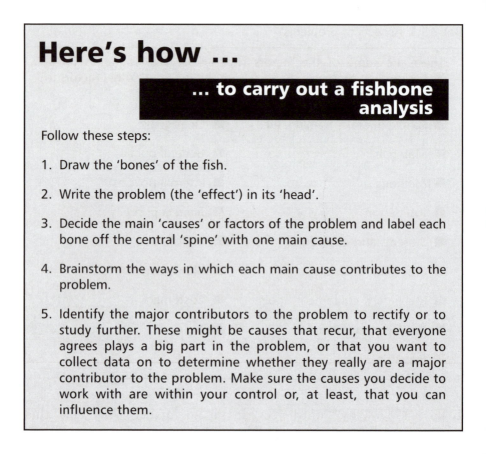

Here's how ...

... to carry out a fishbone analysis

Follow these steps:

1. Draw the 'bones' of the fish.

2. Write the problem (the 'effect') in its 'head'.

3. Decide the main 'causes' or factors of the problem and label each bone off the central 'spine' with one main cause.

4. Brainstorm the ways in which each main cause contributes to the problem.

5. Identify the major contributors to the problem to rectify or to study further. These might be causes that recur, that everyone agrees plays a big part in the problem, or that you want to collect data on to determine whether they really are a major contributor to the problem. Make sure the causes you decide to work with are within your control or, at least, that you can influence them.

Here is the 'Why?' chain for poor induction:

■ *Why?* New employees aren't learning key skills and are not fitting in properly.

■ *Why?* Induction isn't providing the right information and motivation.

■ *Why?* It's too 'hit or miss'—nothing is written down.

■ *Why?* I haven't approached it in a disciplined and systematic way.

■ *Why?* I don't know enough about developing induction programs.

As you can see, by the time you've reached the end of the 'Why?' chains, the solution often becomes fairly clear.

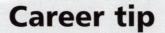

Career tip

Become familiar with these tools and techniques and use them to make sound judgements.

Is/is not comparisons

Sometimes comparing what our problem *is* with what it *is not* can shed light on it.

Here's how ...

... to ask questions for an is/is not comparison

Identity:	What or who is it?	What or who isn't it?
Location:	Where does it occur?	Where doesn't it occur?
Timing:	When does it occur?	When doesn't it occur?
Trend:	How bad is it?	Is it getting worse?

You might want to think about where or when else you might expect this same problem to occur, but it doesn't. Answering these questions often makes the cause of a problem readily apparent and it's then clear what you need to do to fix it. (See Box 15.2.)

Circling

Have you ever noticed that when something goes wrong it's seldom a 'quick and easy fix'? Circling is a technique that can prevent us getting caught in a web of complexity when we're trying to resolve problems.

To tighten up a very broad or complex issue describe the difficulty or concern as you understand it in one sentence. Chances are it will be a lengthy, complicated sentence that describes several problems. Write it on a piece of paper (or flip chart if you're working with a group) and then circle the key words, as shown in Figure 15.14.

Each time you clarify the sentence you sharpen your problem definition. If there is an 'and' in the definition it may mean you're

Box 15.2 Is/is not comparison: absenteeism among office staff

	Is	Is not	Point to follow up
Where?	general office	accounts public relations sales & marketing	Working conditions, hours of work, supervision: What is different about the general office?
When?	most days	no obvious patterns, e.g. Fridays or Mondays	Complete a check sheet to identify any hidden patterns.
Who?	mostly newer staff	not longer-serving staff	Make a histogram of age groups to check this. Check ages and profiles for 'job fit'. Check training and induction given to new recruits. Check their jobs for job interest: are they different from jobs of longer-serving staff?
How often?	about 17% on any given day		Benchmark with local organisations to see how bad this problem is.
How bad?	problem may be increasing	not getting better or staying the same	Check this year's absenteeism rates against previous years.
What?	mostly one-day absences	seldom longer than two days	

compiled by	office service team
date	1 Nov 2002
location	Eastern Central

trying to solve two problems at once (as in this example). Analyse everything you've circled separately.

Figure 15.14 The circling technique to specify broad or complex issues

How to (solve)(customer)(complaints) and (warranty claims.)

Solve = reduce?
        eliminate entirely?
        prevent?
Which customers?
What kinds of complaints?
What kinds of warranty claims?

Checkerboard analysis

As shown in Figure 15.15, a **checkerboard analysis** uses a matrix to analyse a problem. Elements of one key aspect of the problem go down one side and elements of another aspect across the top. Focus your attention on where they intersect.

Figure 15.15 Checkerboard analysis

Problems within accounts / Problems at source	Insufficient information	Inaccurate information	Details incorrect	Processing difficulties at head office	Accounts staff not clear about procedure	Total
Problem: How to speed up the invoicing process to non-account customers						
Form for collecting information confusing and repetitive	✗	✗	✗		✗	4
Staff too 'hurried' to collect details correctly and/or fully	✗	✗	✗			3
Too many interruptions	✗	✗	✗	✗		4
Correct pricing information unavailable	✗			✗	✗	3
Forms not passed on to accounts quickly enough				✗		1
Forms not batched correctly at source				✗		1
Total	4	3	3	4	2	

collected by	A. Smith
period	1–30 November 2002
location	Central administration

The example shown in Figure 15.15 is from a chain of wholesale shops that mainly serve trade account customers but also sell to the public. Problems have been experienced with delayed invoices sent from head office, particularly to non-account (general public) customers. The preparation of these invoices is based on information sent in by the shops. From the information shown in the figure we would probably focus our attention on the form itself and the number of interruptions occurring in the shops as the forms are being filled out. How could the form be improved? What could be done to reduce the errors caused by interruptions in the shops? This might lead us to consider changing the system of information gathering itself. We would probably also want to clarify why the shops are providing insufficient information and the cause of the processing difficulties at head office.

Quantitative methods

Pareto charts, run and bar charts, and stratification charts (discussed above) help analyse as well as identify problems. Look for trends, irregularities, patterns, unexplained gaps or events, things that have changed, deviations from the norm and anything else that looks odd, out of place or surprising.

Of course, you need to use your good judgement. For example, the most frequent problems are not always the most costly in terms of expense or customer good will. To make sure you're not led astray, display your data in various ways. Here are the other main ways to display data to analyse problems.

Histograms

Histograms are bar charts that display the distribution of data. As we have already seen with **Pareto charts**, it is useful to display bar graphs showing the frequency with which certain events occur. This is called *frequency distribution*. While Pareto charts display the characteristics of a product or service, called *attribute data* (defects, errors, complaints, etc.), **histograms** display the distribution of *measurement data* (temperature, dimensions, etc.). This can reveal the amount of variation in a process, help you discover and describe a problem and monitor its solution.

Figure 15.16 shows a typical histogram. The greatest number of units are in the centre, with a roughly equal number of units on either side. A *normal distribution curve*, or bell shape, is statistically what we expect from any process, because every process will vary over time. Repeated samples of any process that is under control will follow this pattern.

If a histogram does not show this pattern find out why. Figure 15.17 shows an example of this where the data are 'piled up' at points to the left of centre. A distribution like this is referred to as *skewed*. Some processes are naturally skewed, but always investigate the reasons for a skewed histogram.

Similarly, if a class suddenly stops at one point without a previous decline in number, check your data for accuracy; someone may have

Figure 15.16 A histogram of a process that is in control

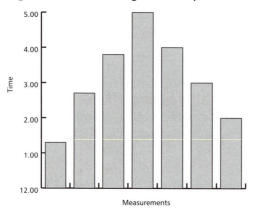

collected by	A. Smith
date	30 November 2002
location	Central administration

Figure 15.17 Histogram of a process that is not in control

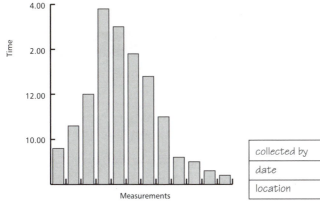

collected by	A. Smith
date	30 November 2002
location	Central administration

made a mistake. If the histogram shows two high points, check whether two or more sources provided the data. If so, go back and get homogeneous data. (Figure 15.18 on page 326 shows how to make a histogram from a frequency table.)

When examining histograms look at the shape of the distribution for surprises—for example, a distribution that you would expect to be 'normal' (a centred bell curve) but is skewed. Are most measurements skewed on the 'high side' or the 'low side'? Look for whether the 'spread' of the curve (*variability*) falls within specifications; if it does not how far outside the specifications is it? Analyse the process further to find out what you can do to bring it into specifications.

Scatter diagrams

Does overtime affect quality? Does training improve results? Does placing an advertisement on the right-hand side of a page affect sales more than a left-hand placement? Does reducing the temperature in a process affect a product's quality? To know for sure, construct a **scatter diagram**. Scatter diagrams reveal any relationships between one variable and another and possible cause-and-effect relationships. They can't prove whether one variable causes another, but they will clarify whether a relationship exists and how strong it is. In this way, scatter diagrams help determine the basic cause(s) of a problem.

The horizontal axis measures one variable and the vertical axis the second variable. Figure 15.19 on page 327 shows a typical scatter diagram showing a positive relationship or *correlation* between two

Here's how ...

... to construct a histogram

1. Gather your data (*data set*) and count the number of data points in your data set.

2. Determine the *range* (*R*) value for the entire data set. This is the smallest data point subtracted from the largest data point.

3. Divide the range value into a certain number of *classes* (*K*), or bars on the chart, using the table shown in Table 15.1.

4. Determine the *class width* (*H*) using the formula below:

$$H = \frac{R}{K}$$

5. Decide where each bar on the histogram will begin and end by determining the *class boundary*, or *end points*. Take the smallest measurement in the data set and use that number (or round it down to an appropriate lower number) as your lower end point for your first class boundary. Then add the class width to your lower end point and this number becomes your next lower class boundary, as shown in the example below.

Smallest measurement in the data set = 7 = lower end point

Class width = 0.20

7 + 0.20 = 7.20 = next lower end point

7.20 + 0.20 = next lower end point

Therefore the first class (or bar on the histogram) would be 7 and would include all data points up to but not including 7.20. The next class would begin at 7.20 and would include data points up to but not including 7.40. The third class would begin with data points at 7.40 and stop at data point 7.60 and so on. Keep adding the class width to the lowest class boundary until you obtain the correct number of classes containing the range of all your data points.

This process makes each class mutually exclusive, that is, each data point will fit into one and only one class (or bar), and gives you an accurate histogram.

6. Construct a *frequency table* based on the number of classes, class width and class boundary, calculated above. This is actually a histogram in tabular form.

7. Construct a histogram based on the frequency table, as shown in Figure 15.18.

8. Use the histogram to diagnose variations and problems in a system. In the example shown in Figure 15.18, the data centre on 7.8 to 7.99, which is close to a normal curve. If the specification were 5.5 to 8.5 with a target of 7, the histogram would show that the process is running high and producing too much unacceptable product. If, on the other hand, the temperature specification were 7 to 9 with a target of 8, our process would be in control.

variables. Notice that the plotted points form a clustered pattern. The direction and tightness of the *cluster* indicates the strength of the relationship between the two variables. The tighter the cluster and the more it resembles a straight line, the stronger the relationship between the two variables. Figure 15.20 shows some other scatter diagrams and how these would be interpreted.

Remember that negative relationships are as important as positive relationships, and that scatter diagrams only show relationships and do not prove cause and effect.

Process capability charts

A system may be 'in control', but that doesn't mean it can meet your needs; it only means it is consistent (it may be consistently bad). This

Table 15.1 Calculating the number of classes required, based on the number of data points

Number of data points	Number of classes
Under 50	15 to 7
151 to 100	16 to 10
101 to 250	17 to 12
Over 250	10 to 20

Figure 15.18 Constructing a histogram from a frequency table

Frequency table

Class	Class boundaries	Mid-point	Frequency (number of data points falling into this class)	Total
1	7.00–7.19	7.1	I	1
2	7.20–7.39	7.3	ℍℍ IIII	9
3	7.40–7.59	7.5	ℍℍ ℍℍ ℍℍ II	17
4	7.60–7.79	7.7	ℍℍ ℍℍ ℍℍ ℍℍ ℍℍ II	27
5	7.80–7.99	7.9	ℍℍ ℍℍ ℍℍ ℍℍ ℍℍ ℍℍ I	31
6	8.00–8.19	8.1	ℍℍ ℍℍ ℍℍ ℍℍ I	21
7	8.20–8.39	8.3	ℍℍ ℍℍ II	12
8	8.40–8.59	8.5	III	3
9	8.60–8.79	8.7	IIII	4
10	8.80–8.99	8.9		0

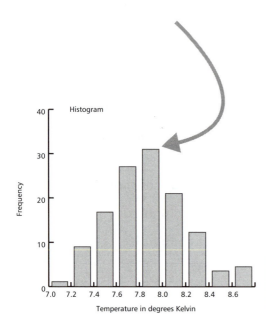

collected by	A. Smith
period	1–30 November 2002
location	Central administration

Figure 15.19 Scatter diagram—strong positive correlation

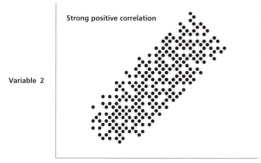

collected by	A. Smith
period	1–30 November 2002
location	Central administration

An increase in variable 2 may depend on an increase in variable 1. If we can control variable 1 we may be able to control variable 2.

Figure 15.20 Scatter diagrams and their interpretations

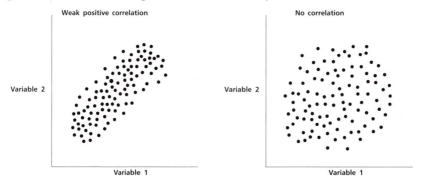

Weak positive correlation

Variable 2 seems to have causes other than variable 1 alone.

No correlation

There seems to be no correlation between variable 1 and variable 2.

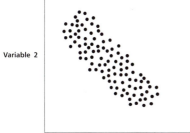

Weak negative correlation

An increase in variable 1 may cause variable 2 to decrease somewhat.

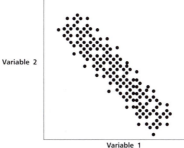

Strong negative correlation

An increase in variable 1 seems to cause a decrease in variable 2. We may be able to control variable 2 by controlling variable 1.

collected by	A. Smith
period	1–30 November 2002
location	Central administration

Here's how ...

... to make a scatter diagram

1. Collect 50 to 100 paired samples of data that you think may be related and construct a data sheet as shown below.

Person	Weight	Height
	kg	cm
1	73	178
2	82	155
3	100	191
.		
.		
.		
50	48	155

2. Draw the horizontal and vertical axes of the scatter diagram with the values increasing as you move up on the vertical axis and to the right on the horizontal axis. Put the variable being investigated as the possible 'cause' on the horizontal axis and the effect variable on the vertical axis.

is where **process capability charts** come in. They will show whether a process, given its natural variation (as established by control charts) is capable of meeting the specifications.

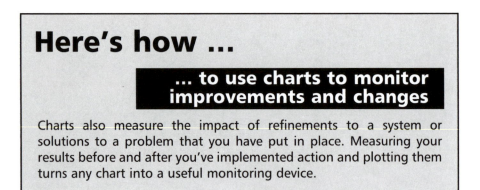

Here's how ...

... to use charts to monitor improvements and changes

Charts also measure the impact of refinements to a system or solutions to a problem that you have put in place. Measuring your results before and after you've implemented action and plotting them turns any chart into a useful monitoring device.

Are your systems and processes capable? If they are, they will meet the customer requirements every time because they are in control and the controls match the specifications.

Process capability charts can also monitor a system and make sure your improvements are working.

As Figure 15.21 shows, capability charts show graphically whether or not your system is meeting requirements by showing the distribution of your process in relation to its specification limits.

Figure 15.21 Process capability charts

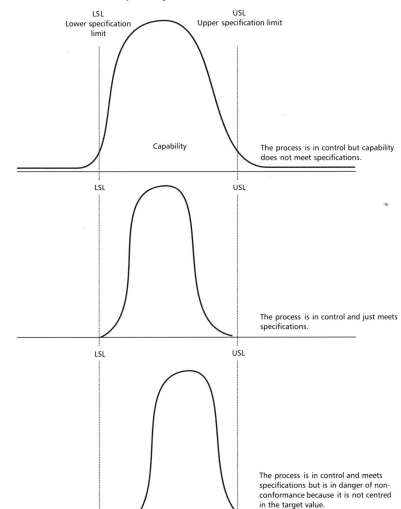

LSL
Lower specification limit

USL
Upper specification limit

Capability

The process is in control but capability does not meet specifications.

LSL

USL

The process is in control and just meets specifications.

LSL

USL

The process is in control and meets specifications but is in danger of non-conformance because it is not centred in the target value.

A process capability index is calculated from the upper and lower specification limits (USL and LSL), the measured natural variation in the process, and the standard deviation in the process. If the process variation exceeds the specification, too many defects are being made or services are not being provided satisfactorily. Even if the process variation is within specification, defects could still occur if the process is not centred on the specified target.

Figure 15.22 Summary of when to use systematic, analytical tools and techniques

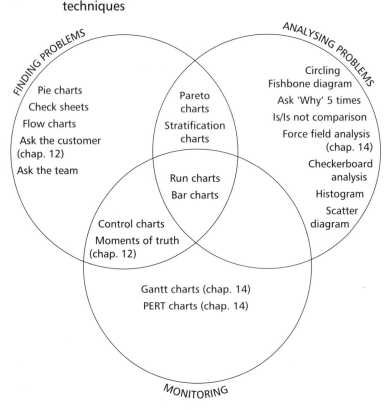

Checklist for success

☐ Don't waste time, effort and money by gathering data haphazardly, randomly or indiscriminately. Focus on information that is useful and relevant and tells you what you need to know.

☐ Sign and date all the information and data you collect.

CHAPTER SIXTEEN

INTRODUCE AND LEAD CHANGE
Planning and fostering change

B y now, the relentless, rapid and revolutionary nature of the changes the world is experiencing must be clear to everyone. Most organisations are experiencing major change resulting from new organisation structures, new technology and new ways of working. The question every supervisor seems to be asking is: *What next?*

More than ever before in the history of modern organisations, we need to be flexible and responsive to the massive changes surrounding us. In fact, organisations and the people in them must adapt and transform, or fail. People must continually update their skills and ways of thinking, and organisations must reinvent themselves not once in a generation but once every three or four years.

Change management is no longer a specialised skill but one that every supervisor needs. Your ability to lead change in a way that helps people flow with it will greatly increase your market value.

WHY DO PEOPLE BAULK AT CHANGE?
Change is part of an ever-present process that every individual and every organisation goes through. It is an obvious and natural thing to do and it is mandatory. Systems that cannot change to preserve themselves stagnate and eventually die.

If change is so natural, why do people resist?

Five good reasons people resist change
1. *People resist what they don't understand.* When we don't understand what is happening or why it is happening, resisting change makes sense. That's why communicating is one of the two most important things you can do to make change work.

2. *People resist what they haven't had a part in creating.* Whether or not we support change depends on whether it is done *to* us or *by* us. You probably like trying out a new hairstyle, wearing a new outfit or discovering a new place to eat, but when a new way to organise your company or your work is announced the important elements of choice and a sense of control are usually missing.

Ignoring people's need to join in with a change effort will cost us their support. That's why involving people is the second of the two most important things you can do to make change work. While people are working together to create and deal with change, they are also creating the conditions, new relationships and new ways of thinking and working that will make the change work.

3. *People resist if they don't trust 'the powers that be' to do the right thing by them.* All too often this describes organisational change. Particularly in the absence of trust in the aftermath of the downsizing frenzy of the 1980s and 1990s, when change was often a euphemism for retrenchments, it's hard for a lot of people to believe anything good can ever come of change.

The less trust there is, the stronger people's concerns will be and the harder you will have to work to allay their fears. If you don't have a trusting working relationship with your work group you won't be able to foster change and innovation easily. They'll never believe the change will be in their interests.

4. *Change often hits us at core levels.* Changes to work groups, for example, usually mean both formal and informal changes. Unofficial group leadership and the unofficial 'pecking order' and established networks may shift. Change often violates cherished group norms and routines. People may be anxious about having to work harder, learn new skills or work methods or become used to new routines or work areas.

People may worry about losing their old job, which they liked, or fear that their new job will be less skilled, less interesting or too demanding. They may resent the implied criticism that the way they have been doing the job is not good enough. They may dislike the thought of outside interference in their jobs or fear loss of control.

Change is personal and this is a large source of resistance. Again, there is no substitute for a continual flow of communication.

5. *When the future is uncertain, it's natural to try to protect ourselves.* We resist the uncertain future that change heralds. Again, communication and trust are crucial.

   In order to make the transition into change, people need to feel safe. The less safe they feel, the more they will resist. If you can calm people's concerns and increase their comfort levels with a change, you'll find it easier to implement.

Two other factors help determine people's resistance to change. The first is: how big is the change? The bigger the change, the more resistance we can expect. The second is: how much does it affect people? The more it requires people to change old habits, ways of working, working relationships and skill sets, the more they will resist.

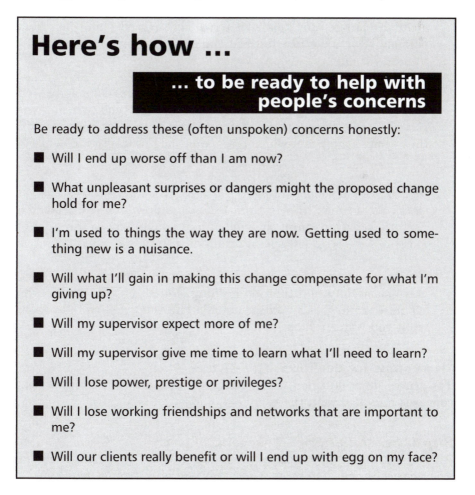

Here's how ...

... to be ready to help with people's concerns

Be ready to address these (often unspoken) concerns honestly:

- Will I end up worse off than I am now?

- What unpleasant surprises or dangers might the proposed change hold for me?

- I'm used to things the way they are now. Getting used to something new is a nuisance.

- Will what I'll gain in making this change compensate for what I'm giving up?

- Will my supervisor expect more of me?

- Will my supervisor give me time to learn what I'll need to learn?

- Will I lose power, prestige or privileges?

- Will I lose working friendships and networks that are important to me?

- Will our clients really benefit or will I end up with egg on my face?

What does resistance look like?

Welcoming workplace change with open arms is rather unusual. Here are five responses you can expect to see:

1. *Passivity.* It's easy to comply with the *letter*, but not the *spirit*, of what a change requires. If you don't show people the personal benefits in taking up the change more wholeheartedly, they'll only go through the motions, doing no more than the bare minimum of what is required. This deprives us of people's energy, enthusiasm and commitment.

2. *Malicious compliance.* Has anyone ever asked you to do something and even though you knew it wouldn't work or knew a better way to do it, you did it their way anyway? That's malicious compliance. People will withhold their good ideas if they're feeling sceptical about a change, don't believe it will be a good thing for them personally or have lost faith in the organisation to 'do the right thing' by them.

3. *Loud complaints.* Some people air their concerns noisily and openly. The question is, will they voice them to you, which gives you a chance to respond and try to bring them on side, or will they voice them to workmates and begin a groundswell of resistance?

4. *Refusal.* Some people simply cross their arms and say *'No, it won't work'*. Sometimes they explain their doubts, which can lead to a useful discussion; often they don't, and you'll need to ask a lot of questions to ferret out the information you need.

5. *Loud agreements.* Have you ever known anyone to say *'Sure, fine!'* enthusiastically and then do nothing? Watch out for people who seem raring to go, then fail to deliver. They may just be telling you what you want to hear.

Three steps for dealing with resistance

The three steps outlined below will help you find out people's real concerns and deal with them.

Step 1: See things from their point of view

Although it might be tempting to smother people's thoughts, concerns and questions or brush them aside, this will only strengthen them.

Here's how ...

... to lessen resistance to change

- Paint a clear picture of why the change is needed, what it will 'look like' when it's finished, how it will be introduced and how it fits in with what people hold as important and dear.

- Specify clearly what you expect, both in terms of the 'whats' (goals and measures of success) and the 'hows' (expected behaviours, any changes to the team's culture and ways of working).

- Make it clear how people will benefit.

- Involve people in designing and implementing the change. Make sure everyone is 'engaged' and has a common understanding of the change initiative: where we are, where we want to be and why, and how we'll get there.

- Manage the transition from the old to the new carefully. Look after people and help them through the 'discomfort zone' of the gap between 'where we are now' and 'where we want to be'.

- Commit the necessary resources—budget, time, communication, training and so on—and direct them all towards the change goals.

- Support and reward the supporters. This will help them grow in number to the needed 'critical mass' for the change to 'take hold'.

- Ensure visible signs of early progress and publicise the successes to encourage people.

- Keep communicating and listening.

Bring their concerns into the open and explore them by asking open questions. Try to put yourself in the resister's shoes. You don't have to agree; just see things their way for a few minutes. What is troubling the person? Accept what people are saying; their concerns are not 'wrong', 'silly', or the result of 'being difficult'.

It is no understatement to say that your listening skills are critical in overcoming resistance to change. Use the EARS formula (see Chapter 2) to understand fully the employee's concerns.

E   *Explore* by asking questions.

A   *Affirm* to show you're listening.

R   *Reflect* your understanding.

S   *Silence*—listen some more.

What do you do when you're listening attentively? You don't gaze out of the window, fiddle with your pen or shuffle through papers! You face the person you're listening to, make eye contact and lean slightly forward. You probably nod your head occasionally and murmur things like '*Umm*' or '*I see*'. This is called affirming. Trying to talk to someone who isn't affirming that they're listening is like trying to talk to a brick wall: people soon give up.

To reflect your understanding, repeat back what you've heard them say, in your own words or theirs. How are they feeling? What exactly are they saying? Keep these reflective statements short—you want to keep the conversational ball in the other person's court. Keep your words and body language neutral—if you disagree or think they are wrong now is not the time to say so. Let the person have their say: no judgements, no arguments, no corrections.

Once you've made your reflective response, listen some more. Hear what else they have to say.

Keep using the EARS formula until you have explored the employee's concerns fully. Often, having aired their fears, the resister will be ready to move on and accept the change. If this happens, go straight to Step 3.

Step 2: Explain the change as you see it
Now it's your turn. Use your understanding of the employee's concerns to decide which aspects of the change to explain. Describe how you see things. Paint as clear a picture as you can of the road ahead and the outcomes you are tying to achieve. Show how the change will benefit the employee.

Step 3: Action plan
When there is a clear road ahead, walking down it is much easier. Agree what each of you will do to implement the change successfully. Try and gain the person's commitment to this.

INTRODUCING CHANGE

According to Harvard Business School professors Michael Beer and Nitin Nohria, two out of every three major change initiatives fail. You can prevent this with a bit of forethought and common sense.

Communicate, consolidate, incorporate and celebrate

Nurturing change is as much about people as it is about goals, new systems and structures and technical practicalities. To achieve genuine change we need to help people's attitudes, beliefs and behaviours to change. In fact, organisational and departmental change often depends on individual change.

If you're tempted to say *'This is the way it's going to be. Now get on with it!'* remember this: forcing change on people leads to either short-term compliance or resistance. Either way it has little impact on people's attitudes and therefore their long-term commitment.

To make change work we must change people's hearts and minds. If we fail to address the people issues, the entire change initiative is likely to fail. The bigger the change, the more important it is to ensure everyone is 'on board'.

This means providing frequent and enthusiastic communication about:

■ the purpose and reason for the change;

■ an understandable and convincing picture of the desired outcome;

■ how the change will take place; and

■ each individual's part in the plan and how the outcomes will affect them.

Explaining a change

Provide a clear vision of the future. Explain why the change is necessary and what you hope it will achieve. Be clear about how everyone in your group will be affected and how their working lives will change. Communicate this picture so consistently and so often that everyone else sees the same picture you see.

People want to know precisely how the change will take place, so explain the steps your department or organisation will go through

Here's how ...

... to avoid failed change

- Don't introduce it in a climate of poor morale and lack of trust.

- Think it through and plan it out properly.

- Set clear and realistic goals and a clear and realistic picture of what the change will achieve and how people will be affected.

- Get your timing right: if change comes too slowly people lose heart; if it comes too quickly they feel overwhelmed and railroaded.

- Make sure people understand precisely how the change will affect them and how you will help them prepare for it.

- Balance, if you can, what people are losing with what they stand to gain from the change. Why should people gladly change if they'll be worse off?

- Communicate frequently, even if it's only to discuss progress and listen to people's thoughts on how the change is progressing.

- Reward people who change; make sure people who don't change are not rewarded in some subtle way.

- Get influential people on side, including the informal leaders in your group, those that others listen to most.

- Involve people as much and as often as you can, in every way you can.

- Recognise and acknowledge the sadness people hint at or express. Give them a chance to 'grieve' for the past or say 'goodbye' to the 'old ways'.

- Provide resources to support the change, for example training, space, equipment, time to consolidate new ways of working, new relationships, new routines.

- Integrate the change with day-to-day working realities and routines so that it's easier to carry on with the new ways than to 'backslide' into the 'old ways'.

- Make change part of people's jobs, not an 'add-on'. In other words, make sure it doesn't add more work and take none away.

to reach your goals. Explain each person's part in the plan and the contribution they will make. Explain what you expect of them in terms of skills they'll need to learn, new roles they'll be expected to perform and the **measures of success** they'll be expected to achieve.

Make sure that you select realistic measures of success that are within people's control and that they are clear and measurable and everyone understands them. (See Chapters 3 and 6.)

Don't push—give people time to reflect on the changes, gather their strength to deal with them, bid farewell to 'the old ways' and come to grips with the new. Aim to strike a balance between making progress fast enough for people to know they're succeeding but not so fast they feel overwhelmed.

Keep the momentum going and celebrate progress, for example by celebrating successes and rewarding the people who change. Cement the change in the department's routine way of doing things once it's working. If you don't do this you're inviting the system to return to its old order.

The bottom line ...

... to introducing change successfully

Communicate, communicate, communicate! It is impossible to over-communicate when it comes to introducing change. Even *'I don't know'* and *'There's nothing new to tell you about yet'* are better than a vacuum of silence.

Never be too busy to put your pen down and lend a listening ear, answer a question or explain how well things are going. Never be in a rush when you reiterate the vision and goals of the change. Never become exasperated with people's questions or ideas. Take a deep breath and explain it all again!

Tell people what they want to know when they want to know it
Should you explain everything you know about a change all at once? Probably not. First, people can't take in too much information at once. Second, they won't be interested in everything. Provide information in the sequence below, or it will fall on deaf ears.

When faced with change, people's first concern is *themselves*. What will happen to *me*? How will *my* life change? What will *I* have to learn to do differently? They know what 'life' is like now; show them what it will be like for them *after* the change. Provide extensive information on how their jobs and duties will change, what training and other support you will provide, how long they will be given to learn the new skills they'll need and so on. Provide as much detailed information as possible so people don't feel 'lost at sea'.

Then focus on the practicalities of the change. Help people build and hone their skills and organise themselves to carry out the new procedures or ways of working. Once they're managing reasonably comfortably, help them make sure their customers are satisfied with the changes. Then, help them to practise *kaizen* (see Chapter 13) to refine the changes and find ways to make things even better.

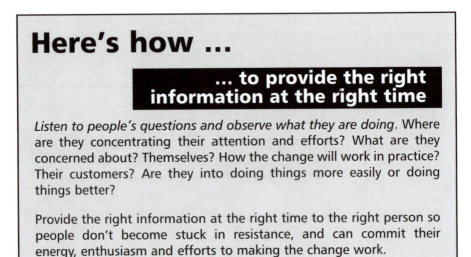

Here's how ...

... to provide the right information at the right time

Listen to people's questions and observe what they are doing. Where are they concentrating their attention and efforts? What are they concerned about? Themselves? How the change will work in practice? Their customers? Are they into doing things more easily or doing things better?

Provide the right information at the right time to the right person so people don't become stuck in resistance, and can commit their energy, enthusiasm and efforts to making the change work.

Helping people through a change

Here are the eight steps to follow when you need to introduce lasting change to your work group (see Figure 16.1).

Career tip

When introducing change, communicate fully and paint a clear picture of what the change will mean for everyone.

Figure 16.1 Eight stepping stones to introducing change

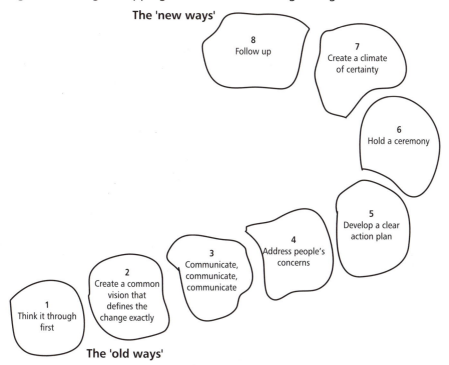

1. Think it through first

Be clear in your own mind precisely what you want the change to achieve and what you expect from your team. Analyse the forces for change and those resisting change (see Chapter 16). What support from others will you need? How will you reward and recognise people for accepting the change? (The change planning worksheet in Figure 16.2 will guide you in preparing for change.)

2. Create a common vision that clearly describes the change

Help people understand the need for change and provide a clear vision of what will be accomplished and precisely how people will be affected. Communicate this clearly and often, to everyone.

3. Communicate, communicate, communicate

When it comes to change it is impossible to over-communicate. When you consider all the questions people will have when coming to terms with a change it's easy to understand why communication is so important. People will look to you, their supervisor, to set the pace and show the way.

Figure 16.2 Change planning worksheet

GOALS

1. What is the goal of this change? What will be different once it's implemented? _____

2. How can you measure whether you have achieved it? _____

3. What is your time frame for introducing the change? _____

4. What specific behaviours do you expect from your team? _____

5. How will you create a common vision and sense of purpose to ensure commitment and acceptance of the change?_____

PLANNING THE CHANGE

1. What resources (time, training, space, equipment) will be needed and how will you procure them so that the change will succeed? _____

2. Does your team have the skills and willingness to change? _____

3. Will the leaders of the organisation model the behaviours required by the change and support it enthusiastically?_____

4. How can you involve the team in planning and evaluating the change? _____

5. Is your action plan realistic? Think about scope, pace, supports required. ____

6. How can you ensure several 'small wins' early on, to get the momentum going and allow people to feel a sense of achievement? _____

7. What formal and informal mechanisms will you use to reinforce change? To reward and recognise people who support the change? _____

8. How will you make sure you consult people regularly and communicate frequently? _____

INTRODUCING THE CHANGE

1. What will be the impact of the change on your team and on individuals? What will they want to know? Who will react, how and why? _____

2. How will the work group's culture be affected? Formal and informal networks? How can you minimise the effects, make them less 'painful' and more appealing to people?_____

3. Who else will be affected by the change (customers, other departments, suppliers, contractors)? How will they be affected? _____

4. What information will you need to provide? What questions are they likely to ask? _____

5. What will be the impact of the change on other parts of the system? On your work team's productivity? On quality? On morale? On particular individuals?

6. Who are the key parties, both formal and informal? Do you have their support? How can you gain it or strengthen it?

7. Analyse the driving forces (for change): task, team, individual, systems, environment. How will you build on them?

8. Analyse the resisting forces (against change): task, team, individual, systems, environment. How will you minimise them?

9. Do you need any further information?

10. How can you build in 'islands of certainty' amidst the change?

11. How will you promote the change to win everyone's understanding and commitment?

12. How will you provide closure from the 'old ways' so that people can let go and accept the change?

TRIAL TEST

Is the change big enough or complex enough to need a trial run? Who should be involved? When should it be carried out? How will it be conveyed to the rest of the organisation? What if it fails? How will it be evaluated? By whom?

KEEPING UP THE MOMENTUM

1. What communication channels will you use to let people know how the change is progressing?

2. How will you maintain momentum for the change?
   - using reward systems, unofficial rewards
   - articulating clear vision/objectives
   - encouraging participation
   - publicising successes throughout organisation
   - using existing power structure
   - integrating with rest of system
   - supporting the supporters
   - providing necessary training
   - communicating and listening
   - tapping into the organisation's value systems
   - using good timing
   - other

3. How will you gather feedback about how the change is working? How will you gather ideas for making it work better?

4. What steps will you take to incorporate the changes into the way your department habitually operates?

Don't let people hear things from the grapevine or any other way—you should be their primary source of information. Even when you think there's nothing to communicate people need to hear from you. You can always give a progress report and reiterate the change goals and vision for the future. Even bad news is better than no news.

4. Address people's concerns
Remember, if people fear for their future they will resist. Although it may take good listening skills and a great deal of patience, respecting and discussing people's concerns will help them deal with them and accept the changes more quickly. Use the EARS formula to bring people's concerns and questions into the open and discuss them.

5. Develop a clear action plan
Involve people as much as you can in developing clear plans about who will do what, when and how in order to make the change work. What specifically must be done to make the change happen?

Create a 'climate of certainty' with a 'path of progress timetable' visually for yourself and the team. How will you know when the steps have been achieved? How will you celebrate achievements along the road to your goal? How will you know if progress slows? Without 'pushing', keep the momentum going.

6. Hold a ceremony
Anthropologists tell us that ceremony is one of the most powerful and satisfying ways to achieve closure. A 'formal finish' allows people to 'let go' of 'the old' so they can begin 'the new'.

If you don't give people a chance to say 'good bye' to the 'old ways' they may yearn for 'the good old days' and never fully accept the change. Some form of farewell, however short and simple, to mark the end of the current stage clearly and welcome in the next helps people separate, let go and move on.

7. Create a climate of certainty
Since it's the uncertainty that seems to cause the most problems build in psychological certainty wherever you can.

8. Follow up
How is the change progressing? Get feedback from employees about what is working well and what needs improving. Who is still resisting? Why? How can you ease their reservations? Reward those who have

changed so that the benefits of change are real and any remaining resisters can see some positive results. Let the group know how well it's doing to keep enthusiasm and interest high.

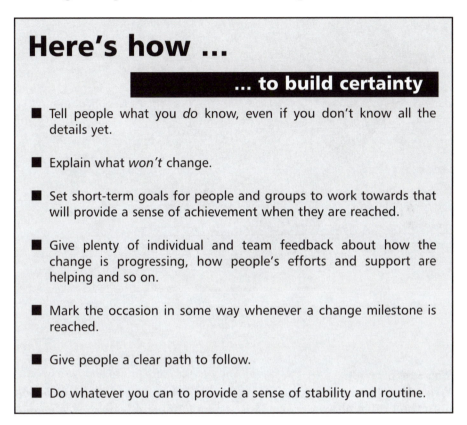

Here's how ...

... to build certainty

- Tell people what you *do* know, even if you don't know all the details yet.

- Explain what *won't* change.

- Set short-term goals for people and groups to work towards that will provide a sense of achievement when they are reached.

- Give plenty of individual and team feedback about how the change is progressing, how people's efforts and support are helping and so on.

- Mark the occasion in some way whenever a change milestone is reached.

- Give people a clear path to follow.

- Do whatever you can to provide a sense of stability and routine.

Crossing the bridge of change

Change is difficult for people, more so for some than others. Figure 16.3 shows the bridge of change, which symbolises the three phases people go through as they come to grips with a change.

Letting go

First they have to let go and make a break with the old. This can be painful, especially if they strongly identify with what they're leaving behind. People commonly experience a sense of turmoil and even dread when faced with the need to let go and move on.

No wonder people resist change, especially big change. Stress that the 'old ways' weren't 'bad' but that conditions (in the marketplace or inside the organisation) mean it's time to move on.

Figure 16.3 The bridge of change

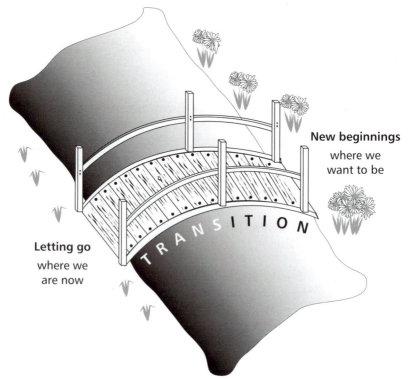

Transition

When people can quell the inner turmoil, they can tentatively move onto the bridge of *transition*. This is like a neutral zone where people often 'go through the motions' as if in a state of shock until they can bring themselves to accept the change fully and work with it. They often feel dazed, confused and swing between hope and despair. The more you communicate, the more you can help people move across the bridge of transition quickly. Eventually, a sense of hope will begin to emerge.

New beginnings

At some point people are ready to accept the change and commit to making it work. They enter *new beginnings* where we finally have access to their energy, ideas and, hopefully, enthusiasm.

How distressing crossing this bridge of transition is and how long it takes depends on a person's make-up, how major the change is and how skilfully you lead them through it.

Some people will be unable to accept the change and will choose to leave the organisation. While this is inevitable, don't treat it too lightly. When a person leaves we lose their experience and knowledge and our investment in their training and development.

When the news is mostly bad
There will occasionally be changes that can't be couched in positive terms. A factory, shop or bank branch may close, for example, or a large number of people may become redundant. The more those affected personally identify with what is changing, the more grief they will feel.

When announcing such changes, avoid blaming anyone or anything or urging people to see 'the big picture'. Be as empathic and supportive as possible and offer whatever assistance you can on behalf of the organisation (counselling, outplacement consulting, further training, etc.). As discussed above, provide some form of closure that helps people say 'goodbye' so they can move forward at their own pace.

Don't forget to learn!
Review the way you introduced and implemented the change. What have you learned? What did you do well? What can you improve on next time? Who in your organisation would benefit from your experience?

This reflection and review helps your group, as well as yourself, learn from experience. If your organisation has a mechanism to store this learning, use it. Otherwise, make sure you take note of your learning for your own future reference.

Invite feedback from your customers and other key players (e.g. contractors, temporary staff, your manager). Sit down and have an informal chat over a cup of coffee, or, if the change effort was a large one, prepare a one-page feedback form that won't take people too long to complete.

Checklist for success

☐ Bring people in on the planning stages so they feel they own the change.

☐ Think through the introduction of the change carefully: get your overall strategy right, establish your goals and know step by step what you need to do.

☐ Make sure everyone shares the same vision of the future and why you need to reach it, and that it has something for everyone to buy into.

☐ Build an alliance of influential supporters. You can't bring about change by yourself. Make sure the power holders, with the resources, expertise, information, legitimacy and political support, are on board and that the key stakeholders who will be affected by and implementing the change understand and support it.

☐ Keep on communicating. Walk around, talk about the change, make sure people are familiar with it to build their comfort levels and gain their approval.

☐ Make sure you get some 'wins' early on, celebrate and publicise successes and steps forward.

☐ Keep change moving forward at a steady pace.

☐ Stay enthusiastic and provide clear direction to overcome any inertia or apathy and keep the momentum in the desired direction.

☐ Keep people in the picture, involved and understanding what is happening so they don't feel powerless and vulnerable.

☐ Put your money where your mouth is: if people need training provide it. If people need time to adjust let them have it (within reason). If people need resources provide them. Don't expect the impossible.

☐ Involve people through training, discussion, question and answer sessions and so on to help them develop new attitudes and knowledge.

☐ Make yourself available to listen uncritically to people's concerns. Find out what's troubling them most and deal with it.

☐ Keep a balance: if you're asking people to take on extra work remove a few other duties.

☐ Monitor progress so you know what is working, what is not working and where the blockages are.

☐ Keep communicating.

☐ Make sure you have enough resources to implement the change successfully.

☐ Pick other people's brains when thinking about how to introduce change. Better still, make it a team effort.

☐ Make sure the environment around the team supports the change.

☐ Persist and persevere. Learn from your mistakes and keep at it until you make the change work.

☐ Share the credit and recognition if you ever want to lead a change again. Recognise and reward people's efforts.

85:15 rule Provided people know precisely what is expected of them and are trained to do it well, 85% of the causes of poor performance and low productivity can be found in the work environment (tools, equipment, teamwork, systems and processes, time, information, job design) and are not the direct fault of the worker. The remaining 15% is accounted for by 'acts of God' and personal problems.

active listening See 'reflective listening'.

agenda A list of the topics to be covered during a meeting, written with verbs to indicate what is to be achieved, or the objective of each discussion (agree X, decide Y, explore N), and the order in which they are to be covered.

bar chart Used to display differences between categories or types of activities.

behavioural interviewing A method of interviewing that focuses on what candidates have done in the past and uses it to predict what they will do in the future, comparing the needs of the job with the abilities of candidates.

boomerang principle We reap what we sow: how we treat others encourages them to treat us similarly.

brainstorm A freewheeling, creativity technique used to shed 'blinkers' and generate lots of ideas for later evaluation.

burnout The 'syndrome of just being sick' first identified by Dr Hans Serle, resulting from unalleviated stress.

cause-and-effect diagram See 'fishbone analysis'.

check sheet A method of gathering data based on sample observations that helps detect and isolate problems.

checkerboard analysis A matrix used to analyse a problem by comparing various elements of the problem with each other.

consensus The process by which an issue is explored, analysed and discussed, and agreement reached.

control chart   A type of run chart showing the upper and lower acceptable limits of variation in a process on either side of the average.

core process redesign   See 'process re-engineering'.

cross-skilling   Increasing the ability of employees to carry out a wider range of tasks at the same or similar levels of responsibility.

culture   The collection of unwritten rules, codes of behaviour and norms by which people operate: 'How we do things around here'.

customer–supplier chain   Viewing an organisation as a series of relationships continuously supplying and receiving products, services or information from each other.

delegation   Assigning a task to an employee, generally to be carried out on an ongoing basis. Useful for training, developing and motivating staff and a time-management technique.

distress   Negative stress or pressure that undermines our ability to cope. (See also 'eustress'.)

empowerment   Providing training and conditions which enable employees or a work team to increase their range of decision-making authorities and responsibilities.

e-training   Training delivered electronically, for example on CD ROM, over the Internet or an organisation's intranet.

eustress   Positive stress or pressures that energise and invigorate us. (See also 'distress'.)

external customers   The people or organisations who purchase or use our products and services. (See also 'internal customers'.)

fishbone analysis   A pictorial representation which helps to isolate the main cause of a problem or helps specify and clarify a problem by allowing us to view it in its entirety. Also called Ishikawa diagrams and cause-and-effect diagrams.

flow chart   A pictorial representation showing all the steps of a process or activity.

force field analysis   A technique that helps ensure a smooth implementation of a plan or decision by highlighting factors working against us (resisting forces), which we should diminish or remove, and factors in our favour (driving forces), which we should capitalise on to move from the current to the desired situation.

framing statement   A short declaration used to introduce and specify a topic for discussion.

Gantt chart   A planning and monitoring aid listing planned activities vertically and time periods horizontally.

group dynamics   The unique pattern of forces operating in a group that affects particularly the interactions between members and their relationships with each other; the way people operate together and their behaviour towards each other which influences how they go about achieving the task.

group maintenance   Looking after the interpersonal aspects of group relations so that people will work effectively together.

groupthink   A phenomenon of highly cohesive groups that occurs when group members would rather maintain a group's agreement than cause friction by challenging ideas, stating an opposing point of view or tabling contrary evidence, thus inhibiting disagreement, constructive criticism, full assessment of alternatives and filtering out contra-indications to a decision or chosen course of action.

heuristics   Unconscious mental routines, some of which can sabotage decision making.

histogram   A bar chart that displays the distribution of measurement data in graph form showing the frequency with which these events occur, to reveal the amount of variation in a process and help discover and describe a problem and monitor its solution.

hot stove principle   Provides advance warning followed by immediate, consistent and impartial discipline.

'I' statement   A clear, succinct and blame-free statement of the effect of another's actions and your preferred outcome.

Ishikawa diagram   See 'fishbone analysis'.

internal customers   People inside our organisation who benefit from our efforts. (See also 'external customers'.)

job breakdown   An instruction tool which divides a job or task into its stages and key points.

job design   The way a job is structured in terms of its specific duties, responsibilities and tasks. An important source of job satisfaction and an influencer of performance.

job enlargement   Expanding a job horizontally, at the same or similar level of responsibility and authority.

job enrichment   Expanding a job vertically, at a higher level of responsibility and authority.

job purpose   A succinct, motivational statement that expresses the main reason a job exists.

kaizen   Continuous incremental, or small-step, improvements.

key result areas   The main areas of responsibility and accountability of a job.

lag indicators   Measures of results after a process is completed; historical measures.

lead indicators   Measures taken during a process; current measures of what is happening as a process occurs.

learning plateau   A period when learning tails off, while the learner consolidates what has already been learned.

measures of success   Key performance indicators that measure important aspects of a job, task, plan or change to track how well it is being achieved.

mentor   A person (often older, more senior or experienced) who takes an interest in someone's career and provide positive help, support, advice and encouragement.

merit principle   Basing employment decisions on people's relevant abilities, skills and knowledge rather than on irrelevant factors such as sex, age, religion and so on.

mindsets   Our often unconscious and unquestioned assumptions and beliefs about ourselves, the people around us, the world and how it operates, that guide our behaviour.

minutes   A record of what has been said and agreed during a meeting. They also indicate the time, date and place of the meeting.

moments of truth   Any contact a customer has with an organisation, for example with a person or electronically.

multimedia conferences   Virtual meetings that use collaborative computing to allow people to meet and work on applications in real-time.

multiskilling   Training across a broad range of skills enabling employees to carry out a wider range of tasks.

networking   Building a web of mutually supportive, informal relationships with others inside and outside the organisation to call on and share help, advice and support.

nominal group technique   A multiple voting system that ensures the opinion of everyone in the group is considered.

norms   The unwritten codes of behaviour people follow which prescribe the 'rules' of 'how we do things around here'.

outsourcing   Divesting traditionally internal functions such as human resources, training, telemarketing, information technology, accounting and administration to external contractors.

PDCA cycle   The Plan–Do–Check–Act process for making and maintaining improvements to a system or process.

Pareto principle   The 80:20 rule of Vilfredo Pareto which says that 20% of our efforts gain us 80% of our results and vice versa.

Pareto chart   A vertical bar chart which displays the relative importance of problems or events, showing the data in descending order of quantity.

performance appraisals   A formalised, systematic assessment and discussion of an employee's performance and their potential and desire for development and training.

performance gap The difference between the expected performance and actual performance, preferably measurable although it can be behavioural (i.e. something you see or hear).

PERT diagram A diagram that shows how planned activities relate to each other and the most time-critical sequence of activities.

pie chart A circular graph showing percentage of the data being studied displayed like slices of a pie.

power A person's ability to 'make things happen' arising from their formal position and/or their personal attributes.

process re-engineering Using technology and systematic analytic methods to radically redesign processes and operating procedures to achieve dramatic improvements in productivity; radically rethinking an organisation's processes, systems and procedures from top to bottom. Also known as re-engineering and core process redesign.

reflective listening Also called *active listening*, this is briefly restating your understanding of the speaker's feelings and/or meanings.

run chart A simple way to graph trends in a process.

self-fulfilling prophesy The process by which our beliefs and self-esteem influence the way we perceive the world and others and guide our behaviour; we tend to perceive what we expect, which reinforces our beliefs.

scatter diagram A way of displaying what happens to one variable when you change another variable, revealing any relationships or correlations between the two variables.

stakeholders An organisation's stakeholders are considered to be: owners, employees, customers/clients, suppliers, the wider society, the closer community.

stratification chart A way to graph and analyse data by breaking them down into meaningful categories, helping to isolate a problem.

stressors Sources of stress.

task What we are trying to achieve. See also 'team maintenance'.

team briefing A systematic process, cascading from the top down, of holding meetings to keep all employees informed about important events and results in an organisation.

team building The process of working with a team to clarify its task and how team members can work together better (process issues) to achieve it.

team maintenance The actions that help people to achieve the task, such as morale building, providing feelings of belonging and cohesion, time out for a bit of fun or humour and establishing a friendly and supportive working climate.

teleconference A meeting between people using simultaneous telephone line connections allowing participants to hear and speak to each other.

Theory X   A belief that employees are lazy and work only for money, leading to leader behaviours of coercion and threats of punishment.

Theory Y   A belief that employees want to do their jobs well and will seek responsibility and challenge, leading to leader behaviours of high expectations and coaching.

trading partnership   The view that organisations and suppliers operate together to achieve mutually satisfactory outcomes; if one 'loses' so does the other.

unity of command   One of the 14 principles of management developed by Henri Fayol which stated that each employee should have only one boss.

upskilling   Adding to people's arsenal of skills and knowledge, usually at a higher level.

videoconference   A meeting held between people or groups in different locations with a 'real-time' video link that allows participants to see and hear each other.

INDEX

Numbers in *italics* indicate diagrams.

London Life, London T-005
HR Training & Development
The supervisor's survival guide
April 20, 2006